THROUGH THE CLOUDS

THROUGH THE CLOUDS

*A Journey of Self Discovery
and the Lessons I Learned
While Flying Through the Clouds*

C. Wes Mercier

authorHOUSE®

AuthorHouse™
1663 Liberty Drive
Bloomington, IN 47403
www.authorhouse.com
Phone: 1-800-839-8640

First published by AuthorHouse   12/30/2011

ISBN: 978-1-4685-3824-3 (sc)
ISBN: 978-1-4685-3826-7 (hc)
ISBN: 978-1-4685-3825-0 (ebk)

Library of Congress Control Number: 2011963733

Printed in the United States of America

About The Author

C. WES MERCIER, OR CASUALLY KNOWN AS CHUCK WROTE periodically to international pen pals, friends, and yes, even Corporate Executives for ten years. At one point even called, "The Letter Man" by his brother from another mother. However, writing as a career didn't occur to him for another couple of years. His gradual rise above mediocrity began when he acclimated himself to the revelation, "If your ship doesn't come in, swim out to it."

Chuck, his wife Shahlo, and their two boys Enzo and Massimo can be found splitting their time between Orlando, Florida and North Augusta, South Carolina. Together, their family enjoys sports, traveling Delta, and all things Disney.

He has operated his own insurance agency for twenty years and has spent twelve years providing excellent customer service at Delta Airlines, and some of her subsidiaries. He is now serving as an aircraft Part Coordinator for Delta Connection carrier Atlantic Southeast Airlines, and a Delta Diversion Specialist for Delta Global.

As always, Chuck loves to hear from his readers. He can be contacted at 8131 Vineland Avenue Box 410 Orlando, Florida 32821. He would love for you to visit his website at www.cwesmercier.com.

Table of Contents

1.

Who Am I?

THIS QUESTION HAS PROBABLY BECOME THE QUESTION OF ALL questions in our lifetimes, and its answer may solve some of the problems we have about defining ourselves. The belief is that if definition can be given to a single object, then that object may present itself to us, in a formatted version of the truth. So where do we actually find a solution then? As for me, I begin somewhere between the road to nowhere and childhood. A road paved with good intentions while entering those peculiar years of adolescence. In high school, I never had the vigor or the self-esteem to finish anything. Yeah, I'd begin it, and with passion that would have William Shakespeare proud. But then as I wondered within my own realms of reality, I'd find the end result was just too far out of reach, that I wouldn't even bother progressing.

North Augusta, South Carolina is a small town for sure. To an extent, it has aspirations to acquire that big city feel while maintaining an ever prevalent quaintness. There's even a hint of fresh air steadily blowing off the banks of the Savannah River. And in those early years, we always found our way down there for aquatic refreshment whether my mother knew where we were or not. I can imagine this particular town being just like many others of its size. With or without the river, I believe every town has its ups and downs. People who are actively involved in just about anything they can get their hands on, and then those who aren't. There were the mothers who couldn't bear to send their little tadpoles off to school. As if they were going to follow them down the halls securing a seat for their kid at the popular table. Oh! And how about the fathers who were at every football practice, whether their son was any good, or not? To me, that was the funniest thing about small town America. They would rather sacrifice any kind of success just to placate an active booster. There were some of us who thought we were talented enough to play. But yet, for some ungodly reason, we were left to sulk into our own sense of stardom on that beautiful place we called the bench. I remember there being coaches who were no bigger than a jockey from the nicely manicured racetracks of Kentucky. You would've thought they ruled the athletic world from what they were saying about themselves.

There on a hot steamy August afternoon, I was sulking that even though I was as big as anyone on the team, I wouldn't play one play. If I wanted to be part of North Augusta Yellow Jacket Football, I would have to do so from where, you guessed it, that all so purposeful bench. I got so disturbed one time that I came home to vent my frustration. Maybe even to quit. But my mother or father wouldn't hear of it. She said, "You chose to start this season, now just finish it, and next year you can do what you want!" Needless to say there was always something about a mother's reassurance that would turn a big boy into the child his mother still saw him as. So doing what I had to do, I suppressed my anger and vested my time within the solitude of that sweltering practice field.

The consensus was that I'd persevere and just finish the season. But life as I knew it was about to change. What I didn't know was there was Coach Long who coached Defensive Line, and he was about to give me an opportunity of a lifetime. A powerfully built defensive line looking man who himself had successfully completed his high school career at North Augusta, howbeit a lot earlier than I. So Coach Long looks at me in those befuddled eyes of mine, and directed me, "Mercier, I want you to come here and play over here." He was pointing at the tackle position on the Defensive line. And as excited as I was to be taken from the tackle dummy position, I still pondered as to why he chose me. Maybe it was because I was so tall and I could knock the ball down in the event that the quarterback threw a screen pass or something like that. To this day, I don't know why. It really isn't important though. But what is important is that I will always be thankful that he gave me that much anticipated time off the dummy's dinger. And then there was the day when those Jockey coaches would see the way I tackled.

We had a scrawny old Head Coach who didn't seem to want us to tackle. At least tackle correctly anyway. I believed that this should be done as to stop the other player from going anywhere. That's the point right? You immobilize your opponent as to keep him from moving forward. So why was this man trying to conceal the art of tackling from us? His belief was this would only be done at game time, and only during game time. The instructions he gave us seemed as if he was trying to hold us back. Wait a minute, I just said us, as if I was part of that group that he would look at, and then bark out his commandments. I have to remember I was the one he would look through just to see someone else. Until that day anyway, I thought I was invisible to this man. Coach Long had strategically positioned me with his starting defensive linemen. Taking what was unfamiliar territory, the all so sacred practice field, I'd look around the linebackers to wave to my buddies on the tackling dummies. As if they were routing me on. It really was a nice thing to see. So, being placed somewhere I thought was so far out of reach that there must have been a look of bewilderment on my face. But I stood there confidently among the giants within my own state of a beanstalk mentality.

So there was our Head Coach, let us just call him Coach Jockey. He looked at the defense and barked in what seemed to be a West Virginian dialect, "All right guys, I want you to go 110%." Excited to be standing there with marching orders in hand and I was free to show them I could play. The belief was that I could actually go full steam ahead when I truthfully never heard these "All Out" words before. It seemed like to me that finally, we were doing what it took to win football games. The offense broke huddle. The first team players placed their hands gingerly upon the ground. Waiting there for the commands from their own signal caller, they would wait patiently. "Blue 32, Set, and Hut!" I heard it as if cannons went off in my head. All I wanted to do was make an impression with Coach Long. I believed that he was the only one on that field who saw something more in me than I did within myself. So if I was going to be successful for anyone, it'd be for him.

Rather than sit there and wait for the offense line to react, I chose to jump over the person who was lucky enough to be in front of number eighty six. Low and behold there was the quarterback that happened to be there when I landed on all fours. So I did what most people would do on a field like this, make sure that my coach knew that I would no longer be their tackling dummy. That my will would be forced upon my quarterback, and ultimately he would fall. I hit him with as much of the 110% percent I had left. After this hit, both of us were there on the ground, he was wondering why he had been hit with such an awesome thunder. I was there knowing that the thunder he felt rattle his bones was me. Then I heard something that sounded like a mouse trying to squeeze through a cheese whiz nozzle. A high pitched whine coming from the mouth of Coach Jockey, I could barely hear what he was trying to say. But from what I could render, he was screaming while grabbing my helmet, "Get up, you imbecile, why did you hit my quarterback?" I remember hearing him spitting those words out as if his madness had suddenly become the chemical compound of water. Otherwise known as H2 Spit, and I wasn't able to tell where his spit began and my sweat ended. Once again, this was the man who never showed anyone on this team how to tackle. And in one instance, this tall lanky defensive lineman had just given his teammates a Smithsonian display of what it means to pummel your opponent into ultimate submission. I promise you that I heard one hundred and ten percent. But apparently what was actually said was something a hundred percent farther down that proverbial line. This Coach said ten percent not one hundred and ten percent. Imagine that!

Here I was in total amazement at how I had just finished my entire season in one snap and we still had ten games left. Needless to say I didn't help the quarterback up from his billowing slumber. I really did hit him with a hundred and ten percent, so I felt that if I'd done what Coach didn't want me doing in the first place, then it really didn't matter if I helped him up or not. Coach Jockey was still losing his mind and his ever increasing anger was more present now than ever before. Feeling totally isolated, I just stood there as if to say, "Just tackling here, might be a thing or two you guys want to learn." He then smacked my shoulder pads and grabbed my grass stained helmet with his hands, "Who is going to play quarterback?!!! You hit him, you gonna play quarterback?!! You see anyone here who's gonna play if you knock him out for the season?!!" His spit was hitting my face as if it were a driving rain. I started smiling as all my teammates began to notice this boyish grin. Then in the beat of a heart, I quickly responded with confidence, "Hey Coach, I'll play quarterback! You ask who'll play, and all I want to do it play football. So if that's the position you want me to play, I'll do it just as long as you let me play." That wasn't something a man who had just seen his star player getting his bell rung wanted to hear. He hit my shoulder pads again, and took my practice jersey in his hands. And then he yelled, "Boy! You see those receivers, get over there and get out of here, you need to get away from me, you flipping idiot!" The emotions I had then were somewhat demure. I had just demonstrated to our team what I thought it would take to win football games. To tackle as Coach Long would have us tackle. With as much authority as it would take to revolutionize North Augusta football, at least to that point anyway. However, Coach Jockey thought I'd be better suited to spend the next couple of months with the Tight Ends. Which was really kind of fun, except for the friends I'd made on those tackling dummies would now be on the other side of the field. For a second I thought I'd be sent to my ruin within the confines of the tackling dummies. But from there I was sent to oblivion, not really knowing where I would play, somehow delegated to what I thought would be a second string Tight End.

Then another incident happened. And number eighty six here was really up to the challenge. Coach Long would always seem to want me back, but never voiced his opinion because of his position. At least that is what I thought anyway. During practice one day Coach Jockey called a play that was designated for me, the Tight End. "This is it, a chance to show this team I can be an

C. Wes Mercier

asset rather than a liability!" I said to myself. I broke huddle and started to line up so that the defense would not know this would be the day the Lord had made for me. The same call that I heard when I played defense I heard then except that I would be the one who initiated the cannon blast. The quarterback roared as he purposely looked over to me, "Hut, hut!" I wish I had really paid attention more to it because this was the payback play. At least it seemed that way anyway.

Before I finish, have you ever heard the old steam engine at Disney World? The sound of its whistle when it blows can be heard basically from anywhere in the park. And sometimes even on the monorail. But once the monorail leaves the park it drops you off at the parking lot. That sound becomes a distant reminder of the fun you enjoyed for the day. When you get to the car, it's the one place in the park where the train can't be heard. Well, I believe that is where I was the day that play was called for me. I was in my car all the way back in the furthest part of the parking lot. Let's just call it the Donald Duck lot because ducks don't have ears and I didn't hear anything. So needless to say, I didn't sense anything. It seemed as if this would be a major turning point in my football career. It didn't matter if I could hear the whistles or not for I was about to take off on my own. All I heard was, "Hut!" I knew that this screen pass had number eighty six written all over it. The center snapped the ball. The quarterback who shall remain nameless except for number seven took the snap. And with a twirling acrobatic move he danced around his center who was preoccupied with a nose guard of his own. I ran what I thought to be the correct route and then every inch of number seven's arm strength was released. A rocketing bullet meant for me, and I was intent on showing these people I was not out of my league. I knew I could catch. All I needed was the ball. Now, they would know and we'd be one big happy family. Yeah right? However, that's when the train came. As if lightning struck right beside me I felt an electrifying jolt that seemed to turn the lights off within my own mind. I knew I had the ball. And I believed there were more yards I could have gained. But of course, the train I'm talking about came by way of a strong safety who just happened to be the best friend of guess who? Really

6

now, is it that simple? Yes it is, it was the quarterback, of which Mr. tackling dummy here, turned defensive line extraordinaire had politely laid out just a couple of weeks before. I didn't see it coming. But it's as if this Coach Jockey had set this up just to show the other tackling dummies that when he says ten percent, that's what he means.

The smell of Bermuda grass is a wonderful smell in the middle of summer. Having just mowed the lawn, it glistens with a soft fragrance of mist. The grass I'd become so acquainted with while mowing it, smelled altogether different that day. Not as soft. Actually after that though, I don't remember much, but here I was, a boy on his back who didn't know where he was at the moment. Then, like the sun would seep through the fog, I could hear distinct voices. Some sounded like tiny birds chirping, others sounded like mice nibbling on a mound of Gouda cheese. Then there was a discrete laughter. And I wasn't at all amused. Dazed and confused were the emotions on tap for that minute. Coach Jockey stood over me with a precarious smile. Along with the other offensive coaches, they were all overly excited to see that this strong safety had made contact. I don't remember if they even asked me how I was doing. But as if the light switch came on and the light began to creep back into my head. I asked, "What are you guys doing in my room?" I felt that I accomplished something because I still had my fingers wrapped around the ball. And yards were gained. It was ultimately a success. I'd now become part of this team.

So for the rest of the month we practiced hard. I was relieved to know that I earned my way on the second team. I thought that for five games anyway. We were playing at home against Greenwood and it was midway through the second quarter. I was procuring my original place on the bench, and I stood up to start walking around. You know in mid-September, the Gatorade is really cold when you're not moving around. So I had to start moving for nothing more than the sake of staying warm. The yellow jackets were swarming and gaining ground. Catching something out of the corner of my eyes, it made me jump up out of my own little comfort zone, and run over to Coach Jockey.

The starting Tight End had been injured. And I was the second team Tight End. Number eighty six was finally going to see game time. On the home field as well, this was sure to be one heck of a good day. My helmet fastened tightly upon my chin, and I waited patiently for Coach Jockey to usher me in with the play. I thought it'd be the same one I had gotten my bell rang earlier in the season. But I didn't care, I just wanted to play. He turned around, looked at me ready to go, and turned his head towards another direction. One in which had me confused. The seconds that I stood there seemed like hours but I was standing there ready to take the field. The direction in which he turned was nowhere close to mine. He turned to the second team quarterback and asked, "Dodge, do you know these tight end plays?" This was a moment that made me feel as if I was the only one in the stadium. I looked at him angrily and in absolute disgust. As to why he would call someone other than his second team Tight End was far from the current answers that I knew. But he did.

That moment defined my future with the Yellow Jacket football team. It was one of those moments where you could picture yourself taking off those bulky football pants, the jersey that remained clean week after week, and yes that helmet that had become a symbol of failure. Feeling stunned by what was transpiring, I imagined just turning around to the two, maybe three thousand people in stands, waving goodbye, waltzing across the field while the other players were still on the field playing. Nothing but me, my fruit of the looms, and my pride, or what was left of it anyway. But rather than embarrass my mother and father who were in the stands, I chose to turn around and place my downtrodden hind parts on the place that was most familiar with me, the bench.

Miami Vice was one of those shows that transformed me from that state of failure to a level where I enjoyed most. My father and I would eat a steak together while watching Tubbs and Crockett take on the bad guys. Every once in a while, my mother or brother would sneak through to see us pounding a massive sirloin into our mouths. Now those Friday nights were fun. This would start for me immediately following the football game. I'd skip out on the shower with the team just to be there in time for Vice. I'd ask myself, "What did I have to wash up for?" I was already clean. I never even broke a sweat standing there on the sidelines.

I went home intentionally after that God forsaken night to tell my parents I was fed up with the political rat race. I was tired, worn out in fact, to be part of a team that would use me as nothing more than a manikin for displaying the number eighty six jersey. Still there were no takers on the quitting theme that night or any other night. I wanted to quit, now and not later. But they wanted no part of it. So I'd stay on the team to complete the season.

I learned something that year. It was that I'd continue to define who I was by these events. Such circumstances that would curtail me from my own desire to be in the "It" group, I'd find myself finding comfort with what brought me there in the first place. My best friends never once cared about how much I played on this football team. They would only care if I'd be drinking the big glass or the small glass of milk he'd have for me at his house. Whether or not if I was going to eat the Oatmeal pies or the seven layer bars his mom made the night before. These were the good ole days of my youth. It was in those days that I began to ask, "Who am I?" Never would I come up with a definitive answer though. Somehow, it was always the same. I was me, and no one else. To accept the definition that everyone else would give me was just easier. It could be harder for me to try and figure it out myself, so I'll just be who I am based upon what everyone else thinks of me.

I wanted to be a millionaire in those days. Maybe it was the Ferrari Crockett used to speed around Miami driving those thoughts. I think it goes back to where living in a small town had its disadvantages. Everyone it seemed had an agenda. To seek out and destroy the moral of anyone who did not fit into a certain mold. In the sixth grade, I was made to feel that wearing the Cuga brand of shoes was so past funny that it made me feel I didn't measure up to the "Cool" kids ideals. If I didn't wear Izod, and yes, it was Izod back in those days too; I'd be laughed at and ridiculed. So what does anyone who has any pride left to do? He chooses to apply the Izod rule. What is that? It's the fact that if everything you wear is Izod, then no one, and I mean no one will laugh at you. My father was not a rich man but he was a hard worker so I would persist that I could buy the "Cool" clothes. My brother didn't seem to care who or what Izod was; it was okay with me that he felt that way. However, I didn't want to be left to feel this way again. I wanted to define how I saw myself with the clothes I wore. If someone were to see me in something other than Izod, it just wouldn't happen. I wanted to be in a position where Izod defined my being. So that's exactly what I did.

The reasons I'd give myself would provide shelter from my own feelings of low self-esteem. So then how does one provide an answer to the question, "Who am I?" It can be blazingly simple or completely complex. It is really a single movement within the mind. One man's choice to initiate ideas that may have shaped the way he sees himself. I sat down one day and asked myself that same question. And I found out that I really didn't have an adequate answer. For myself anyway, I wanted change. I wanted to be sure of who I was as a person. No one would ever define who I was as a person based on the fact that I wasn't a star on the North Augusta Yellow Jacket football team. Nor would they define who I was based upon what I wore. And what I drove would never be used again to provide meaning for myself. I knew that it was in these moments that the ultimate power to be self-defining grew more intense within my own being.

And that power would be the fuel that propelled this rocket of confidence until the time I was given had expired. So what did I do? I chose to define what I thought of myself. I would not be held to what others defined in me. I'd be walking down the road, and my mind would be racing towards finality. That I was who I was because of who God chose me to be, and I knew that he wasn't finished with me yet. I believed everything . . . to be an opportunity for perpetual growth.

Going back to those seconds that Coach Jockey turned around and asked for someone else other than me to get on the field I made a decision to do something that'd be helpful. Not one that would tear down the very fiber I had instilled within myself. Do not misinterpret this statement. I was hurt, but I was not battered when Coach Jockey did this to me. He was doing what he thought to be best for his team. I was seeking out what was best for me. The most important events in life can truly define where you will see yourself ten, twenty, maybe even thirty years down the road. So does that leave us to chance? No, I think it comes down to where one must decide what they feel about certain things that have happened in their life. Anthony Robbins said, "It is in the moments of decision that your destiny is shaped." Only then can you truly experience power. I began this life as someone who accepted definition by someone else. Hey Mister Man, you're not a good football player. You're not a good singer. I would hear those words that would pierce my soul and it truly affected me. I felt that I had to wear name brand clothes to be accepted. So in essence, I was being defined by the clothes that I wore. If it was a brand new car, like a Mercedes, or whatever class of new car, the definition would still dive deep within my bones. Even though I drove a Nissan pickup truck back then, it was something that was defining me by someone else. And I chose to let those definitions stick within the confines my own mind.

So where does definition come from? It comes from the depths of your soul that you have to go looking for it. Searching for it as if you were searching for the lost treasure of Blackbeard the Pirate, only then shall you find the answer to the question, "Who am I?"

I made a decision not long ago to define every area that I felt that I needed to in order to become a better man. I knew that God defined me as his child, and I was happy to serve him as such. But as for substance thereafter I was empty. So then, I made an effort to change what or how I saw myself. Never again would I see myself as a failure as a direct result of the football program at North Augusta High School. I was a member of a team that had one win. That is it. I defined my success based upon the success I enjoyed not the failure I experienced.

In fact, most of the greatest minds today are defining different aspects of their life all the time. I imagine that Mr. Gates would not define how he would see himself in a business meeting. What would be the result had he not prepared in this way? Disastrous at best, I'd imagine people do not plan to fail, they fail to plan. Have we not heard that before? It's still true today. How do you not fail to plan though? Well, I would make statements that truly define who I will be once success is achieved. I'd begin to ascertain several ideas that would define what I would feel once the goal is attained. It makes for a smooth transition when definition is given, and given with as much detail I chose to give it.

My question to you is, "What are the things in your own life that may have shaped your destiny?" I went through my experience with the team. And I know that it is important to you to find the answers to your own questions. Otherwise, I don't think you would have read this far. So you apparently want something more in your life. Be true to yourself and apply definition. Give meaning to the most ridiculous events in life, and you just may find out that you really have never given anything much thought at all. And once you begin to dive into the meaning and interpretations you have, it'll be then and only then can you see how things change.

One last thought is that there may be certain events or items that don't need defining so do not waste the time. But I'll take you back to the Izod rule. If it may change the way you see yourself then redefine it. Define things that have the greatest emotional impact, and I am sure that you will experience noticeable results. Be happy about this natural progression through this process, and always remain thankful to have lived through it.

2.

The Picture Of Mediocrity

THE SUNNY DAYS OF SUMMER JUST ABOUT ENDED WHEN WE registered for classes at the University of South Carolina in Aiken. And hey, it was only a short drive away from where I actually wanted to go to college. You see, I had this crazy idea I wanted to major in music. And it seemed to me a lot easier to go to a school in which I'd become so acquainted with. For one, my voice teacher was there, and even my piano instructor was there. Both of which were professors at Augusta College. I can't say for sure that I was excited to be anywhere else. But my father was headstrong about me going to college in a state where I lived because of lower tuition cost. So I now had been registered to go to a public University within the state of South Carolina. For about a week it gave me great heartaches to be going to Aiken, when I had my heart set on being in Augusta. That's when my desire to finish my voice classes began to drift away. As well as piano, I just didn't want to continue. I felt like a piece of balsam wood being tossed to and fro within the frolicking rapids of a bending river. I settled in though, and did what always seemed natural to me which was to continue on without showing anyone my true feelings. The truth though became more evident to me as I pacified myself, "Hey, at least you got in."

That was the thing. I breezed through high school on a song and a prayer. And there were teachers who saw I had more to offer but was intently holding back. I guess I'll never know what I could've been in their eyes. Painting myself as a complacent child just happy to be moving on, while my teachers saw me

13

more than number one hundred and seventy one in a class of three hundred and forty two. The exact half, I knew I could never be called a nerd, nor could I ever be called a complete idiot. And that's where I felt most comfortable. Safe, if you will. A cocoon of sorts, except that this worm never knows he's supposed to be a butterfly.

Computer class to me was an absolute blast. I'd learn how back in the fifties, computers would be the size of an entire floor in a corporate office. However, I should've listened more to Mrs. Davis. She was a kind woman who would complement me on my accomplishments in class. But as I danced through compliments, it was within those moments when I became the Plot Point guru. She would progress through her daily lessons, and I wouldn't even lift my head to let her know I was there. This one particular day we started graphical placements. And I loved it. I wanted to draw using these two points and really lost interest in whatever followed in that class. My favorite band Journey had just released Raised on Radio and I took a picture of the album cover and designed the radio station on my computer. Now remember, the rest of the class would move on to other subjects. But I was comfortable in my own zone. She must've been frustrated to witness my obliterated failure to pay attention. I didn't really follow what her current lessons may have been at the time. Even in the midst of my defiance for cumulative knowledge, she remained cordial. However, I do remember her being stern enough to tell me to open my book. That much I'd give her. I believe she deserved that courtesy at least. My friends would ask me to design their names in these plot point illustrations. I obliged because it would get my mind off the fact that I still had to go to this stupid class.

Some years later, I saw Mrs. Davis around town and she asked me how I was doing. I told her that I was doing well. And how I'd begun working for my father in his business. She told me that she always thought I'd end up doing something with computers. I started laughing. And she was surprised by my response. "Why aren't you?" she asked. I wanted to make sure she knew I wasn't laughing at her. So I told her, "Mrs. Davis, I failed your class. And how could I ever think I was smart enough to do something like that?" Rather than agree with me which most people would do at that point just to get away from the subject. She amazed me with her response. In a clear voice I heard her say, "You were one of the smartest people I ever taught." Did I say clear voice? Yes, that's what I meant. She said this in as much of a clear voice that I was stunned to hear her say something so positive about me. Sad to say, but yes, I did hear her but really didn't think too much about it. Happy to hear it, but truthfully I just didn't believe her.

That's why college seemed like a cake walk to me. Some of the people I went to high school with joined me in Aiken. The familiarity with some had me in a position of comfort once again. Core classes are what every student must take when he enrolls in college. Well, guess what? Due to the fact that I was planning to enroll in an entirely different school, I arrived late. Meaning only one thing, the core classes that I was supposed to take had been taken. Every class that I needed to take was full. So I did the only thing a man of my stature could do . . . southern studies.

I had two professors in this class. Both of them acquired doctorates early on in life so I felt I was safe learning what it meant to be a southerner. It was really a fun class. We learned how to cook southern style barbeque. We were taught how the traditions of the south still play major roles in how we define our culture today. But their talents were much more than that. And it was something that moved me more than anything else in my life in those days. These guys would teach an hour and ten minute class, and then would make their way to the gymnasium to play the game of life . . . basketball. I'd walk through the gym on many occasions but mostly during the times between noon and two. I sometimes wished I would've never seen these guys playing. Because it only did one thing, it brought out the one thing that always made me happy. The idea was if I was playing basketball; I could disappear where nothing else mattered, and to me, it really didn't matter. Most college students do everything but study in their first year, and I wasn't any different. I enrolled in classes but rarely saw the inside of a classroom.

The two doctors of whatever, I really didn't know what their doctorates were in, but the thing I did know now was that they played basketball after class. So I did what I did to make sure I could play. I joined in. There were more professors playing. But now, I'd be playing on a level field with people who were intellectually superior to me. This game of basketball seemed to be an equalizer of sorts. From that point on I would play on Mondays, Wednesdays, and Fridays. Except there was one catch, my two doctorate professors would have to teach my southern studies class. And then they'd come to play at the gym. But who do you think wouldn't show up to class in order to get there at eleven fifty? I knew that at twelve ten, they'd be ready to play. What happened is that I'd meet them after class. And the first thing they'd ask, "Where were you? We didn't see you in class young man." In my all so simple way I responded with complete confidence, "Hey Doc, I was here. Waiting on you guys." They'd shake their heads and act as if it didn't bother them. Somehow though, I think it did. So I pacified them and showed up for a couple of classes just to take the test. It wasn't supposed to be this way in the first year of college. Nevertheless that was me.

Falling into what my mother always said about me, and I have to say that it really never bothered me to be this, "You're the complete picture of mediocrity." But as I look at it now, maybe it really did bother me. If I settled for second place all the time then how would I ever experience a successful life? Would I ever know what it feels to win and win big? How clear did it have to be for me?

I've always been a fan of the Los Angeles Lakers. In my younger days I'd watch Magic and the boys round out many championships together. Could they have ever done anything like this if they were the same pictures of mediocrity I was? Envision Magic in nineteen seventy nine or eighty saying to his coach, "I'm only going to play point guard. I don't want to play center, or forward, and Love it or leave it, this is me!" What would've happened? Probably Kareem Abdul-Jabbar would have said the same thing, and then what? Time would've pretty much stood still. The banners you now see high above the Staples Center floor wouldn't have the championship they won that year.

Why? Because Kareem got hurt that series and our boy Magic came to the rescue. Remember now, that this was his rookie year. And he came out in roaring fashion to rise above mediocrity with an enticing boyish grin. That night Mr. Johnson played all five positions and led his Lakers to a world championship. That night the world knew who Irving "Magic" Johnson was, and quite possibly who he'd become.

Do we have a spark inside us that could lead us to such extraordinary performances? I believe we do. And it goes along with what we defined about ourselves in the early developmental years. Changing those definitions can be a long and tedious task. But to complete the transformation you'll need patience, and an apparent mental fortitude. How did I realize that being this model for the middle would cause me to lose a lot of precious accomplishments? How would you?

For example, take Mrs. Davis' computer class experience. What could I have seen then that would've revolutionized my life? There was a girl in my class with a brother who was a magnificent and accomplished artist. Both were highly intelligent, and not taking anything away from the sister, but I want to talk about the brother here. He wasn't in this class, but I'd play basketball with him too. So I knew him quite well. He would draw, draw, and draw. And his illustrative art was something else. The rise above his mediocrity was a smooth ascension to where he is today. I use this class for an example because I was doing the same thing he was doing except on a miniscule level. I'd draw, draw, and draw; except my drawing would be on a computer. His masterpieces would begin on pieces of paper. What was it that made him so different? Well, I think it came down to decision. I chose to go to a small college near my home where not going to class was easier than going. He went off to Winthrop University, and then finished his degree at Texas AMU. Yes, I could've done well had I escaped the mediocrity bit. But once again, it was where I felt most comfortable.

Steven graduated, and moved on to California. What was the difference between his decisions and mine? It's easier just to sit here and talk about my failure rather than to realize the opportunity was there for both of us. It was inevitably up to us to make that move. In those days of computers for me, and paper for him, we didn't know where it would lead us. But now, my friend who kindled his talent for art on paper has turned his gift into a colorful Computer Generated World. Truly, I never saw my mediocrity for anything more than a way of life, while he grabbed life by the horns and ran with the bulls. Why can I say this? Because Steven's natural progression through mediocrity has been a wonderful gift that almost everyone in this country has enjoyed. You say you haven't enjoyed it. Yet, if you have seen certain movies by Pixar, you have enjoyed it. You see, my friend Steven is an Animation Scientist for this corporation. And it seems that this company has a knack for presenting quality family entertainment. Personally, I think in part because of him.

So what if I had risen above it? Where would I be? Let me say that I'm totally happy for anyone who has risen above his or her own mediocrity. And I strive now for this type of excellence every day. I don't choose to straddle the fence anymore. I either do it or I don't do it. To paraphrase a Bible verse, let your "yes" be "yes", and your "no" be "no". In other words, be definitive in the pursuit of your own plan for life.

What happens if you don't have a plan? Then the plan will have you. In other words, you'll settle in to your own definition of mediocrity. You'll walk around town as if to say, "Oh, ho hum. Ho hominy hum" Never being noticed by anyone except yourself, you'll be safe for sure. But what if you feel that being something else is what you really want. Then stand up now and do something about it. First of all, define who it is that you wish to become. Then draw a map. Back in the days of Blackbeard the Pirate, do you think he would've gone one day without a map as to where he hid his treasure. No way. In fact, he'd probably peruse around the coast of the eastern United States to look for interesting landmarks to set those maps in motion. In Georgetown, South Carolina it's been said that Blackbeard actually spent a lot of his time there. How true it is, I really don't think we'll ever know. However, we might be able to discover his many treasures if we had that map. Clearly defined by Blackbeard himself to illustrate what it'd take to find it. Does one exist? Only time will tell. But that's not what's important here. What is though is the fact that even people long ago detailed how they'd rise above their own mediocrity. Howbeit, by treasure or even by the invention of bifocals, we know that our lives are made better by a sudden rise from the depths of oneself into a meteoric and monumental giant. Made possible by desire and determination, people who have surpassed greatness show us that their excellence is just as obtainable. But where do we acquire such tenacity?

After many years of basketball within those walls of my University, I finally chose to leave and try working for a living. Whether it was by my own design or by being forced to leave really isn't relevant. I realized that if someone plays basketball with the professors and doesn't go to class, he excels in one area of Academia. By the score on a scoreboard I could've won every game, but ultimately I would've lost everything in my educational pursuit. What happened is my grade point average took a nosedive. In my first semester, I think I did well. Hey, a two point nine was better than average, right? Of course that was before basketball. As soon as I realized that professors do more than teach, my grade point average suffered. But you think I cared? For me, I was somehow comfortable within my own degree of mediocrity. So that is an affirmative, "No!" I didn't care. I should've, because who knows where a successful campaign within the college ranks would have led me. The only logical conclusion to my dilemma was how would I explain to my father my complete failure at this educational level? Here was a student who was probably closer to being a smart mouth than he was to being a smart man. In most cases parents pay for tuition. Some of these costs are offset by scholarships, and I know with absolute certainty that I would've never qualified for anything out of high school. So my father paid for everything. I think that was the major reason I found myself going to an in-state University . . . to save money. When my father saw with his own eyes that I brought a point six grade point average down from a two point nine, it wasn't a good day. He went absolutely nuts. There were never any chairs thrown or anything like that. Let's just say that he was so angry that he said to me, "Son, you're going to pay for your own school! I am not going to reward you for complete ignorance!" In my most coy way I smiled and quickly responded, "Hey dad, I just got put on the academic suspension list. So no one has to pay for anything." That wasn't something you want to say to make a situation better. He just shook his head and looked at my mother as if to say, "Woman, that's your son." My mother didn't say much except to say that I was again, the most complete picture of mediocrity she'd ever seen. I just took her word for it, because up to that point that's who I was.

Going through this adventure, I wanted to be something more. I guess you could say that I had delusions of grandeur. I was always thinking about things that other people were doing successful. My thought was that this just wasn't me. Guessing somewhat about the boat I'd dreamed about hadn't come in yet. Best friends were buying Mercedes' and others were buying sports cars that only a select few could own. I would think how would I ever be in the same social economical class these friends now enjoyed? There was never a depression factor because I really didn't want to be in that state of mind. It was closer to being an anxiety problem. No medicine was needed because all I wanted was answers to the questions I was asking myself.

Who am I? What are things in life that are most important to me? Am I going to be satisfied with this current progression of life? And what if my boat never comes in, what would I do? It was easier just to set under the star laden sky to consider what options I may have had. And never did I think about a romantic rendezvous with a woman. I knew I had nothing to offer. I was driving a late nineteen eighties Ford Taurus. Which I believe there is nothing wrong with. However, you just didn't want to pick up your date in that kind of car. My life was an utter disaster. A freight train bearing down on one of those Fiats stuck in the middle of the tracks, I felt about as small anyway. It was about a man who had grown out of his boyhood in the anatomical sense only. I needed answers because time moves faster the older I'd become. So where would I go to find them.

Some years went by, and I still felt as though my wheels were spinning needlessly. I spent my time thinking that I was an insurance salesman when in reality I just put on the tie on to look good. Impression to me was more productive than action.

If people saw something that looked successful, they'd probably assume as such. Every time I looked in the mirror, I wanted to throw up. The life I led was a complete farce. Then in an instant, I believe God spoke to me in a way that moved me. His word was not only part of my life; it gave me instant inspiration when I felt there was no apparent direction. Well then, what did I hear?

"Hey, if a man doesn't work, he doesn't eat." as loud as it could possibly be. I heard it as if he was there with me. And guess what? He was. But how did it speak to me personally? Well, I've always been large but since I wasn't playing as much basketball I'd become fat, or in nicer words . . . oversized. I thought possibly I'd go hungry. As infantile as it was, I wanted to do something about it. The decision was pretty easy. Either I would eat and be happy, or not eat and not be so happy. Then I sat down and started drawing my own treasure map. I took pieces of ordinary paper and eliminated all the obstacles. If something seemed like it'd be difficult, I didn't care. I'd survive. As I dabbled along this paper I realized one integral piece of information. That I needed motivation, and where would I garner enough courage to crack this eggshell of complacency? The discovery was quite amazing. I needed a quotation but I didn't want someone else's to define my life. So, what did I come up with? Well, late one night I was trying to get some sleep and it hit me like a ton of bricks. Bam! No more mediocrity.

I jumped out of the bed and said it where anyone who was in the house could have heard it, "If my boat doesn't come in, I'll swim out to it!" The realization was that as long as I was moving towards something positive, then something positive may move towards me. Reminding me of the story I'd learned when I was a child at Sunday school about Paul. This man had things in his past that could've paralyzed him. But he used them as motivation to move into a better relationship with his risen Lord, Jesus. God allowed him to look at his surroundings and cultivate an amazing life. I don't want to quote it directly because I don't want to mislead someone, so I'll just paraphrase. Never stop praying, and always be joyful. Be thankful in all circumstances. There it was. Laid out for me in clear black ink was the exact number of steps that I had to take. So I did what any man would do to remember, I drew my dotted line out on my personal treasure map. I knew that if I'd forget about the notions of mediocrity then I would experience personal growth like never before. Continue to do the same things that would net positive results became my motto. I wanted to be successful so this started out pretty easy.

For someone who may have had a similar occurrence there are a couple of serious notions that you must consider. The first thing you need to do is to make a treasure map of your own. Make sure that you've documented every step. Imagine if you have worked on this treasure map and you missed fourteen steps. You'll shovel yourself into oblivion, never knowing where the treasure was laid. Hey, you're only fourteen steps off the mark. But you're still off the plan, right? You'll sweat yourself to death and find a whole bunch of rocks and dirt, and quite possibly, ending up on the Cantonese side of China. None of which would bring you anything of wealth. Why not get it right the first time? If it's clear that you must walk fourteen paces, then walk fourteen paces. Maybe you have to turn right at the old oak tree. Follow the map to a tee and don't deviate from it. It's your key to escaping personal mediocrity.

Secondly, fix your thoughts on what is true, and honorable, and right, and pure, and lovely, and admirable. Think about things that are excellent. You've set priorities by allowing yourself to draw a map that will lead you to your own personal treasure. Now, it is just as important to keep your mind set on the prize. If you're always thinking that your next opportunity is never going to come, then it may never come. But if you set yourself in motion through a persistent mentality, you should be in prime position to accept that opportunity when it does come. There was something else that I chose to do. I'd maintain focus and never react in an erratic way. During Braves games, I'd watch Tommy Glavine pitch and I noticed that this tendency was unbelievably helpful for him. It didn't matter if he was down by six runs. He would still act as methodical as if he were up by six runs. By being noble and forthright you never know what kind of blessings may come your way. And if they don't, act as if they did. In that case, you just might find yourself walking into something that goes beyond anything you've ever imagined.

In essence, be ready for anything. Lightning could strike. Not literally but figuratively. Something that changes your life could literally be just around the next corner.

Learn to appreciate the time you're given. What do I mean by that? Well, I'm about to stumble upon my twenty something high school reunion. Those that are planning this event set up a web site to facilitate a most spectacular evening. On this site they prepared a link titled . . . In Memory of, so I clicked it, and started browsing around. Some of the people I knew died, but some I didn't. It was disheartening to see so many faces that I fell into somewhat of a sad state. A couple of these guys never saw their twenty fifth birthday. It was truly kind of depressing. But needless to say, I didn't delve into it too long. I moved on and realized that I must be thankful to be able to live every moment to the fullest. To know that God has given each one of us a talent or maybe even multiple talents to be used for his glory should give us all extreme confidence.

What about the fact that God gives an appointment to be with him one day? Everyone alive when their days are done will face our creator. Be appreciative of this time that he's given you. Never knowing when the talent or talents that he supplied you with may be deemed complete. The one thing it'll do is free your mind up so that you can strive for perfection with absolute absurdity. Almost a reckless abandon, so you may never see that mediocre lifestyle again. Kiss it goodbye. Never to be seen again. As if it was catapulted to the ends of the earth.

And finally, keep swimming. What do I mean by that? I was stuck in my own demise when I made a dramatic revelation. Swim out to the boat because that boat was never coming to shore. I looked at it this way. When Jesus began his ministry many people were healed. He'd teach and many people listened. His disciples were pursuing a better understanding of his ways. He spent a lot of time with these guys. And boy, did they ask a bunch of questions. They were given special gifts to heal so they could if needed. But Jesus would stop whenever he heard someone ask for him. You could say He loved them enough to ask something like, "What do you want from me?" And in their most fragile way, "I want to be healed." When Jesus was about to heal someone of their peril, he always asked them to do something. Numerous times he'd tell people, "Take your mat and go home." I look at this as a command. One that if I'd just follow God's lead. I too, could be healed. Yes, I would take my mat and go home. Which means that I must keep swimming, no matter what, I need to tread water long enough to wait for my boat to float right up next to me. I became the dock that it'd tie up to. So there you have it, you have to be definite in drawing a treasure map. Be appreciative for having this time to move past any trace of mediocrity. And then, keep swimming until you reach your own boat. By doing so in this fashion you will be in a positive position to adequately handle anything that life has to throw at you.

3.

Yeah, That'll Be A Table For One!

I WAS SINGLE AND FRIENDS TO FOUR PEOPLE OUTSIDE OF MY IMMEDIATE family. There were my best friend Robb, Brian, and my other best friend Tommy. All of us had someone join us later in our lives and his name was Marty. More on him later, but for now I'll let you in on a secret. I was about as single as a man could be.

A couple of years after I graduated high school my parents decided that they'd purchase a recreational vehicle. My mother was in this "I want to see the country from an RV" point of view. And my father was up to providing her with that point of view. I have to tell you that it was pretty funny to see my father climb up into this twenty eight foot home on wheels. Let me just say I know now where I get my extreme lack of patience. My sisters were ecstatic that they'd experience a new view of the open road mapped out ahead of them. So this mobile vacationing adventure would be just that to them. However for me, I'd experience this beast in a whole new light. It was Spring Break two years after we graduated. The boys and I were headed to Orlando, Florida with the top down if you will. We weren't prepared for what was about to happen. We left Augusta as fast as we could. I thought it'd be best if we went down Route one, but the others wanted to pass through the woods to the interstate. These small towns were plentiful as far as police cars go, and I didn't want to get caught. So even if we navigated through those towns, we'd do so with tremendous caution. As it is in most early summers, the sun was coming down to signify the end of the day. We'd have to put the visor down to make sure that the rays that were peeking through the trees wouldn't blind us. Those Georgia pines were lit up as bright as Christmas trees in the middle of December. The sunlight found its way upon our faces but it was never enough to hamper our pending vacation. We were loaded with fuel, and almost as loaded on fudge rounds and Slim Jims. There were enough beverages in the refrigerator to eradicate the thirst of a small army. Of which I thought we could be considered. I was a big boy, I say boy loosely because even though I was old enough to be a man, my mentality was that of a small boy who'd never been let out the house.

I was set on driving the entire way down to Disney. Directions were never a problem for me. I believe God gave me a great sense of direction. Lost was never a word I used. It was something that even if I was stuck in the middle of nowhere I was somehow going to make the right turn and find my way out of it. Think of it this way. Just keep making right turns until you find your way. This night began with the wildest of expectations. But as we turned off those country roads onto interstate two ninety five in Jacksonville we realized one thing. The inside of our cabin was lit in this darkness but the road was not. We decided to pull off the road and check it out. Here were three of the smartest dumb guys you've ever met in your entire life looking at each other saying, "I see the light in here, but I don't see it out here." Dim as it was, we believed that this would be okay to proceed because we thought it was lit enough to deter the police from pulling us over. None of us wanted a ticket. Especially from Florida's finest Highway Patrol, we liked the color of their cars but we didn't want to see it parked behind us with the lights on, if you know what I mean. Besides, we knew we were only a little more than an hour away from Daytona Beach. I was tired of driving so I asked if someone else could drive. No one wanted to drive because they'd never driven something so big. But as straws would have it, Marty drew the shortest. And that's where Robb and Marty began their dancing escapade on the front window, even while we were still driving.

Robb and I were always the funny ones in our group. So knowing that, you must think about making laughter first, right?

There's a bridge on two ninety five that spans somewhere close to three miles, I think. The Saint John's River carves its banks through Jacksonville and even further southward towards Orlando. This bridge ensures safe passage for millions of passengers each year. It was somewhere around ten o'clock at night so it was really dark. But this particular night it seemed to be darker than most. And a slight steady wind was blowing in from the east. All of us could feel the camper being tossed around. Marty was already whiter than white but he started turning to a paler shade of white. There was white and then there was his color white. The only difference was this big old boy had round rosy cheeks to let everyone know that he was scared to death. Robb and I started laughing. Maybe we laughed because we thought he wasn't serious. We thought maybe he was joking. Here was a six foot one three hundred plus pound man driven almost to point of tears because we were going over this little old bridge.

That camper hit the beginning of the bridge with a horrendous thump. I was ready as if I'd never been before. To make things worse, fog began rolling sideways where it was hard to see the side of the bridge. You've got to know that fear was being magnified because back then it was a two lane bridge. And this is where we trusted a novice Ford Tempo driving mama's boy to make it across the river. Robb and I were taking things in stride. Swaying from side to side we were acting as if we had done this before. That's when my best friend Robb got a wild and crazy idea. Let me let you in on another secret, it is never a good thing when Robb gets a wild idea. It might be funny, but I guarantee you, it isn't going to be good. I saw him get up and move to the back of the camper as close as he could get to the bed without jumping in it. He started running towards the window, and leaped sideways catching himself between the dash and the window. He started screaming, "We're gonna to die! O Lord Jesus save us all, we're gonna die on this bridge tonight. Help me! Help me!" Because I knew what he was going to do, I wasn't scared at all. But the boy in the driver's seat was about to pee his pants. He started yelling back, "Get off there, I can't see a thing!" I tossed Robb the flashlight and told him to light the road for Mr. PeePee pants over here. We both started laughing but

Marty wasn't having a good time at all. He said that if we didn't stop, he was going to pull over and we'd have to drive the rest of the way. Neither Robb nor I wanted to do this again so we'd try to remain quiet so he could complete his part of the driving bit. Robb handed me the flashlight and said for me to stay on one side of the camper. Then he did it again, landing squarely on the window and flapping around like a fish stuck in between a window and the dash. The end was near for this bridge and Marty knew it. He looked at us and said, "I can see houses so I think we're near the end." I knew we were but I wasn't about to say anything because Robb had already caused this man child to soil his only pair of pants. And low and behold, just like he said he would, he pulled over on San Jose Boulevard and yelled, "You guys want to play, play with one of you guys driving then." I told Robb that I'd driven most of the way down here and I wasn't going to drive until the next day.

Robb was like me, he was okay with whatever. He jumped up in the driver's seat and started to crank up the camper. Marty went back to the back to call his mama. That's when we really started to laugh. We couldn't believe that this mammoth of a man would want to talk to his mommy at this moment. But truthfully though, we tried to be nice. It's funny to us that to this day we still call this event, Death Bridge Eighty Nine.

Without incident we made our way to Daytona and stayed at the Marriott there. Yes, I know we had this big camper to sleep in, but I was a big comfy bed kind of guy. We even tried to stop at a gas station and drop the camper off to see if we could get it fixed. But we weren't fortunate enough as for them to fix it then. So for the night, we'd try and relax to forget about the day.

In Daytona, it was senior week so there were a lot of people there. Some of which I knew from home. We perused the boardwalk for most of the night daring each other to do that bungee cord thingy. I chickened out by telling them I thought I was too big and for sure that cord wouldn't support a big old boy like me. There were a lot of people drinking out there so it was pretty loud. And I was beginning to feel the results of the long drive. So I excused myself to the confines of my bedroom.

Trying to sleep that night, Robb and Marty came in after walking down the boardwalk. Wine coolers in hand, how they got them don't ask me, because all of us were too young, but they did. Robb was still picking on Marty for the camper comedy act he pulled earlier in the trip. Then out of nowhere, Marty stood up and put his hands in Robb's chest and started yelling, "Let me tell you something, you keep doing that, I'm going to make sure that it stops. I'm tired of it. All I want to do is call someone to come pick me up." Let me just say that Marty had no idea that Robb was carrying a package that didn't need to be opened. But he stood there with his overbearing frame thinking he could take Robb who stood a little over five nine. That package, I believe would've been unleashed had I not been there. You see, Robb was a state champion martial artist and I know with certainty that Marty would've been pummeled beyond any confidence he may have garnered while poking Robb in the chest. It would've been fun to see, but I chose the side of peace and told them, albeit from the other side of the room, "Ladies, why don't ya'll stop that because Marty, I don't think you want to do what you're thinking about doing. It might be the last time you do it. Robb, hey man, just let him call his mama." Marty was calling everyone he could to pick him up, shoot, even his distant cousin Jake, but ultimately we told him that we'd behave so he decided to stay. Needless to say, Robb slept on the other side of room from Marty for the duration of the trip. It's almost as if I had to sleep with one eye open to see if either one of them decided to beat the other one while he didn't expect it. An adventuresome night I'd say for sure.

Waking up to the sun blazing through the curtains, it was another day to tackle the problems we had with the motor home. I thought it was the battery. So after our talking about it for several hours, we decided to stop at the next gas station that we saw. As funny as we thought we were, the man sitting on the chair at this station would take the funny man prize. We drove up into the driveway and he didn't even stand up. We all rolled out and walked over to him. Robb asked, "Hey man, you got a battery you could sell us?" I started smiling as this man was laid back on this chair leaning up against a wall of batteries. He spit through the gap in his teeth and told Robb, "Main, I ain't authrized to sell no battries." My smile never left my face when I said, "Then wouldn't it make sense to get someone who is authorized?" He didn't move. His response was such that it looked as though he'd sit in that chair for the rest of the day, and to me, for the rest of the night. I bet if he'd stood up there'd be an indention of his butt cheeks embedded in the chair. Nonetheless, he never stood up to show us.

Back in those days Wal-Mart wasn't as visible as they are today. So getting a battery quickly was something of a problem, I think in part because we were in the middle of the country. Robb wasn't happy, and Marty was still talking to his mama on the phone. I'm just kidding, but it did seem like he talked to her an awful lot after Death Bridge. I guess it was important to call mama if you soiled your pants two times in less than an hour. I really am just kidding. He didn't do anything like this, it just kind of seemed that way.

Darkness began to fall and we knew that we'd have to at least get batteries for the flashlights. If we couldn't get one for the camper, we'd try our luck with the flashlights. A short hop over from Daytona, it's only about forty seven miles. So, we loaded up and started driving. Marty and Robb holding both flashlights to light the road, I think their arms were getting tired. Just by the looks of it anyway. And we only had ten miles or so to go. And we made it without one policeman pulling us over. That was a good thing. Especially when we didn't have any extra cash for unforeseen occurrences such as getting tickets for speeding or whatever the officer deemed appropriate.

Bent for Disney we finally made it. It was only the second or third time that I'd set up the camper so we crawled out to try and figure that thing out. We set the stabilizer and made sure the power was connected. We all felt that we were missing something but that's where we all heard the sounds of Space Mountain calling us from the distance. Changing in a flash, we set out for the park. Riding as many rides as we could before the sun would come down. The day wasn't going to hold us hostage. Suppertime was rearing his head and screaming loud boisterous chants to eat. Of course, with me and Marty, it was always time to eat. I was truly a hungry man when I was younger. We looked for a place that was good for everybody. This diner we all agreed on was right next to Frontier land, and while we were looking up at the menu, Robb was busying trying to find us some dates. This is where my being stupid single surpassed all normal understanding.

Robb was one of those guys who had the gift of gab when it came to talking to women and almost all the time, they'd be quite receptive. Me, on the other hand was more of the hit man type. I'm very observant about everything that happens. Whether if it is a napkin that falls on the floor in the right corner of the room, or if someone is drinking from a Mickey cup, I'd be the one in the group who notices. I may seem uninterested but really I am just aware of my absolute surroundings. Robb was over by the ketchup and mustard dispensers talking to some girls from Vanderbilt University, at least that's what I presumed because of the shirts they were wearing. They began moving towards us and I heard Robb introduce us as I looked at him, with bewilderment. Now remember that I was a single man who really didn't have many girlfriends in my life so it was hard for me to tell if someone liked me. Robb lifted his hands and was like, "Hey man, these nice ladies want to join us later on tonight!" In my most sincere expression of single Dom, I said to him with complete obliviousness, "There's nothing to eat here." He was blown away as he dropped his head and nodded, "What!" The girls thought I may have said something about them so their interest died almost instantaneously. I was still unaware of anything that I said because I was still preoccupied with the menu.

Robb has never been more upset at his best friend than at that moment. Here were a trio of beautiful college girls who were going to come over and hang out with us and Mr. Me decided he didn't see anything there to eat. You know, there's a saying somewhere that says, 'The best way to man's heart is through his stomach." I think I was more interested in the hamburgers and fries than I was with those girls from Nashville. However, I was informed that if I wanted to be something more than just single for the rest of my life, I'd have to shut up and let Robb do the talking. He wasn't forceful or anything like that, but he did let me know that these girls were in the palm of his hand. And now they'd flown the coup because of what I said.

I thought being single was probably where I'd stay. Because of this kind of unawareness, I was creating such a formidable wall to climb when it came to meeting someone of the opposite sex. Call it what you want, I called it fear. Maybe it was the constant rejection that I served notice to myself that I'd be okay with being single. How would I ever make a decision that talking to someone didn't mean that you had to marry them? I was that guy who really didn't want to get involved unless I knew it was safe. Safe for me and for her, my thoughts were that I wouldn't want to involve someone into my objective point of view. The desires I had were stable. My core values were not going to change, and I wouldn't change for anyone. Don't get me wrong, I wasn't a tyrant but if a woman would date me, they'd know that they were special. Being a fan of the love movies I guess you could say that I was building my ultimate plot point except I was in the middle of a massive writer's block. Every time I felt that I was getting close to someone I dove right in to make sure that my movie mirrored something out of romance novel.

When in reality, this never happens, and I mean never. People try to recreate romance and find that it may work for you but it doesn't work for the other. What happens in that instance is that you have a woman walking faster away from you than you could ever run to her. A creation of the perfect little dream relationship within the realm of your own mind when again, in reality you've found the thing that drives you apart. Does one ever recover from a bad relationship? Sure they do, but how? They change what they think about that "couple" word. Transforming couple based statements into the one and only, "single" statements. "I am single and proud of it." You will hear those words more than others. Justifying to themselves that they are and will be always happy being single, it's a façade used to create a boundary between a wounded heart and a strong will. Possibly even confirmation that a man who is single may be happy being single, however he may also be covering the shame he feels because of the desire to be loved in that relational sense by a woman other than his mama. He wants to feel the love, and give it too. Rather than slipping into depression he or she may choose to think something else about being in a relationship. And by their doing such, they'd be generating a confidence in establishing themselves as a single person.

Why is being single a pertinent step in personal development? It is simple to illustrate. How would one know the things that they like personally? Or how about the way they react to a situation? I really was okay with being single. Being honest though, maybe even that's a lie. I'll offer you another story for example's sake.

It has got to be that my confidence was so shaken that I'd give someone the three strikes rule. What is that? Well, I'd ask a girl out, and they'd waffle around and not be specific about their intentions. I was alright with this because my patience would allow me to wait at least two seconds. If I was told no, I'd leave as if I didn't hear anything so that it wouldn't hurt so much. After a couple of days, I'd gather my thoughts so that my feelings weren't shown and I'd ask her again. Still the same result, I'd wait again for a couple more days. Then that was it, I didn't care if she was the one to walk up to me and want to go out, I wouldn't give in. So many times, I'd invoke the rule and it was evident that my heart was strong. I hated rejection even though it looked as though I was solid as a rock.

There must be something about a woman having the ultimate power to say "Yes" or "No" to a man who is an inch away from begging her for a date. Sometimes the women that I'd asked out but were well pass the third strike would come up to me and ask if I was free. Let me just say that I was never mean when I'd say "No." But I did it, sometimes with regret. I wouldn't let my rule be broken. Three strikes and that's it.

There was one day when I was in a local Bank of America and there was a beautiful blond hair hazel eyed woman. This point in my life I was ready to date . . . so I thought anyway. Robb had just met the woman who would become his wife, and this woman was my bank teller's friend from childhood. Robb's future wife Mandy told me she was already dating an officer from the South Carolina Highway Patrol. I was one of those that if I needed to garner confidence, I would. This day wasn't any different. I pranced up to the counter and asked her if dinner and maybe a movie would be a viable option for her. She said she wasn't sure but she'd let me know something tomorrow. So I did the best thing I could . . . wait for tomorrow. The next day around three o'clock I walked in to see her but she left sick for the day. I was kind of upset to say the least because when a man builds up the courage, he wants to get it over with as soon as possible. But I wouldn't be deterred from asking again. Remember now that I viewed this to be the second strike. And being on Friday, I knew I'd have to wait until Monday to ask her out. The whole weekend I'd talk to Robb and his future wife to see if she was even interested. Robb's fiancé thought it'd be best if I just forgot about this one particular girl. But here was stubborn old Chuck looking to conquer another fear.

I did what any red blooded man would do if given the opportunity. I went in Monday about Noon. She looked at me with a look of wonder, and I was ready to hear anything. The counter where she worked felt as though it was a million miles away. And her greeting was appropriate for a professional relationship. "Well" I said inquisitively. Her reply was not as positive as I would've liked. But I still think she was cordial enough. She whispered, "I . . . I mean . . . Well . . ." Sensing some uncertainty in her voice, I told her it was okay if she said, "No." I was relieved to hear the words, "It's not that . . . It's . . ." Trying to cover some of my insecurity I retorted, "You know if you say No now, I could be in L.A. by ten." Immediately she said, "It isn't that, I think I am beginning to see someone else." I played off the fact that he was a lucky man. And I was okay with him having this wonderful opportunity. So here I was, left to My Delta and being single. I say Delta because I worked for the airline as an operations agent. So being was something I was truly okay with, really, well, maybe I wasn't. But let me just say that if you are sulking in your own sense of singleness, the Los Angeles Lakers can sooth that loneliness. I did make it to L.A. is what I'm trying to say. And hey, even with a smile on my face.

The funny thing that happened with this girl was that Robb and his fiancé would get married within the year and we were both part of the Wedding Party. I was the best man and she was the Maid of Honor as fate would have it. All the way through the Wedding I'd just smile and make small chatter. Robb's father even made a comment that she and I would make a good couple. I just laughed, not at him but at what was being said. Needless to say the reception was a rolling adventure. I asked her to dance and I was pleased to say that she said, "Yes." But that was it, small chatter just to pass the time and nothing more, I guess.

Then after the reception, I was kind enough to walk her to her car. And she asked me, "What are you doing tonight?" Quickly I told her, "Nothing much except going home to sleep. I need to be at work at four." Puzzled is the emotion that I'd clarify at that moment for her. Nonetheless, she went her way and I went mine.

I still had Robb's Tux so I wanted to see him off before they left for the honeymoon. I walked up to him and said, "Guess what just happened to me?" Without hesitation he asked, "What?" To define my state of mind, I'd say that I was probably shocked. I said, "Our girl just asked me what I was doing, and I told her I was going home to sleep." Mandy about jumped over the car to ask me what I said. "Well, are you guys going out?" I turned to her and mulled it over for a second before I answered, "Nope, third strike, remember?"

Robb emerged from the back seat to tell me one thing, "You know she was asking you out don't you?" I was this naïve man who really couldn't pick up on these kinds of things so it was nice to have a friend who could notice when a girl is trying to suggest something. Emotionally I was set, I didn't react positively or negatively. Rather I chose to remain neutral. "She was?" is what came barreling out my mouth. Robb looked at Mandy and nodded. "Coochie Man, you did the right thing." You see Robb told me that going out with this girl was like going through a torture chamber. She'd use me and then when she was finished, she'd throw me away to the dogs. Believe me, I'd been there, done that. So, I didn't want to travel the same path I'd been so many times before. Guess you could say that I wasn't going to be taken advantage of anymore from anybody. Robb had a way of always protecting me whether it was my heart or my body. So, I guess that's why he was so adamant about me not going out with Mandy's friend. Ultimately I would've been lambasted with a woman who really didn't care if I lived or died. And that is why to this day I still love my best friend. It's rare that someone gets to keeps his friends throughout his lifetime. But I've been blessed to have the same friends I had since childhood.

I waited a couple of months before I thought about asking anyone else to dinner. I concentrated my efforts on flying mostly. I had a wonderful schedule where I was off four days a week. It made flying off to Europe a breeze. I could leave on Saturday night on the five o'clock and make it there by mid-morning. The thing about being single was that I had absolutely no tie downs. There were extreme positives to this type of lifestyle. You'd just flip a coin to pick where you going, and the next day you'd be off to where it landed on the map. There was an acquaintance of mine who was living in Nashville. And I was supposed to go up there and work with him and his buddies on writing some music.

There I am sitting in the Atlanta airport and the Nashville flights were filling up. If you know anything about non-revenue travel but an employee can only fly free whenever there's a seat available. No seat, no free fly is how I looked at it. There was the list to all of those Nashville flights and I was somewhere in the middle. I was sure that my name wouldn't be called for Nashville that day at least. I called the friend up and told him that the coin I just flipped landed on Shannon, Ireland. Rather than going to Nashville, I'd be going to see where they had filmed Braveheart in Ireland. I cannot say if Wicklow or Lake Blasingale was prettier than anything I would've seen in Nashville. I just think it was different. Surely it was greener. The greenest greens I'd ever seen. And now, I wasn't going to limit myself to a specific time to spend on any such landmark. I'd try and spend as little time on each one to maximize my trip. What is being single do for a man in an International country? It allows him to browse through at his own pace. He doesn't have to stop and trivialize every rock. It may sound as if I am complaining about being single. But truly, I loved it. I could talk freely with girls in International countries and learn about their cultures and how they lived it. Somehow

I wasn't as bashful when I knew there were thousands of miles between me and the closest relationship.

In actuality after I left Dublin, we had to make a flag stop in Shannon to pick up more passengers. That was just the way Delta would do this particular route to Ireland. We deplaned to give the ground crew long enough to load cargo and other things such as fuel. I sat down next to a pretty little Irish girl. She began to talk to me. "Are you from here?" That was funny to me so I started to smile. "No, I am just on my way back home to the states." Later in our conversation she told me she was from a town outside of Wicklow. I was intrigued how people live with those single lane winding roads. I think I made her laugh because she smiled as if she knew exactly why I asked her this question. "We just drive ya noa, pull ya caar ova, and just drive dowan de road." in her most prolific Irish accent. I didn't know if it was okay to tell people that I came to Ireland just to see the place where Braveheart was filmed but I did anyway. Her eyebrows reached to the heavens with excitement as she wanted to talk over me rather than waiting for me to finish, "My fathaa brought de horses dowan for de battle scene ya noa." That to me was exciting but at that moment I was called to board. I told her that I had to go. She was sitting in the back, but because I was an employee and there was a seat available in Business Elite. Well, you know where I sat. So I told her that it was a pleasure to meet her and I boarded my plane. That experience let me know that I could talk to women if I wanted to. No fear of rejection there, huh?

I got to talk to lot of people in those days. I traveled every week to a different country. Growing up we were blessed enough to see the entire eastern seaboard but I'd never been to Europe before I started working at Delta. So this was a benefit that I was using and using with absurd frequency.

The only single man in my family meant that Christmas was always a blatant reminder I was single. What does a man do when he feels like he is the odd man out in the midst of couples? I left. I wanted to make sure that I wouldn't be there when the couples began to celebrate. Even though Christmas time was a good time of year I didn't want to be around if I was the only one that wouldn't have a counterpart to share it with. It was Christmas 2004, a brisk cold winter as I can remember. We were never used to snow these times of the year and this time was no different. There was weather forecasted and rain would be the norm for the next couple of days. I knew it was getting close to the time when most people would get together with their families. So I started planning where I'd go next.

The twenty fifth was just around the corner. The flights on holidays are always light so I wanted to act fast. I went to my mother's house and exchanged gifts on Christmas Eve. I knew I wouldn't be there the next day, so I left other gifts for my extended family. And then I went to the Augusta airport to leave. I was going to fly to Stuttgart Germany and spend Christmas day there, and take a hopper from there. They have a low cost carrier called German Wings that took me from there to Prague. Because ultimately this is where I was headed, I knew I had to take something out of Stuttgart but it worked out because I thought I was going to have to go through Frankfurt in order to get to Prague anyway. It was rather funny because when I first saw the billboard advertisement for German Wings, I thought it was just a different flavor of Buffalo wings. It was funny enough to run their operation like they were Southwest, except we did not get any chicken wings on our flight.

The flight had no incidents. And as we began to descend below the clouds the turbulence was normal. Not too bad, not too good, it was just okay. I was trying to see the city but it was overcast so I really couldn't see a thing. The wheels screeched and we firmly landed. After the entry process I made sure that I'd have sufficient money for a taxi. And not just money but their type of money; bank machines are a miracle when it comes to currency exchange. Stick your card in and boom! A hand full of cash in whatever the currency is for that country. Summoned by a taxi driver to take his taxi, I was pleasantly surprised when I climbed into a Mercedes. Over here in the states, we consider these types of automobiles to be luxury automobiles. There, they are taxis.

Whenever I'd arrive at a city that I'd never been before I'd always be amazed at the difference in the styles of architecture, and Prague wasn't any different. My eyes were locked upon the buildings that lined the streets on the way to the Hilton downtown. My language skills were nothing more than an occasional thank you or maybe a hello here and there. But most of the bigger hotels like the Hiltons, the Westins and the Sheratons were English friendly so I was safe. In those days I was a high level member in Hilton Honor's program so I when I checked in to hotels I was allowed to go the "Special Member's Desk." I wasn't prepared for the room they gave me. Being able to upgrade, I thought I'd be allocated to a one class room upgrade. I was given the center room facing the Charles Bridge and the Prague Castle. And this is where I'll tell you that the thoughts of having someone to love hit me hard. I saw those purple lights reflecting off the castle walls. And the bluish purplish lights reflecting off the Cathedral. It was stunningly beautiful. I remember telling myself, "Man, you need a woman to share this one with!" And I meant it at that moment too.

Before that, I was comfortable seeing romantic things by myself. But it must've been something about seeing the Castle and the Cathedral sitting atop that hill with the Vltava River flowing down below that ignited the embers of the romantic fires within me. My imagination ran wild. I'd plan out in my mind how maybe one day I'd have a moment to share with the love of my life in places such as these. But that night I knew the vision I saw wasn't happening anytime soon.

Totally exhausted from the flight over, I chose to shut the curtains and go to sleep. Tomorrow I'd tour the city. The plan was to stay there for two nights. I don't know what it is about curtains in hotels but on most of the ones I stayed at in Europe. The sun would slip through the tiny crack and seem as though it was sawing it in half. Only to wake me up at the break of dawn, and I was ready for the town. So all day long I walked through the city and learned different things about that 1300 year old Cathedral that amazed me. How the Charles Bridge got its name, and many other things I took in as if I were a sponge. I noticed an authentic Italian place on the side of the road and it was some place that I knew I wanted to eat that night. I believe it was named Don Corleone. I guess I was worn out from all the walking because I didn't want to go there as the day drew more to a close.

I went back to the hotel and asked the concierge, "How much is it to ride the dinner cruise on the Vltava River?" He started looking past me to see if I had anyone with me. "Sir, that is two person dinner table, who will be dining with you?" with an obviously perplexed expression. And me being the smarty pants I am, "Well, then, tell them to take one side off the table and set it for one." He wasn't amused. This man took his job serious. "I do not tink dat is possible, sir." in a semi forceful Czech tone. I wasn't about to get embarrassed because there were people now gathering behind me. As I thanked him, I also whispered that I'd talk to him later about the boat thingy.

In the elevator on the way up to my room, I remember asking the Lord, "Why can't I have someone to share a nice dinner with?" Most people that follow him know how he'll answer that one too. "Son, you know that's what you wanted. But as for your question, your time hasn't come yet." as if he were standing right beside me with a megaphone blistering my ear drum. The door opens and here is a family that is on their way out. Discerning that the Lord was trying to show me something, "Be sure you know what you want before you open your mouth!" I started to laugh at the fact that I knew he was right because he's always right.

The door of the elevator closed and I was speed walking down the hall. I couldn't wait to get into my room. That view was intoxicating. I'd saved my appetite for the boat that night so to say I was hungry is an understatement. But the concierge downstairs ruined that idea. I opened the door and the phone started to ring. "Ting!" like a light bulb was levitating over my brown spiked hair, I had an idea. When I was walking through the city I remember seeing advertisements for an escort service. But there was a problem with that idea. I was a Christian and didn't want a sexual encounter. All I wanted for the evening was companionship. Next I answered the chiming phone and I was greeted cheerfully from the "Special Member's Desk" to make sure that I had everything I needed. Mentally bruised from the concierge, I told her I was okay with just the chocolates they left on my pillow.

Hanging up, I grabbed the telephone book to look for different numbers. I started at E for Escort Service. When I came across an ad that I liked, I started dialing. I was surprised to hear a woman's voice on the other end. "Hello how can help you?" she asked me. I told her that I was a Christian and I wasn't interested in a sexual adventure. But rather I wanted to have someone join me for a dinner cruise on the Vltava River. She wasn't impressed. "How much is an escort for about an hour or two?" I continued. Without wavering she spoke in a soft but genuine accent, "That will be two hundred American dollars." My mouth dropped to the ground because I didn't expect it to be so high. "Listen, I don't want to have any kind of physical contact, I just want to go out to dinner." I concluded with absolute certainty. She almost laughed at me on the phone. You know when you can hear someone's voice change as if they're about to laugh. This is what I heard. She sneered, "I tell you what, you pay two hundred American dollars, and you can do whatever you want with her or to her!" Let me just say that I was very nice to her as I quickly hung up the phone.

I learned another lesson that day. Once again, I was naïve enough to think that this truly was an escort service. When an ad says that I can have a knowledgeable woman who knows the city accompany me as a guide of sorts, I thought it could be just that. She and I enjoying dinner, and not have any expectations for a sexual encounter. The reality was that this just wasn't going to happen. I can tell you one thing though. That club sandwich I ate at the hotel that night was awesomely Devine. Granted it wasn't a dinner cruise on the Vltava but I did have a bird's eye view of an incredibly beautiful city.

I would have to say that lessons were being learned all over the place. Before this trip I was intent on being a single man living my life in the air. Happy as a lark perched aboard the wings of my Delta Air Lines, I'd rather travel than settle down. But it worked for me and I didn't try and push my lifestyle on anyone else. That's when I decided that each person must decide what is best for them.

But what do I mean by that statement? If a man is entirely comfortable being single then leave him alone. However, if a man decides that he should find a mate. That too should be okay. In fact, it is biblical. It is said in Proverbs chapter eighteen verse twenty two . . . The man who finds a wife finds a treasure, and he receives favor from the Lord. Even Adam was alone for a while. But we have great power to be in the position that we are in. That position of choice where we can decide if single Dom is the place we really want to dwell.

One needs to be certain. One needs to be absolute. Never wavering about the decision, because if the wrong one is made it could turn out horrific for the other person involved. Think about this. They've given their entire being to you and the relationship you have with them. So, choose now to be single or choose now to be a couple. Either way, single or a couple, be certain. A single man can have multiple options at his disposal but not have anyone to share his options with. On the other hand, a man who chooses to couple with someone may have limited options but a plethora of opportunities for development within his own love life. So actually, what is being said here?

I was content being who I was as a single person. I think maybe because I had the ability to fly around the world for free. Who knows where it would've taken me had I not had Delta? Paying for tickets would have severely changed the variables. I can't say that there weren't times when I thought about having a family. As a matter of fact, there were times when I would go see my nephew play baseball and the cinders of desire for a relationship would flicker. But I realized that seeing all of these people that I went to high school with and their kids didn't mean that I had to be depressed. What could a man be depressed about when he is at the center of the diamond watching one of his favorite sports? This is about the only time in the states that I'd think about being single. So what did I do about it? I left and did something else too. I started thinking about the things that I do have. Rather than thinking about things that I didn't. I knew that my release was the flying. Whenever the thought would come that I didn't have a child that I could teach the game of baseball or basketball to, I'd reclaim focus and board a plane to the vast lands of Europe.

By midday the next day I was so shocked that I was able to fly free, and oh, did I mention, I could eat free too? Maybe that's why I am still overweight to this day. You know how much starches are in airplane food? These thoughts or maybe even desires for having a family would float away as if they were a sailboat that disappears into the horizon. I felt more and more relieved the higher the plane got off the ground. I always feel at thirty three thousand feet in the air as though I am the only one up there. Just me and God, I am free and free at last. Free to do whatever. Whereas those people at the baseball field were not. Not one of those people in the bleachers could be where I was that day. Maybe they could monetarily but not physically. Limited by only time and money, I was on God's good graces. Whereas they were limited by their responsibility to their family, they weren't allowed to take off anywhere but to work the next day. And so I didn't want people to see me waffle between being alone and being single. One is destructive, and one is liberating.

What I wanted to do was to be absolutely sure I was ready for a relationship. Most people refer to the "Sowing my Wild Oats" philosophy when they go through this type of transition in life. I can't say that I had wild oats to sow because being a Christian meant I define wild a little differently. I went wild in other areas. Because at that present time I'd much rather be in the air. To me, the best thing I did was pen some things down to remind myself that I was okay with being single. And then I'd scribble side notes that would provide me adequate motivation for when the time was right to find my special someone.

I knew that when I was ready I wanted to have something impressive to bring to my relationship. I didn't want to have any lingering reflections upon my single life when I landed safely within the arms of a woman. What does that mean for the single man? Make sure that when you fall in love, you fall in love with the idea of having something to present to that relationship. It is good to never on purpose remember anything about the single life. You should provide the love of your life everything they need.

Not want, everything they need. There is a difference you know. I can tell you that when I examined myself. Pieces of paper had become notebooks, and scribing what I thought I could bring to a relationship became a habitual occurrence. I didn't care if it was attainable, true or not. I wrote it down. I'd worry about the details later. I didn't limit it to a specific time frame, believing this to be really important. A couple of days later I would dot a few more things down. Somehow I knew the next stage of my life would be relegated to pursuing a relationship that would create an equilibrium shared between myself and the one I was pursuing.

So there you have it. The most pertinent obstacle that one must overcome is oneself. My best friend Robb used to tell me, "The only limitations that you have are the ones you give yourself." You may or may not decide that being single is the way for you. So, here at your fingertips is the future. Keep in mind that you have the ultimate power to shape your destiny. And given that power you can either share your destiny or horde it for yourself. This chapter was all about me being content with my being single. I would have to say that it was also about my wanting to share my moments whether they were romantic or even trivial. Truth is there were crossroads that I vectored around in the Czech Republic. It was then that I decided to chase something more than single Dom. And finally by doing so, I was given the prospect of defining what I could bring to a relationship. In the course of it all, I intricately discovered that in my life, it really doesn't have to be a table for one.

4.

The Covered Dish Delight . . . And What Do I Bring?

Most Southern Baptist churches have services on Sunday mornings, Sunday evenings, and even on Wednesday nights. My mother always made us go to prayer meetings then. And she made sure that my brother Tony and I were in RAs, short for Royal Ambassadors every week. And that, being a biblical learning class for male students. Sunday though was the most important. So if we were brave enough to try and skip out on Wednesday there'd be no way we'd ever miss Sunday morning. She'd make sure she had one eye on me and Tony, and the other on the pastor.

We lived nearby so the walk to church was almost effortless; sometimes I was even sidetracked by people playing on the softball field. And you know how kids are. Wherever there was a ball being thrown, most of the time they want to dive right in. Knowing this, my mother would clock us to make sure that we'd make it to church on time. It made it difficult because there were playgrounds from an elementary school across the street. And I don't know if you were anything like me but if someone was outside playing, it was hard for me to concentrate on what was going on inside. What I'm trying to say is that I think I had Attention Deficit Disorder before it was ever called Attention Deficit Disorder. Not so much a wild and uncontrollable child but rather one that couldn't focus for an extended amount of time.

Although, I did believe that I was a normal child for a boy my age.

In the pew of the church I would hear the preacher say those big old fifty cent words, I tried to listen but eventually I'd just doze off. Especially when he'd have those extensive prayers I'd find myself slithering down between my mother and the cushion. Then lightning would strike at what I thought to be fire and brimstone but rather it was my mother's two fingers coming together with thunderous fashion to pinch me right in the tender part of my underarm. I really didn't think I was that loud when I exclaimed, "Owl!" But from the sound of it and the looks of the people turning around staring at me, it must have. They were glaring at me as if I'd bellowed from the depths. And all I was doing was trying to rest. They should've been staring at my mother because she was the one who started this whole deal. I'm just kidding. She was only doing what God gave her the ability to do, being a stern and instructive mom. Needless to say, I got the message. Sometimes I feel as though I still have that whelp on the side of my arm. Oh, it doesn't hurt anymore so I think I'm going to be okay.

The older I got the better I listened to the pastor. Those fifty cent words became more than just change to me. I began to actually know what they meant. As a child, I always wondered why someone who was trying to preach the gospel would use words that were so hard to understand, much less try and pronounce. But with age comes wisdom as they say. Now when a pastor says something about the vernacular, I actually know what this means. I guess I'd owe them gigantic appreciations because had I not heard these words I don't think I'd actually know what most of them mean today. Maturity is a good thing in the Lord's house.

The funny thing about those services was that sleeping wasn't relegated towards us younger chaps. There were the cigarette smokers as I called them that would drift off into the slobber lane. Why do I call it the slobber lane? Imagine a middle aged man who had just finished his shift at the plant and while in church, he'd doze off for a minute or two. Just long enough to have the slobber hit him right in the hand, he'd almost fall over in order to guarantee no one sees him. But guess what? Here I was, Mr. Lookin-at-Everybody sitting patiently, staring at him, and just waiting for him to fall flat on his face. I never understood why older people wait until the preacher started preaching before they'd fall asleep. Let me just say that I've never been directly or indirectly part of shift work so I can't say that I would understand what these guys actually go through. So I tried not to be so judgmental when I was told by my father the kind of job that these people had. Trying to be funny though, I'd always create a stream of slobber trying to immolate these guys. Neither of my parents thought it was funny, but Tony would. So, I would joke a little to make him laugh then I could get back to what we came for, good Southern Baptist preaching.

I was never involved in any other denominations so I'm not aware of the activities that they'd have. But In my church though, we'd have business meetings every quarter or so to vote on issues or activities that would arise during the year. Sometimes these would become pretty heated. Deacons who were supposed to be nice and ordinate were not so. Arguing over such trivial things that still to this day, I remember their facial expressions. However, I don't think that it was traumatic enough to wound me forever though. You'd think that these people were Scotch Irish the way that the color of their faces turned red. I thought this was the time when Jesus went somewhere else to church.

Not really understanding the workings of this type of meeting, I'd try and do something else because it got loud. One meeting in particular became the reason why I won't go to these meetings to this day. It was as if the Hatfield's and McCoy's reignited their age old feud. One side of the church was the "Nay" crowd and the other side was amazingly the "Yay" crowd. A proverbial line separated them as if it was one of those football sidelines chalked right through the middle of the church. As if Rodney King himself was in the back yelling, "Why can't we all just get along?" People were shouting things that must've sounded like our church was splitting apart at the seams. The thing that was driving some crazy had something to do with the kids in our youth group. Some of them weren't fortunate enough to pay the full fee needed for youth camp. And it actually blew my mind that here was a bunch of Christians yelling at each other and it seemed, even at me. They definitively weren't acting as Christ would. I know money is hard to come by but these "Nay" say people need to know that there are some who've been blessed. And to horde God's gifts isn't good. Some parents thought that some kids didn't deserve to go to camp if they haven't paid. "They'd enjoy it more if they paid their own way." is one of the things I heard coming from the back of the church. You'd hear the other side in animated fashion, "So what if these kids don't pay, will they not experience the same Jesus either way!" I wanted to stand up and tell them both that I was getting a headache listening to their constant ranting. Among the confusion I remembered a verse that I learned as a three year old child so I stood up and asked if I could say something.

Bashful but affirmatively, "Do not let any unwholesome words come out of your mouth, but only what is helpful for building up others; that it may benefit those who listen." Judging from the way these guys were gawking at me I thought maybe I'd overstepped my bounds. None of them were happy that I almost single-handedly called them out. So having the "Go for the Jugular Vein" mentality I continued, "Here in this church we have people who are visiting from other places, and I know what I would think if it were me listening to this, so agree or disagree. Please, please! Let us do so lovingly, so that maybe, just maybe these guys will come and want to be a part of this great family we have here." I can't say that everyone was receptive to this kind of rebuke but it seemed as though most were heeding those words. Cooling down a temperate crowd I posed what seemed to be a redundant question, "We are family aren't we?" Problem solved right? Not necessarily, the result of that meeting was that we voted to facilitate half of those requesting assistance. How about that for limiting God's blessings? After the way those people looked at me I chose to just shut up and listen. You see I had never liked being the center of attention. I was someone who needed to be in a somewhat quiet place. And up to this point, it was as loud as Times Square on New Year's Eve. But for now, I was happy to see that those who were yelling were now peaceful, I felt as though we may have damaged the image of our church to those visiting. I'd have you know that later on, at least two of those families trying to find church homes found comfort within our body of believers.

Not all of the memories I have were as horrific as this one. And remember that these business meeting were only held quarterly if that. There were times when we'd celebrate events throughout the year. Instead of Halloween, we'd encompass a fall Festival. And Easter was always big. We'd have a different Jesus resurrecting every year. And then there was the time when I did it. I always ate healthy and really didn't think I was that fat, but being thrust upon a cross in nothing more than a loin cloth would change your definition of being fat.

I was asked if I could play the Jesus part by the music minister. They were planning a Cantata for Easter and no one wanted to play Jesus. To tell you the truth I was flattered. I love him more than anyone in this world and I thought I'd represent him well. Except for one thing, I had a pouching buffet eating belly. And knowing Christ would be in optimal shape on a cross meant that in order to play him, I too, would have to be there as well. Praying for a miracle I chose to go on a colossal diet. I think it was close to a month to go before show time. I was ready to prepare for this part. And I really didn't want to be seen by anyone at the time so I started right out of the gate. My diet consisted of cutting out all starches right away. There was one other problem though. It was that I was from the South which meant there are only two drinks, there is sweat tea and there is coca cola. Both of those had to go. Do you actually know I was surprised to find how much caffeine there is in both of these two?

After three weeks I noticed that I wasn't sleeping well. But somehow I'd lost close to twenty five pounds. I didn't eat steak and I think I was ready to gnaw someone's arm off. I wouldn't even need salt, nor would I need pepper. The only thing I needed was for someone to get close enough for me to open my mouth and chomp down on anything resembling meat. I know they weren't doing it on purpose, but it appeared as if people placed hot dogs or hamburgers on their plate just to drive me nuts. I'd fend off the urge to snatch it from their grasp. There was hungry and then there was where I was. Every time someone mentioned food, it was me who proved Pavlov right. Salivating from every gland in my mouth I just wanted something to eat beside carrots, broccoli, and cauliflower. I guess that's how people remain skinny. They eat vegetables that cause gastric tendencies. For me, Cauliflower wasn't any different. I felt as though I was the paper factory that produced foul smells when you drive through Brunswick, Georgia. If you've ever driven there, you know exactly what I'm trying to say. But I remember having to tell myself that I wanted to be the best Jesus that the church had ever seen. Smelly as my gastric explosions were, I'd beg forgiveness from those who were in close proximity. "For Jesus" is what I'd say. And they were quick in their response, "How could something so sinful be for Jesus? How about this brother? I guess we'll pray for a speedy recovery based solely upon that horrid smell."

All in all I lost close to thirty three pounds in a little more than three weeks. I know this isn't a healthy way of doing things but it got me to where I wanted to go in the amount of time that I wanted to get there. The Cantata began and ended with success. I think I quoted the Beatitudes twice though. Nonetheless, it was still a success.

In one scene, I was supposed to run to the back of the church in a loin cloth. And in the early part of spring it was quite an experience. It rained earlier and it was kind of slippery. Which means only one thing; I was the one who slipped. Coming in the back door I was scripted to walk up passionately towards the cross. That was momentarily hampered by the fact that I had to clean grass off my leg.

Props are a vital part of movies, plays, and any other form of visual media. So being the graphic minded person I am, I wanted blood. I knew it would make an impact in people's minds. I knew conclusively the blood of Christ on the Cross would've been visually and potently overwhelming. For Christians anyway, it's the total sum of our existence. Before the Cantata, a friend and I went to a local store where special effects could be purchased. We acquired wax that had the appearance of skin. My friend wanted to make it look as though the skin had been torn and blood would ooze from the wound just as it would've happened with Jesus himself. So having everything that we needed for the presentation, we were prepared by having this makeup applied before the start of the play. No one would notice until I disrobed. At least that's what we thought anyway.

The script laid out when and what I was supposed to do once I entered the church. The grass had been cleaned and I had disrobed. My friend put a fresh tube of faux blood where it would materialize as if I'd been the one to be beaten to within an inch of his life. The doors were shut so no one knew what I was about to do. Songs were sung during this time and they were about to wind down, and then sound effects were to be played. Whips popping, skin being torn and shrieking screams were the most prevalent effects heard. As the doors opened, everyone turned around and there I was in my loin cloth covered in blood. There at that moment the church was united in what they felt for the Lord. Members and visitors alike were able to see firsthand what Christ did for them. What was most amazing to me was how sometimes things happen that you don't expect. I walked through the aisle symbolizing Calgary and was nailed to the tree. Spending my time upon the cross to find myself quoting our Lord and Savior, "It is finished." But that wasn't it. It was when I was taken off the cross. The blood that we wanted to make an impact did make an impact. The Lord allowed blood to be stained upon that cross with my faux skin mixed into it with an appearance that it had been torn. And the blood just streamed down the cross. To me, it seemed that it would've happened with Christ the same way that it happened that day. A collective, "uh" bellowed from the crowd. When asked what I thought about their reaction later. I responded humbly, "To represent someone who loved me that much was a life changing experience."

I believe the church changed that day too. Yes, there were more mid-week business meetings but the fighting appeared to vanish. I guess we learned more about love and sacrifice that day at the Cantata. But even the meals we shared became an event. Covered dish or otherwise, it was like we all had died and went to heaven.

What do I mean by saying that? One day my pastor preached about the difference between Heaven and hell. Our congregation used to act as they were part of a feast except that feast was being served from the depths of hell. The preacher said the major difference was that there were two feasts. Same food and the same decorations were placed upon the tables. One served in hell, and the other one served in Heaven. This story was being told by someone who was permitted to view both perspectives. He noticed no variations between the two tables. Even the color of the flowers was the same. Imagine that, flowers having color in hell. I thought that down there everything would be black. But for this story anyway the flowers were the same. Everyone was yelling and screaming obscenities at each other. Their arms were locked at the elbow and they weren't able to eat. So basically, they had their own little fight club down there. Battling each other for food, they were extremely hungry. And the devil sat at the head of table with a smirk that illuminated, "This'll be all . . . my food . . . you bumbling fools."

The man who witnessed this was afraid that he too would be rendered a delicacy so he fearfully asked his guide, "Hey, can we got out of here, isn't there something else you want to show me?" Dramatically we were holding on to the edge of our seats. "Now in Heaven it's completely different!" the pastor exclaimed. Remember that you've got the same setting but the major difference the man noticed was that this was a peaceful and loving event. There was no fighting. There was no profanity. But what was going on would astonish you? The man realized that the same problem had befallen these people but they handled it perfectly. Their arms were locked at the elbows as well. But rather than fighting for food, they were sharing. By feeding each other from across the table, they were capable of having their full of this feast. It was like each one of them was related somehow. The guide asked the man, "So, do you see the difference?" Totally amazed, "Yes, these guys are family. Brothers and sisters alike, it's as if they love first rather than fight like the goons downstairs. Even though their elbows are locked too, they can eat well because of their love for each other." Are you asking yourself, "Why do I tell you a story like this?"

It is because of the fact that all churches are a part of a family, and we're all part of the body of Christ. Each member has a function to perform as an arm of that body. Before there was fighting among us, enough so that it may have scared away some vital prospects for our budding church. But given the opportunity to explore the differences that we've been given. We are allowing ourselves the ability to feed someone else while we are being fed. Sometimes through weakness, we are made strong. Each one of those guys at the supper table was truly interested in creating an environment for a thriving body of Christ.

That is when the covered dish supper became the most anticipated occasion within our church home. What was it about this supper that made it such a desired event? I think in part because it allowed us as members to free up our hectic schedules and let ourselves go. "Fellowshipin" as they call it down South. Almost everyone who was able would come to showcase their specific culinary art. The idea behind the concept was for each church member to bring a dish, covered mind you, to the supper. It didn't matter what it was. As long as it was enough to feed your family, which was about the only rule we had. Mrs. Johnson's Fried Chicken had to be the fan favorite. But my guilty pleasure was the Pecan Pie or maybe even the Chocolate Delight the older ladies would bring. My mother always made us eat all the vegetables before I dug my fingers into that pie. But the point is that this was always something that I wanted to participate in. I wanted to bring my best because I was given the best. It seemed as though whenever these were planned I wouldn't eat so much the day before. And did I forget to mention that there were deviled eggs? Without the devil of course, he wasn't welcome in God's house. We prayed him out when we said the blessing. We wanted this to be as heavenly as possible.

What actually is the Covered Dish Delight? I always called it the Delight because it was always a toss-up between the pecan pie and the Chocolate delight for the best desserts. I'd pound as much food in my mouth without choking to death. Pulling myself away from the plate to jump at the table where desserts were placed. I was always the first to get to the Chocolate Delight, but I think my brother beat me to the Pecan Pie almost every time.

Needless to say, it was about as much fun for us as children as it is today for us adults. Nice people became nicer, and those that were more reserved somehow came out their shells to join us in this magnificent affair.

I thought about something one day when I was involved in this covered dish thingy. How could I use the concept in a relationship development program? I came up with a major point of interest. In life, we're always presenting gifts to our partner. And this would be no different. Think of the best that you could bring to this banquet. Would it be the Chocolate Delight? Maybe even the Pecan Pie? Whatever it is you'd do your best to be present and accounted for, and then you'd make sure you had something to eat for others. To maintain a successful relationship you are presenting yourself as the best dish on the table.

Can someone actually be compared to a dish? Yes, they can. Think about ordering a pizza from Papa John's. They pride themselves on having the freshest ingredients, right? Envision yourself as having those superior relational ingredients. I'm not saying anything negative about the other major Pizza chains. But what I am saying, "Be proud about having the freshest ingredients." Ask yourself a couple of questions, "What can I bring to this supper?" and "What do I have within me to present to my partner?"

I asked myself these same questions and had quite the epiphany. Then I did what I always did. I took a pen and a notebook and started writing stuff down. The answers materialized as quickly as I started writing. Girlfriends were about as far from my mind as they possibly could be, but what I wanted to do was initiate principles that furnished me with the tools needed for a wonderful relationship someday. And using foods such as Chocolate Delight and Pecan Pie seemed like the perfect metaphor.

Knowing that my best would be what was required. I didn't want to settle with a woman who didn't want to give me her best. That's why I think I remained single for so long. Most girls weren't ready for a relationship where it was necessary to give up something in order to gain mutual admiration between partners. Please don't get me wrong. I said, "Girls" not "Women" and there is a massive distinction. Girls are not ready for that once in a lifetime roller coaster ride called love. However, a mature woman will grab it by the horns and not let go. It'd be like running with the bulls in Pamplona except the woman just grabs hold of the horns and gets dragged through the ringer alley knowing conclusively that is what she wanted. In essence, she knows because she brought her Covered Dish Delight to the banquet of a lifetime that she now shares with the love of her lifetime.

Why is important that her Delight is well received? It's the fact that here was a man who ate about as much as he could and then when he was ready, he dives right in to the dessert. Consider that for a moment. It all goes back to where one must define what they see in themselves. Make sure that the ingredients that are being applied are the freshest. Which means one thing; it is for all time a good idea to be spontaneous. How can someone being spontaneous be a good thing? Well, ask Mr. Papa how he applies fresh and he would tell you, "You have to order every day, change out the old, put in the new." Let me tell you that I didn't ask him this, so don't quote me as saying such. I just love his pizza and it's evident that his pies are the freshest. You can look at my belly as verifiable proof.

As you define your own boulevards for personal development you shall detect variations in the way you bring the dish. The end result should be the same either way. The fellowship hall doors open up and the fragrance of a mighty meal hits you square between the eyes. You know what you brought. You know what she brought. All you have to do now is eat as fast as you can as healthy as you can to find yourselves living at the dessert table for the rest of your lives.

What I found was that I had all the answers to my personal Covered Dish Delight but what I was missing was the application. Through the years there have been numerous happenstances that occurred formulating another question within my mind. I thought if I did everything just right, love would find me ready and willing. What happened was that I found myself asking over and over again, "Am I Mr. Right, or Mr. Right Now?"

5.

Am I Mr. Right, Or Mr. Right Now?

HAVE YOU EVER FELT AS THOUGH YOU WEREN'T WANTED? HOW about feeling that you didn't measure up to a certain standard? Most of us are insecure anyway but to add this to it can be pretty demoralizing. For me, it all started in the fifth grade. I moved to North Augusta from New Ellenton, South Carolina somewhere close to the end of third grade. My father worked a lot. So having all the latest fads was not the way I'd been raised up to that point. But from the first day of that year I knew this would be a different school in which I'd have to acclimate to. The classrooms seemed so incredibly large. The cubby holes outside were so tall. The kids were cruel. So much so, that I really didn't get used to it until the end of the second or third semester.

New schools were always weird to me. There was everyone staring at you when you walk through the door, gawking, as if you're the one who is going to steal their girlfriends. When in reality you're the one who just wants to finds his desk and sit his happy butt down. As you begin to settle down and realize that this wasn't the worst thing that could've happened, there were other students gaining an extended confidence in you as a classmate.

It's amazing to me that this confidence they gained was also the same confidence they utilized to insult me. My father always made sure that we were well dressed. Warm clothes were provided if it was winter. And In the summer, we were given clothes that would allow us to easily cool down in those hot afternoons. Back then I wore a brand of shoes named "Cuga."

56

Most of you guys who are older know exactly where I am headed with this one. Yes, remember that I was the one who was made fun of because I had these shoes. The old blue ones made with canvas and so easy to get dirty, I had that kind. Kids in my class were vile. Making me the brunt of all the jokes, I spent the entire first semester trying to figure out how I could be different.

Imagine this, a fifth grader walking home every day trying to outline major psychological changes that he could make to fit in. I remember asking myself, "How can I make this stop?" At ten years old I was sick of it. Everyone at some time or another has insults hurled at them. But this was ridiculous. Why were they picking on me? I thought it all came down to what I was wearing, whether it was the shoes or the shirts. It didn't matter that my father worked hard for what I had. Verbal abuse rained down upon me as if it was falling from the clouds. The wheels in my mind kept turning though. I knew I had to come up with a plan. Strategically, I knew if all these people kept pounding me I'd be finished socially. Not one girl would ever talk to me if I wasn't confident enough to defend myself.

I had to make a move. But moving meant I had to make drastic measures. For an entire school year I took it, but the fifth grade was a turning point in my life. It's where I learned how to work. After hearing these guys beat me to death I wanted to do something about it. But what could I do? My father was always working, so I thought that might be why he didn't have any adverse circumstances hit him in the gut like I was getting pounded so relentlessly here at this school.

That bell sounded just like it did all the time during that year. But this summer would be different. I'd be working. I started out by walking around the neighborhood trying to advertise my services. I must've been a chip off the old block. Because I was able to mow lawns like my father sold insurance. Let me just say that my dad is a machine when it comes to selling life insurance. I was mowing grass from morning till night. I remember being twelve years old and having a couple hundred dollars. It doesn't sound like much but as a chap that young, it was a fortune.

But what was the purpose? I believe I was driven by the words I heard that year. If the problem was my inability to fit in because I didn't have the uppity clothes, I knew I had to do something in order to be able to buy that uppity apparel. Mowing grass gave me the motivation and the monetary means to compete. What actually, did I come up with on those long walks home though? I had to immolate what the cool kids were doing and what they were wearing. Otherwise I'd be left to my own demise wearing the not so cool clothes.

I remember coming home telling my mother what some of the kids were saying. And she was always supportive. Trying to comfort me but somehow it just didn't work. I wanted more. My father would get home around nine every night. And there I'd be waiting for him right by the door. Second handed Spaghetti was the meal of the day, and I had already eaten so I wanted to ask him something, "Dad, I've nailed my problem at school. I have to get some new clothes. So this weekend can you buy me some Izod?" He smiled responsively, "What is Izod?" With not so much an ounce of retail excitement, "Dad, it's the only thing I need to make it in this school." My father was not one of those kinds of people who would wear something just because he felt it'd help him with the "in" crowd.

As in most father son relationships, learning from your father is an everyday thing. I was used to it. If he said it, it's what I believed. I reconciled within my mind that I'd be able to find a girlfriend once I became the person hiding within the inner walls of my mind.

I will have you know that on the first day of sixth grade, I was dressed to kill. I had mowed grass throughout the entire summer. Therefore, I had loads of cash to go school shopping. And I became the reason that my dad called me the Izod kid. I had enough shirts for everyday of the week for two and a half weeks straight. One of the things that materialized on those walks was if I were to dress better than anyone in the school. I could eliminate the reason they were making fun of me. Now, it came down to the shoes. Nike was the choice fad in those days. So as I chose to be the Izod kid that my father saw, I also chose to have Nike shoes for at least three days a week. Three pairs of brand new shoes would guarantee my passage in the cool zone. But it was funny that I really didn't feel any different.

You'd be amazed at how party invitations were rolling in. I did it. I successfully transformed myself into one of the people in that Elementary school who no one could make fun of because of what he was wearing. My philosophy was that if I had clothes that cost more than most things you would find roaming those halls. I'd be free from ridicule. But you know what? Somehow it didn't matter that I had become an accepted member of this school. During the summer, I developed friendships with my neighbors that to this day are still my best friends. He lived two houses down from me. And to Brian and Tommy, it didn't matter what I wore. I could be their friend with no strings attached.

I believe that my time in the fifth grade was a point in my life where I wanted to be Mr. Right to everyone in the school. Being placed into an environment where you are lost. You didn't know what you did wrong. All you knew was that you were in the right place at the wrong time. I learned that through my hard work it had a direct correlation between being Mr. Right and Mr. Right Now. It became abundantly evident in the sixth grade. The transformation that took place over the summer was nothing more than aesthetic. I changed what people saw in me. By doing so, I realized that I could manipulate the insults where it was like I was the mirror that would reflect their own insecurities back at them. They would insult me before but when I eliminated the words they'd use. I gave them nothing to talk about. Therefore, I was the epitome of Mr. Right Now. It was funny to me how people would want me to join in their little clicks as though I didn't remember what they said to me a year before. Personally though, I don't think it's healthy to use bad experiences as motivation for change. I do think that being comfortable with yourself is as important a step that you can make. I learned that I didn't have to be someone else to be accepted at home. I could hang out with my best friends and not really feel that I had to make more friends at school. Don't get me wrong I was nice to everyone. But I just didn't get involved in their lives. It worked for me. I didn't have to worry about being Mr. Right or Mr. Right Now. I was Chuck to my friends at home.

Brian was shorter than I and he was two years younger. That didn't matter much to me or him. Kickball was kickball, so to have him on my team was fine by me. We were close but there was a time when we moved into that next stage as friends. It is the time where loyalty would characterize our friendship forever. I was in the tenth grade and Brian was in the eighth. And he was always smarter than I on most subjects. I always told people that I was the brawn and he was the brains. We complimented each other well. Every day after school I'd go over to his house. For milk and oatmeal pies, we'd watch cartoons until his mother and father came home. As a matter of fact, when Brian went off to college, his father said his grocery bill went down a couple of hundred dollars a month. His father somehow blamed me when they were missing seven layer bars. And rightly so, it was I who would go over there and make sure that the oatmeal pies and seven layer bars never spoiled.

One day, Mr. C came home early from work, and Brian had just made his best friend one of the biggest Chocolate milk glasses that he had in the house. It just happened to be on the day his dad would come home early. "Boy, you sure you got enough milk there? Can I go to the store and get you another gallon." barking loudly. I just looked at him and pointed towards Brian in the den. Words weren't finding a way out of mouth because I had them blocked by the most wonderful piece of seven layer bar in the entire world. Did I mention that Mrs. C could make the most glorious seven layer bars you'd ever put in your mouth? I believe when one dies and goes to Heaven, they'll be handed one of Mrs. C's seven layer bars. Those were the days where we'd sit around and talk about things that happened at school.

Girlfriends were hard to find because I was so into building forts in the woods. Tommy, Brian, and I were getting lost for hours so that we could build bridges across the creek. It was those summer months that we'd discover new ideas for the fort. None of us had girlfriends until I started ninth grade. I started going out with a girl who was a member of our church. She was in the same grade as Brian. So, we began our relationship innocently. Her name was Sharon. And she was in the seventh grade, so for her, going on this church's sponsored trips must've been a whirlwind. We'd go to the movies with my mother and my mother's best friend just so we could spend time together other than being at the church.

You know how first loves are, don't you? You invest so much and you feel as though it isn't enough. The flowers are more colorful, and the air you breathe is even more delightful. When love is in the air it is as if you can levitate. Feeling like you can never do any wrong. It is just you and her forever. In the hallways, you walk proudly with your book covers out so everyone can see by the writing on your book covers how much you love her. To go through this is about as developmental as going through puberty. I know because I was there loving my Sharon until death. So I thought.

After completing the ninth grade, it was my last year in Junior High. A natural progression would put you in as a sophomore for the tenth grade. Leaving one school and moving to another. Therefore, I left the gratification of being the big man on campus in the ninth to be being the lowly sophomore at North Augusta High School. It was like being in the seventh grade all over again and one of those things where you had to earn the respect of your elders once more. The thing I found most comforting was the fact that now I had three hundred and seventy students who felt the same way I did. Whereas in Junior High it was only half that much, and now there were two schools being combined to form our sophomore class. More so than that though, I was being torn from the grasp of my loving girlfriend. To me it was a troubled emotion. Here I was in a brand new school with more options than I ever had before. What was I going to do? So many questions were running through my ever changing adolescent mind.

Sharon was in the eighth grade at this time and really had no idea what I was going through. Our relationship was tenuous at best. So after we dated eight months she decided that it'd be best if she saw other people. Then she'd come crawling back. Two, maybe even three weeks later, it wouldn't take long. And being the kind loving guy that I was took her back without any reservations. This happened four times too many. You know how those bugs always seem to keep flying towards the blue light. That was me. I was comfortable in my surroundings. But what happens when bugs gets too confident? They fly right into a mask of electrocution. Falling to their death from the heights of the blue sky, merely to be found wanting at the top of the bug pile. Only to be swept up later by the humans, they'll never have a trace of confidence again.

What does that mean? If someone breaks your heart and uses the disguise of needing more time, then take into consideration that you should give them another chance if they come back to you. However, if it happens again and again, you need to remember what happened to your buddy when he was flying blue sky high. Zap! That was it, your buddy burnt beyond recognition because he thought he was in love enough to sustain multiple breakups. Once again, that was me. I thought that if I loved her enough that I would always have her as my girlfriend. We always went to church. Activities were always planned around that. And I thought we had so much in common. But most of it was the fact that the only major time we did spend together was at God's house. But that is what Brian did for me. He told me Sharon was going to break up with me for the fifth time for some other guy in their grade. "Brian, I'll call you back in a minute." I said upon receiving his call. Needless to say, that night was the last time I talked to Sharon as her boyfriend.

Have you ever been so busy being Mr. Right that you flew right into the bluest of blue lights? Electrocuted beyond the ability to see that you really were Mr. Right Now, henceforth, because of stubbornness you find yourself falling to a certain death. Even among all the others it didn't feel any better to know that you were on top of the bug pile. You were still dead as far as love goes. But you learned as I learned. That everything you go through can be used as precious information to be used later when you go through a similar experience. Recognizing that most of the time you will be Mr. Right Now. You have to realize that maybe it'll only be one time in your life that you find your soul mate. So truthfully, I realized this very late in life. I'd go through relationships thinking I was Mr. Right. And then be stunned by the words, "You're like the brother I never had."

Imagine thinking that you and the one you are trying to court are an item. Then you call her up to ask her to a romantic lakeside picnic, right around sunset mind you. And those stunning words become like daggers to your soul. Can I say, "Been there done that." Thinking it was only going to be you and her there and then two people get out of the car. Not a good day because I invested so much to set this up. I made the sandwiches just how she liked them. I tell you that I wasn't prepared for another man to show up on our date. But he did. It's at that second that you verifiably know that you are and were always Mr. Right Now.

My college years were similar to my experience there at the lake. The Baptist Student Union was a group of Christians at the University who met for Bible study once a week. For the better half of my freshmen year I'd go and try to become a vital member. We'd sing praise and worship songs, then someone would give a testimony, or a message would be preached. The first day I walked through the door I noticed a girl wearing a uniform from our college cheerleading team. She was beautiful enough to gain my attention. The way she gazed at me I thought possibly I had a chance. Being the red blooded man that I am, I tried to find a seat next to her. Smiling at her as I sat down, knowing that she must've been sweet on me. This girl's name to this day escapes my mind. So, I'll just call her Melissa.

Afterwards I hung around and chatted with some of the people in the group. I was intent on getting to know the girl who kept smiling at me. Don't ask me why but there was something about dating a cheerleader. My motivation, I guess was a little selfish. There were some that were going out to eat at a local sandwich shop. Nudging me to go with them, I obliged. And guess what? You have to know where I found my seat. I sat right next to the amazing Ms. Melissa.

We began our night with small talk and after about an hour or so I'd walk her to her car. At that time in my life I wasn't interested in finding a mate. So to me it was more for fun than anything else. But what I realized was that I found myself talking with her after class. We'd almost always go somewhere to get something to eat. Getting to a point where the local restaurants started knowing our names. What I am saying is that we went out a lot. To me it was a date. To her it was a free meal with a friend. One night in particular, playing the Mr. Right card right down the middle of the deck, we stayed out all night under the stars just talking about our future endeavors and where it'd take us. I thought we connected on so many levels. But what shocked me the most hadn't even happened yet.

After those long nights where we tried to solve the world's problems in a night or two. I noticed that she never said anything about us, as in a relational sense. Why I didn't notice before I can't say, but this night I did. Having some doubts about where we were going with this thing, I wanted to ask her what she felt for me. That night, I didn't have enough courage to even approach the subject. A couple of days went by and something pretty bizarre took place. I was walking away from her dorm one night, and she informed me about a paper she needed to write. I don't even remember what she was trying to write about. But I think it was something I knew well enough to help. Remember me, the oblige everyone who I think likes me, and get burned by the very flames that I am trying to fan within their heart. That was me. Again, I was happy as a hippo to help her with her paper. In fact, as I recall, she really never even did anything but talk to me while I wrote the paper. Call me blind because I thought that I was offering time for my girlfriend. But what was really happening I'd find out two days later.

Thursday nights was always Baptist Student Union. It was a ritual for us to go and then eat somewhere afterwards. This night, like any other, I walked in ready to see her. There before my eyes was the leader of the Baptist Student Union and her wrapped in a warm and cozy embrace that I'd only dreamed of up to that moment. When she realized it was me who was walking in she stopped immediately. I could tell from her expression that she felt something else for this guy that she didn't feel for me. I stood like one of those guys who had been hit so many times with a baseball bat that they don't really blink much. Talking wasn't an option. I just wanted to leave.

As the meeting drew to an end, I approached her with question marks posted all over my forehead. But before I said anything she blurted out, "I am so sorry you had to see that!" Never have I been one to hide my feelings so I retorted, "What do you mean?" She really didn't know how to respond but she tried, "Me and Caleb, you know we've been dating for about three weeks now." There is being blown away, and then there was this tornado induced coma that I was in when she told me that. "Where you guys together when we stayed out all those nights?" was the only thing that came to mind. She never hesitated, "Yes, and did I forget to thank you for writing that paper?"

It was always funny to me when I heard the final whistle blow, but not ha ha funny. You know when a train whistles it is usually a couple of toots then an extended whistle. The final straw if you will. That is usually when I'd recognize that I'd been playing the Mr. Right card to myself. I was an audience of one with the implication that I was everything to her. When in actuality I was her Mr. Right Now from day two. Why wasn't I on day one? Because I guess I wore my "take me for a ride" shirt that day. I was so used to being the guy who was compared to a brother that yes, I was hurt, but not destroyed. Another one bites the dust was my motto. I just wished that I hadn't missed two nights of sleep in the process.

Desperately I always wanted to be someone's Mr. Right. I didn't want or even desire to be the Mr. Right Now that so many girls saw me as. And I wouldn't wish on my worst enemy to be labeled, "The brother I never had." How brutal? Makes you want to scream to the top of your lungs. But I guess sensing it much better would've led me to just bow my head and walk into the sunset. If only it were that simple where the end of relationships was equivalent to the ending of an amazing love story. The tears you shed would be of the joyous type rather than those relinquished from the "I'm never going to find someone to love me" ducts. But I heard it and I moved on. The unstable emotions were raising the hair on my arm. But why was it?

I was the one who didn't notice the things that were happening. I don't blame her for what she did. Being one who knows that if I allow something to take place and it does, then I should be the one held responsible. She did what she had to do to get her paper done. Me, I was the one who didn't detect what was happening. Maybe I was being blinded by my desire to date a cheerleader. I don't care to know that I could have been that ignorant. Some would blame the boyfriend thinking he may have been in on the whole plan. Not me, I just wanted to disappear. Imagine if I had Delta back then, I probably would've ended up in Europe for three weeks trying to get over that.

I handled it the best way I could at the time though. Which for me was to go somewhere else except Baptist Student Union, I'd leave school as soon as Basketball . . . I mean class ended. And maybe it was then that I began bidding adieu to my college aspirations. I did play basketball a whole lot more after that though. One of my strangest characteristics I have is that when the going gets tough, I get going. People say that I am running away from my problems. But I don't see it that way.

I change my perspective. The problem to me seems bigger if I am standing beside it. However, if I go on vacation, I can look at it objectively. I can see it from all sides. I believe that is how God sees us. He is omnipresent and omniscient. Meaning he is all present and all knowing. He sees us in our current problems and amazingly, he sees the result. Why can't I take a page from his playbook? Never will I know everything, or be everywhere at one time. But what I can do is to look at my problem in an entirely different perspective.

Take a freight train rolling down the tracks of your life. You have the engine, the freight cars, and finally the little red caboose. Comparatively, when you're born your engine is created. Your brain and body serve as the leading force to pull the rest of the load for the rest of your life. The cars you connect are the experiences that you'll go through in life. Each car symbolizing what kind of shape you were in when you went through it. If you ever observed a train passing you on your way to wherever, then you know that most of those cars are never brand new. Some have writing painted on the side. And then finally you see the caboose. I see that as a resting place. It is where you'll find refreshment after a long journey. The place where you would find ice on an intensely hot day, I believe it's the best place to be when you are riding in a passenger train. With a swiveling chair, it's the only place on the train that lets you see where you're going, and where you've been.

God sees it another way. Because of his ultimate power, he is translucent. Able to see the entire train at the same time, he knows where we are going ten years down the road. He sees the engine, the cars, and even the caboose. Knowing the pain we'll experience. Crying beside us, he feels as we feel. You want to talk about love. I guarantee that you'll never experience love like that. Why this analogy though? Because it is imperative that one changes the perspective if they feel they are going through something that is disheartening. If God sees the whole train, depend on his guidance to direct your actions while you're connecting those freight cars to your own train.

What you'll find is that you'll be able to disconnect anytime you see that you got that nasty gang affiliated writing on the side of your cars. In a sense, you'd be able to cleanse your life experiences of those dirty side effects. Pull this card out from the middle of the deck when someone tells you that brother thingy and it is liberating. You don't take it too hard because you know you're so much closer to the love of your life. You know beyond any doubt that these types of things would never be said by them, because you are the closest thing to Mr. Right that they've ever seen.

My suggestion for anyone who may have been in a similar position, learn to observe the traits you yearn for in a partner. It's easy to get blinded by desire. I believed that if I am busy being Mr. Right I'd be given the unconditional crown of her loyalty. What happens is that confidence you obtain in the beginning is the same confidence that leads you right into that blue light to electrocute you beyond all breath of life. I'm not telling you to find a love that overflows life and then ship it off in the largest FedEx box you can find. What I am telling you though is to make sure that it's reciprocal. Sometimes you end up running right into that love of a lifetime you've always dreamed of. And after all those years that you will share with her, you'll be thankful to have gone through every experience, to have connected every cart to the train of your life, and have truly been blessed enough to have lived every minute of your love with her.

To me, it is one of those moments when you're sitting in the Tuscan swing outside on the porch, hand in hand with love, and you're still gazing into her eyes as if it were the first time. Amid the falling leaves, running fingers through her hair, you let her know intimately, "To have gone through all those times when I was never Mr. Right to anyone, it was worth every heart ache I endured, I'd do it all again just to land here within your arms tonight." What happens next? It might be something like she romantically melts within your embrace to say, "Baby, you're my Mr. Right, you're my Mr. Right Now, and my Mr. Tomorrow's Tomorrow." So, there you are within the brightest of days knowing that you have finally found a love that overflows even your own life. But for now, you're left to fend for yourself in an ever cruel world while asking that age old question, "Can this really be love?"

6.

Can This Really Be Love?

A T TWENTY THREE YEARS OLD, IS SOMEONE REALLY READY FOR A massive change such as marriage? The answer is dependent on who's actually getting married. What expectations have they built within themselves? Is it something they're doing to justify to themselves that they want something more than being single? Mostly, it comes down to fear. Some marry just because they're afraid that they'll be single for the rest of their life. And rightly so, if you knew the statistics implying that people are remaining single longer it is rather alarming. Furthermore, divorcees are choosing, maybe by their own choice or perhaps by someone else's, to remain single.

My massive life change happened so fast that I barely had time to blink. Did I fall in love, or did I fall into win-loss like mode? You may be asking yourself, what in the world is that? Well, writing from a man's perspective I can tell you that sometimes in his mind he'll eliminate logic because of his desire to win. I called it as Pink Floyd writes it, "A Momentary lapse of Reason." Except that moment turns into a lifetime if you marry the wrong person. And taken into account that you don't believe in divorce, it could be a lifetime where you desperately want to find that blue light somewhere, someplace. Who wants to live like this?

Ponder Proverbs in the Old Testament for a moment. Here was a man named Solomon who asked God for wisdom and was granted so accordingly. You want to talk about someone who really knows what to say when he'd been bombarded by women. He said many times in different ways, "It's better to live on the corner of a house than to live with a quarrelsome woman." How do you think he knew this? He must've had personal experience, you think? Imagine opening that big old door at your palace and you have a thousand women staring at you. You better come up with something better than, "How ya'll doin?" But that's exactly what he did. He had a bunch of wives and a bunch of concubines. Somehow, I'm thinking he knew what to do with this wisdom thingy that he asked for.

Beginning in the eighth grade, I used this particular book as a perpetual roadmap for my life. Trying to pull straight from Solomon's wisdom, I thought I'd be able to garner some of my own by simply emulating what his tendencies were. And you want to talk about my own roadmaps. How about navigation through a Biblical illustration of what a wife is supposed to be? All of this if she wants to obtain a noble character far past what she'd already obtained. It's amazing that even though I had all of this instruction, and even had traces of second handed wisdom being thrust upon me. I still wasn't competent enough to listen. Application by error almost to the point of insanity is where I'd categorize myself.

Birthday wishes were in order and all I wanted was Lobster and New England Steamers. It was a family tradition for us, and every member except for my mother would be in for this annual celebratory meal. We drove to Orlando for the millionth time and I was single and ready to eat. But this time we weren't observing mine but my mother's December birthday. I think she only went because we all wanted to go. Nevertheless, we all ate until we were sinfully stuffed. The thing about this trip was I was supposed to leave early enough so I could make it back in time to go skiing. My mother wasn't happy but she obliged anyway. In order for me to make it home, we had to drive most of the night because Brian was adamant about leaving early the next morning.

We were headed to Sugar Mountain in Boone, North Carolina. You know how you go somewhere and really don't expect something exciting to happen to you? Some days I wish I'd never gone. Nothing happened with the guys. It was all good with them. But we were skiing along and we met up with some girls from North Augusta. Sugar was one of those places close enough to us that you could almost run into someone you knew at any time. All of us were invited over to the girl's slope side ski-in ski-out condo. They had this crazy brained idea for dinner and a movie. But the thing is; only two of us went. The other guys had their own pursuits of women to deal with. And it had nothing to do with us because there were only two of us and two of them there girls.

Scott and I went over to the condo with no intention of hooking up with anyone. However, I think Scott liked one of the girls. Remember me? I wasn't looking to hook up with anyone. But after dinner, one of the sisters lost a button on her ski pants, and I was summoned by her father to help her fix it. And fix it in front of everyone. The plan was for me to grab where the button used to be and where it was supposed to go. We were going to fasten it together with a safety pin. Her father beckoned me from the table on the other side of the room, "Hey, just stick your hand further down so you can pull it closer." I was like, "What did you say?" Here I was in front of God and everybody with my hands half way down a woman's pants with her father routing me on. The expression on my face was classic. Her father wasn't a sick perverted man but why was he asking me to do this? Do I do it, or just pass on it and let somebody else do it?

I guess his being a dentist he was used to sticking his hands in tight places and where maneuverability was limited. But as for me, I wasn't happy about what he was asking me to do. Furthermore, what would happen if I touched something that wasn't supposed to be touched? Do you know what I mean? I just shook off whatever fear I had and dove right in. I'll have you know that it went over without a hitch. I didn't touch anything but what I was told to touch. Somewhat embarrassed by the whole ordeal, I only did what was asked which was to hold for the pin. Afterwards, without incident, we watched a movie and finished off whatever dinner was left.

Her mother felt as though she was part of us. Young at heart I guess. Or maybe it was the fact that she wanted to keep a watchful eye on the boys and girls downstairs? Either way, she stayed there with us until we left about ten o'clock. The next day it was pretty much the same. Scott and I skied with the girls for the day. The plan was for Scott to ski with the shorter sister, and for me I'd be hanging out with the taller one. Both sisters were pretty so it didn't matter which one we ended up with, it was all good. But then Scott and I decided to go faster than the girls and told them we'd meet them at the bottom of the mountain.

We took off as if we'd just been shot out the gate, going about as fast as we could. Jumping over every mogul we were trying to gain more speed. Racing each other in a most amateur way, you know how guys are when it comes to winning, all out for the "W" right? Well, that's when I saw this boy about ten years old come out of nowhere. He wasn't looking at me. And truly, I didn't see him until it was too late. His body was facing the opposite direction and he had no idea what was about to happen. On the other hand, I knew full well that I had no other option except to plow on through this little man. I turned my body sideways trying to miss him, even lifting one leg up where I was skiing on one ski so I wouldn't hit him. Ultimately though, this kid was toast. Knocking him almost unconscious, I thought I killed him. He was positioned face down in the snow, skis were heaved way beyond his reach, and his poles were bent past repair. My eyes scanned the mountain to see if he had family nearby. But I wasn't getting a response from little Mr. Face-in-the-Snow here. Doing the only thing I could, I grabbed hold of his jacket and pulled him up. Trying to get him to walk it off, I asked him, "Have you got any family here? Are you with a church group? Are you okay?" A deer glazed over by the headlights of an impending collision with a freight train is the best description I can offer to describe his expression. This kid was helpless and then all of a sudden, it was like he slowly came to and then he answered, "I'm okay, but where are my . . . my . . . poles?" Relieved as I was, I was still looking around the area to find someone where he could find comfort. I creamed this kid like Ray Lewis would hit someone in an opposing team's backfield. But now, I was relieved that he was okay.

By the time the kid started skiing off the girls had reached us. They were concerned because as slow as they were they still beat us down the mountain. Scott came back to help as he witnessed the incident first hand. He gave his best illustration of what happened. And the girls were taking up for the kid. It was kind of hard for me to believe since I couldn't do anything to miss him. Shrugging my shoulders was always my response when I didn't particularly agree with something or someone. So I did just that. Once I was certain that the kid was skiing regularly and truly was okay we were free to ski on with the girls. It was pretty much the same for the rest of the day and night; we skied, ate, and watched movies for the rest of the evening. And yes, mother was still in the room with us as we watched those movies. A thin slice of weird I thought. But hey, we were all having fun. So I didn't say anything. I knew the next morning we were leaving early and I just wanted to enjoy the last night. But to tell you the truth, I really thought it was it as far as spending time with the girls.

Scott, Chris, and Todd had to be back because they were still in high school. Starting in early January is not what they preferred but it was what it was. The girls were their age so I guess all is fair in love and war. At that point I actually thought I wouldn't hear from them again because of hectic schedules. But the next Thursday night, the shorter sister Gina was heartbroken from a breakup she sustained when she returned from the ski trip. And her mother being the nosy, in your face mother she was, called me. That is right, me. Why'd she call me was the biggest question in my mind. Nonetheless, she still called. Being somewhat shocked by what she was asking for me to do, I hung up with her and started dialing for tickets.

The boys and I were going to see Michael W. Smith that Friday night, and her mother wanted me to take Gina with us. I wasn't thrilled about it because Scott, I thought was sweet on her, and I didn't want to interfere. I tried to get out of it by telling her, "I don't know if I can get tickets, but I'll try. That's all I can do." You could hear the tone of her voice change as she responded, "I'll pay for all of your tickets if you can find her just one." That part sounded like adequate motivation to find her a ticket. I did try to throw a disclaimer in there though, "Hey, you know we won't be back until Saturday afternoon? We are staying the night at Tommy's place, in Clemson." I thought for sure I'd be told that she didn't want her going because she didn't want her spending the night. It didn't happen as I would've liked, she still went.

The concert was awesome and everything we did surprisingly turned out to be loads of fun. She and I ended up talking a lot more because the rest of the guys seemed to think I'd set this up so they wanted to give me time with my new found friendship. "Hey, Thanks Guys, for nothing." is what you could hear me say numerous times. Being that age, your maturity hadn't reached a point where you felt grown up. So hanging out with buds carried more leverage than hanging out with some girl. Don't misunderstand me. None of us had issues; every one of us loved women. But we also loved the time we spent with each other because it wasn't that much due to most us being in college or high school.

The whole trip was a learning experience. I had no intention of falling in like but that's eventually what happened. It being the first time that I can remember asking myself, "Can this really be love?" As if it's too early to decide, I chose to ride this wave out to see how far I could go before making it back to shore. We courted for a couple of months and found our lives to be a gradual progression towards each other. I was an assistant youth counselor at Grace United Methodist Church in North Augusta. My duties had nothing to do with leading anyone but rather to be a helper to the youth minister. Gina and I grew closer just by the long talks that we'd have. One night after youth fellowship, we sat out on the stairs, and would enjoy hearing different things about our lives.

I don't know how it came about but she was saying something like, "I heard that I was adopted. What've you heard?" I really didn't know how to react to this so I said the only thing that came to mind, "I kind of heard that too." As much as it was true I think it was wrong of me to even imply that I knew anything of her being adopted. Her mother called that night to let me know that I should've never told her she was adopted. You want to talk about a fire breathing dragon. Her mother probably is still smoking to this day. I quickly and affirmatively responded, "What are you talking about woman, I never told anyone anything. I told her I had heard she was adopted." There is one thing I hated and it was to be accused of something that I didn't do. Here she was . . . doing just that. Can you say, "happy happy?" She kept on and asked me, "What if I told your sisters that they were adopted? What would you do then?" This was funny to me and I started to laugh. As soon as she finished I blurted out, "My sisters knew they were adopted the second they walked through our door! What's your excuse?" It wasn't a healthy conversation. I knew that it couldn't continue because my mouth was on the verge of losing my religion . . . literally. So I chose to play nice and just hang up.

From that call on I wasn't allowed to see Gina or even talk to her. It was frustrating because we had developed what I thought to be a love relationship in our most recent conversations. This is where I found out what kind of mother this girl really had. I keep thinking things are over and bam! They take off in an entirely different direction. This bulldog of a woman called my University and obtained a copy of my transcripts. She was trying to prove I had lied to them about the hours that I actually had. Among other things she was trying to ruin my life. And I didn't like it one bit. I may have been young and immature. But I wasn't going to stand and let her get the best of me. I was taught if something is bothering you, cut off its source and you eliminate the problem.

Brian and I were over at Tommy's house talking about the big bad bulldog. They suggested I handle it by cutting off totally from anything resembling Gina. That to me sounded like a definite win-win situation. I asked Tommy for his keys to his Pulsar and his cell phone. He threw me the keys and told me, "Cell phones in the car, dip wad. Go end that @#$%." Tommy was always colorful in the way he said something. She lived maybe two miles away so the drive was short and sweet.

I pulled into her long sloping driveway and hit the brakes. The smell of burning rubber must've permeated the air. I ran up the stairs as I was met by the devil herself, "What do you want?" My response was always super swift, "Nothing from you, I just want my necklace and the key to my apartment back!" Then in a flash, Gina pushes her mother out of the way, "You're not leaving me here with this crazy woman." I was bewildered when she even threw me back to run towards the car. Following close behind her, I got in the car and noticed that she was truly serious about getting out of there. That to me, was the second time I asked myself, "Hey man, can this really be love?" A million things passed through my mind on the way back to Tommy's. Internal dialog so intense, it was blaring like a horn in the midst of a dense fog, "What in the world are you doing? Are you as crazy as this girl's mother? And if so, how is this going to end well?"

A little more than two minutes later, I opened Tommy's front door and heard from the back of the house, "Well, did it go as you planned?" As those words were flowing like a river out of Brian's mouth, Gina came around the corner. Floored by who was standing in front of them. They weren't prepared and were truly at a loss of words. Brian turned to me, "What's she doing here?" Without the desire to blame Gina I responded, "We don't really know." Both of us felt awkward being in a place that so many questions were flying around the room. Trying the break the tension I went into the kitchen to get something to drink. Tommy's father was loading the dishwasher. Looking up, he raised his eyebrows and whispered, "Don't come in here looking for sympathy, you made your bed, now you'll lie in it. We love you, but this is something you're going to have to go at alone."

Pleased to have his honesty hitting in my face I responded so that Gina wouldn't hear me, "I tried to end it, but she jumped in the car. What was I going to do?" Grabbing the last plate he turned completely around and said, "The thing you left here to do. That would've been best, don't you think." I wasn't angry at him because I knew what he was saying was true. I left their house with a manly mission but returned with a massive manly problem. What happened to me was a variable that I never planned for. I just wanted it to end.

That night she stayed at the apartment in a different room. And the next day I wasn't prepared for the full court press her parents and family friends would render. My phone rang off the hook the whole day. I finally answered it about seven o'clock that night. And with a boisterous voice, "Where is Gina? You need to bring her back here now." This coming from a family friend who was calling on behalf of her parents, I was telling them all the same thing. My apartment is located on so and so street at so and so intersection. Please end this for me, by coming over here and getting her. I was intent on it being resolved amicably and quickly as well.

Nothing happened for the next couple of days, the calls subsided, and I was trying to figure out how someone in my position at the church could get out of this thing without any major spiritual ramifications. She was an eighteen year old girl who wasn't bending either way. She didn't want to leave. So I drew strength from a place I still to this day think was somewhere close to the hot place. I should've left this girl alone, but I let her know, "Listen, I'm involved in the church, and I'm getting flak from the youth minister. The only way out of this is to get married." She said she wanted to make sure she didn't have to go back to her mother's house ever again.

My mother was supportive even though she was still healing from some of the things the bulldog did to her. We told her our plans to marry and she began to lose that smile as quickly as the words tickled those little hairs in her ears. Happy, happy she wasn't. But she said she'd help if we needed her. We planned for most of the week and negotiated a place where we'd hold the ceremony. As hard as it was to put this thing together I should've known that God was placing every roadblock in our way so he could deter us from doing what we were planning. Remember God knows best . . . always. Listening to him would've saved me a couple of years of wasted life. But I didn't listen, so now I have a story to tell.

We were married on the sixth of August in nineteen hundred ninety three. Her father was told that we'd be married in Thomson, Georgia when in reality we'd complete our matrimonial mayhem in the quaint little town of Edgefield, South Carolina. After a honeymoon trip to Nashville, we arrived at the apartment to begin this new life of ours. From the second we walked through the threshold I noticed that this woman I married was beginning to paint her true colors on the walls of my life. Insulting me became a habitual offence. And I wasn't used to being the brunt of such horrific attacks because I hadn't been abused verbally since I was in the fifth grade.

One afternoon we were invited over to Marty's mother's house for supper. This was the thing about Gina, it didn't matter where we were; she felt it was the thing to do to make me feel as though I were nothing. Sitting on the couch across from his mother, Gina began pounding me as if I wasn't there beside her. Most of what she was saying was based upon my not working a nine-to-five job, it was demoralizing. Especially in front of Marty and his mother, I could tell that they didn't like it either.

Charlotte was as supportive for me as she was for Marty. And I could tell that she was on the verge of letting this girl know that the man she married was a far better man for listening and never responding to the incessant badgering. Marty was always kind of passive anyway but this was getting on his nerves as well. I think I took more comfort in the fact that they knew that I wasn't as horrible as my new wife believed. I could sit here and tell you that it didn't bother me but I think I'd be lying. The only way I dealt with things like those was to disappear and go somewhere else in my mind. Protecting myself in a shield like manner I ensured my peacefulness. A state of mind that I believe everyone should live in for extended amounts of time. Why? Because if you are in a constant state of peace, bad things can be said, bad things can be done, and it just won't matter. God allows us to beckon him when we need comfort. And even in those times where we are bruised and battered, he invites us to his soothing embrace. Jesus knows the pain you may suffer. He's been there done that too. So always know you've got a friend.

Even though I wasn't actively involved in a church I still knew where my Jesus was, and I wasn't afraid to seek his refuge. Being the subject of that much ridicule was hard to take. I'd let my head fall further into my hands and just go to that next place. Then to try and cut some of the personal attacks, Charlotte gave Gina a job at a bookstore where she was manager and it seemed to settle down a little. It was a blessing for me because I didn't have to see her that much. She was working forty hours a week. And I'd choose to work the hours she wasn't. So, that peace I was praying for was found within the confines of my own home.

This job allowed Gina to achieve a fresh relationship with her parents. I thought it to be a good thing. Except now, misery had company. Remember the fire breathing dragon otherwise known as her mother? Well, I thought if the peace I had acquired was going to remain I needed to be more forgiving. Never have I been one to tell anyone what they could or could not do. Therefore, I told Gina that it was fine with me if she went over to her mother's and tried to rekindle a relationship with her family.

She did so and it was a good thing. Except for the fact that after a couple of weeks, the dragon started breathing fire into her daughter's ear, and I didn't want to see this happen again. I worked with my father's agency selling life insurance. That was my job because college was no longer an option. Being what my father would want is what I chose to do. Her mother on the other hand was scheming towards inevitable disaster.

I'd leave everyday about four or five o'clock because that would be the time that most people would get home from work. Being in the insurance business, you have to catch both the husband and wife at home. Otherwise you'll hear objections until Jesus comes back. So, one night on my way to Orangeburg for an appointment, I noticed a car that didn't look familiar parked in Tommy's driveway. As soon as I drove past his house this car pulled out rather quickly, I sped up not thinking too much about it. He ran the stop sign and started following me. Noticing this man wasn't showing any sign of slowing, I did something kind of funny. Have you ever done something to verify to yourself that what you believed to be true was in fact true? That's exactly what I did. And guess what? He was following me. Knowing this to be a fact my next move would drive this man crazy. I chose to drive around the neighborhood numerous times. Virtually making a circle around the neighborhood I was most familiar with. I knew where the turns were and he didn't. Good for me, not so good for him. I lost him on the second time around. At that moment I called Gina's mother and told her passionately, "If you going to hire someone to follow me, then get someone who can actually stay with me. Otherwise leave me alone."

I was then informed that she thought I wasn't being faithful with Gina and she was going to prove it. I was so fed up with the harassment but I still said nothing about Gina having a relationship with them. I just let it go. Almost two years of this and I really wanted something else for my life. This was the last time I heard, "Can this really be love?" Because that is the exact moment I knew it wasn't. Love is obsession, something you can't live without. And with this woman, I was all about being somewhere else but with her.

Conveniently, she started going to school to be a hygienist. I worked later and later so that I'd protect myself from any further abuse. I can't say if this was the moment where Marty became more infatuated with Gina and less friendly with me. But it seemed as though they were increasingly secretive. Remember now, this was a three hundred pound man who all of sudden lost forty or so pounds. He said it was for his health but he never changed what he ate, he only changed the amount. In Ryan's Steakhouse one night, he ate a handful of green beans and said he was full. I rarely laughed at him but I couldn't help it, I started laughing. And both of them looked at me with those devil eyes of theirs. They didn't seem to think it was funny. My question was why he was losing the weight. Gina had a bicycle, Marty got one. It was like he was no longer satisfied with being the third wheel on this cart we called a friendship.

To be honest, I was relieved that I didn't have to involve myself into her life. Yes, I was married but in a relationship I wasn't. My father and I started traveling a lot more. Marty and Gina started going out more on innocent jaunts. Bike riding is where they'd be when I'd get home from work. Afterwards they'd find themselves cutting the rug at the local night clubs. Lord have mercy, it was fine with me because I didn't have to see her anymore. Peace to the power of ten! The hours I worked I was unable to help her with her homework and Marty was more than helpful. What was happening was that I was growing further apart from my wife and her new best friend.

An afternoon conversation truly defined where we were headed as a couple. I came home early and noticed Marty's car parked where it was always parked. I walked in and observed that Marty and Gina were doing homework closer to each other than normal. I asked Marty to leave so that I could talk to Gina.

On his way out the door, he gave me a glance as if to say, "Why are you doing this now, you've never done it before?" But I actually think he was afraid to say anything. I guess he could tell by my demeanor that I wasn't in an answering questions mood. Waiting until he drove off I then went into Gina's room to talk. She had her own bedroom because she said that I froze her out of ours. I thought from experience that man and wife should sleep in the same room for the rest of their lives. This wasn't the way it happened with my marriage. After two years she moved into the other bedroom. I was happy about having the king size bed to myself but not so happy about having to be in it alone. After opening the door she looked like she was angry at me. How did I know? This was an everyday occurrence so I knew it quite well.

She said, "Why did you do that?" I knew why she said this so I responded, "Listen, I need you to curve some of the time you're spending with Marty. Cut it out. I mean this is ridiculous. I am tired of having to defend you guys with everyone asking if you two are dating." You want to talk about someone being just like her mother, this girl starting puffing like an angry lioness. Yelling at the top of her lungs, "You're not doing that to me, you're trying to take the best friend I've got!" Dazed by her response I retorted, "I thought I was supposed to be your best friend. Your husband is me not him, remember?" She stood up and started taking her index finger and poking me in the tendon that connects my arm to my shoulder. If you've ever been hit in that spot you know exactly how it feels. It hurts. After telling her to stop I countered, "Hey, Hey, look . . . you want to have him, have him but I'll no longer be your punching bag." She ran towards the front door, "I'm leaving and you can kiss my @#$!" Being the smarty pants that I am I started laughing and said, "If you do, remember something, that'll be the last time you see the inside of that door. You better take what you can because everything you leave behind will be ticketed for the trash bin!"

Leaving is what I thought she was going to do, but what she did was surprising. She stayed home and just cried. Here was a man who was fed up with the whole situation but he still felt he needed to apologize. As kindly as possible I did just that.

You'd think that her reply would be the same wouldn't you? But as soon as she heard me say, "I'm sorry." She was on the phone with Marty telling him everything that had just happened. Shaking my head, I started smiling and just walked off. As always, I'd disappear within myself at 7:05 pm. That's when the Braves came on. It's a good thing that they were playing that night because I didn't want to think too much about what had just happened.

It was the beginning of the end I presumed and I was right. Two years into an unstable relationship and I was ready to be something else to someone else. Except for my belief that divorce wasn't an option, I actually thought that I'd live in this God forsaken marriage for a lifetime. But God has a way of taking you out of a situation that he knows to be fruitless. Even though we were dumb enough to jump into a bad state of affairs, his ever sufficient grace rescues us from becoming the eternal idiot. There would be more that I thought God wanted to teach me so I tried to be more receptive.

Settling down for a couple of weeks, if Gina and Marty were together, it was with me. I guess they hid it well other than that. Then one evening Gina sat me down to ask me a favor, "Can I go to Florida, or can we all go to Florida I meant?" She was serious. I thought about going and then took into account the electric bill. "Our electric bill is two hundred and ninety five dollars, how are we going to go to Florida and enjoy anything with that hanging over our heads?" What she said almost knocked me off my feet, "That is your bill. It's got nothing to do with me and Marty." Nodding to her sarcastically I cried out, "Oh! You think so do you? Well, I can't go then." Saying something like this you better be sure that you're prepared for what follows, "Then Marty and I will go. You can stay here and pay your bill. That'll be fine with us." Puckering up my lips with total amazement, "Let me get this straight, the woman I am married to is going to go to Florida with an unmarried, single man?" She never even wavered, "Yes, is it that hard to understand?" I was like, "What?" You know I was okay with them doing stuff around North Augusta but to have to defend their actions some three hundred miles away was a little more than I bargained for. I, being the one who never told anyone to do anything said, "You know what, you want to go with Marty, then go, but to me, I think you need to call the dragon to let her know what you're doing?" All those inquisitive looks on my face were finding their place on hers now as she asked, "Why should I call my mother?" As if she wasn't getting what I was trying to say, "I am so sick and tired of having to defend you guys to everybody that she needs to know that I knew what you guys were doing. That way she can't blame me for something I didn't agree with in the first place."

For most of the day she continued to be a royal pain in the buttocks. Checking with Marty to see if what she was saying was okay with him. I really did think I was invisible. And finally, she got fed up with the conversation and screamed, "Fine then, we're leaving and I don't give a #$% what people think, you can tell them what you want." Being who I was I started smiling when I didn't like something. I guess I'm always trying to find something funny about it. Or maybe it's the fact that I feel I can't do anything about what is happening and just grin with chagrin. Either way it happened about as fast as they could close the door. In fact, Marty already had the car cranked, so she jumped in, and they drove off.

Left there with an entire pocketful of "what-the-heck just happened" I called my father at the office. We talked about it for a minute or two and he told me he was coming to get me and we'd go get something to eat. Over dinner we laughed about everything that was going on with Marty and Gina. As soon as he dropped me off at the house, I walked in to hear the phone ringing. I thought it might've been Gina telling me that she was half way there. A shrill voice that sounded a lot like what a dragon sounds like when they're about to spit fire, "What in God's name are you doing? You let them go to Florida? It blows my mind how you are so . . . so . . . I didn't raise a Vegas whore!" And that coming from a mother who was hell bent on destroying my life, inside and out. I did what I always did, which was to laugh. Not a ha ha thing but just a smirking laugh, one that says, "Who is this woman to call me and ask anything?" Feeling that she was trying to find a way to blame me I come back with, "I didn't let them go anywhere, I told her that I didn't want to go and she went anyway. So, you can't lay this one on me now woman."

It sounds as though I was disrespectful to my elder but if you knew everything I had been through with my mother-in-law you'd understand why I talked to her like this. Maybe you will see those stories in another book. Maybe the title will be, "My Journey through the Hot Place, or how to slay a fire breathing dragon with your mouth." But for now I'll just tell you that I endured many things with this woman.

Marty and Gina went to Florida but returned early because of what Gina's mother was saying. Mad beyond measure Gina started yelling at me from the time she hit the carpet in our living room, "Why did you tell my mother what we we're doing?" In my recliner I pulled my head away from the television and told her, "I didn't do anything, you want the truth, call her and get it yourself." We were three and half years into a marriage that was nearing its end. I gave her the shortest answers possible. Less is more is what I thought. She wants me to give her reason to blame me rather than where the blame actually goes, her lovely mother. It didn't matter one way or the other, the fact still remained that she had gone with Marty to Florida. I was pretty much over it and was resolved to be at peace with the situation.

Almost like the calm before the storm she treated me better for about two weeks. Then she approached me for another trip to Florida. My monetary situation had changed a bit and I told her that as long as I had someone go with me to the Boston Lobster Feast in Orlando, I was game for Crescent Beach. So we left with Marty in tow. As if we were going anywhere without him, and if you needed to ask, I drove most of the way down. We even passed Death Bridge eighty nine once again. However, it wasn't as eventful this time around. They added two lanes so Marty wasn't scared to cross it. After stopping twice, we arrived somewhere close to nine o'clock. I was worn out from driving so we went to sleep.

I woke up in the morning to the sun beating down through the curtains like it always did. But the only thing different was that Gina was out on the balcony. Not by herself but with who? You guessed it, that jolly old Marty. I can't say I was mad because it was as if I expected it. All day long I hung around the beach. And they never moved from their chairs on the balcony. About four o'clock that day I was getting hungry so I went in to get cleaned up. After which I asked them, "All right, which one of you guys are going with me to the Lobster place?" They looked at me and Gina started sneering while looking at Marty, "We don't want to go, we just kind of want to stay here on the balcony."

Shaking my head, puckering my lips, and even smiling a bit, I told them, "This is funny to me, I came down here to get some lobster and steamers and you guys are saying you won't go. Why did you tell me that you'd go when you really had no intention of it?" Borrowing a reaction from me they began to laugh as Gina replied, "Yeah we did, but that's the only way we could get out of North Augusta without my mother riding my back."

Driven to the point of frustration I left as swiftly as I could. The sun that was bearing down on me all day now had been hidden behind the clouds. And those clouds were now filled with the wet stuff. By the time I hit interstate ninety five which was about twenty two miles away. The rain was so intense that I could barely see out the window. I remember talking to God and asking him to protect me from an accident because it was pretty scary. It took like two hours to complete an hour and ten minute trip. The lobsters and steamers were Heavenly though. You know I didn't mind having to eat alone because the food was really that good. Dipping lobster in warm butter will make you forget your name sometimes much less the fact that you just happened to be eating alone. I left around seven back to the condo after eating myself into oblivion. The rain had subsided and the drive back didn't seem as treacherous.

I pushed open the door and saw a pizza box on the table. From the looks of it they were gone, but then I heard talking. These two nutcases were still . . . yep, out on the balcony. This puts them out there for like thirteen or fourteen hours. As I past the couch, I slid the balcony door open, "Hey guys, you still out here, huh?" Verifying to me that they were full from the pizza I asked them if they wanted to watch the rest of the Braves game with me. I was told that it was okay if I watched it but as for them they were okay with sitting out on the balcony overlooking the ocean. The game ended well for the Braves, but not so good for me. I went to sleep knowing that it was a total waste of time to even ask Gina to come to bed. It was an adventure that I am happy to say that I lived, learned, and navigated successfully though.

How do I judge success? During those long talks out on the balcony, that is when Marty and Gina planned how to leave Mr. Me here. It all works out for good, I thought. Less than two weeks later, I came home from a business trip in Orlando and walked in to find that my house had been literally cleaned out. Marty moved Gina into an apartment and was now comforting her in this difficult time. My brother had a wild hair and wanted to prove this by recording them together on video but I wasn't interested in finding a reason to bring her back. When Robb found out what happened he said, "Hey Coochie man, let me do this, I can beat him in three different languages and no one will ever know." I'll have you know that I didn't let Robb do anything. Both of us are Christians, so this would've been as close to backsliding as you can get without stepping in it. But the thing about this was that truly I felt like a burden had been lifted off me. Free as a bird left to conquer the skies in front of me, I felt I'd learned the things that God was trying to show me.

But what did I learn? And how could I apply it to the life I had in front of me? There were a couple of different answers to all the questions I was asking. God's timing has nothing to do with us having a watch. It has to do with us being watchful. When you're hurt by someone that you think you love . . . it really does hurt. However when it continues, you become calloused. I started taking everything Gina said with a grain of salt. I expected insults to be thrown at me as soon as my eyes would open in the morning. It was like, "Ho hum, another day in paradise." Someone asked Billy Graham one day if he'd ever thought about divorce, and he responded by telling them, "No, but I have thought about murder." Laughing of course with his wife Ruby by his side she agreed with love. I have to let you know now with absolute certainty that they were joking. They weren't serious so don't take that as a pass to go and kill your spouse.

Everyone who knows God's character knows that he may lead you to a place where you feel broken. And just in time, he'll supply you with the rope to pull yourself out of any quicksand that you may've found yourself in. I called on him to somehow get me out of a bad situation and he did. Not on my timeframe but his. To this day I'm not mad at Marty, or Gina. Being the best friend that he was, he did me a favor by ending my misery. I didn't believe in divorce and I would've stayed in an unhealthy situation but through Marty, I was given enough rope to free myself from a certain death in the relational quicksand that I stumbled upon.

I didn't want anyone going through what I went through. So I designed a cheat sheet for people who are a lot like me. Maybe the kind that wants to be the Prince Charming to a damsel in distress. They want to play the village idiot and jump into something they have no business jumping into. It is a virtual force field for the heart. A barrier around your capacity to love, that's protecting you from undeserving abuse. But what is it?

I was taught by experience that if you S . . . L . . . O . . . W . . . down you'll be able to notice when something isn't right. Had I taken the time to listen to some of the things that Gina said in the beginning of our relationship I would've known that the ending would have looked a whole lot better sooner. What would've happened if I'd left her at her mother's house? If I slowed down I would've known that this girl was in no shape to love me in the way that I wanted to be loved. That's why this needs to be the first step of anyone who is beginning a new relationship with the desired result being marriage.

1. SLOW DOWN—I learned to look at things objectively because I was able to slow things down. It's the same thing as leaving on a mini vacation. You're able to look at all angles of the situation and judge for yourself if it is truly . . . the way you want to go.

2. When SLOW, be ALONE—It's not enough to slow it down because your relational motion can be sped up at any time. Take yourself out of the moment. And don't invite anyone else to come along for the ride. That way there will be no additional variables being thrown at you from a different perspective. Maybe one, but it'll be from someone totally unfamiliar with what you're going through.

3. Ask yourself, "Can this really be LOVE?"—I asked myself that question a couple of times before I got married and truly should have answered it before I walked down the aisle. Do you remember in the movie Field of Dreams when Kevin Costner was told, "If you build it they will come." That is the same thing as knowing when its love. You have to build it first and it'll come. Take the time in the beginning to see if what you believe to be true is true indeed. Otherwise what you end up with is a once divorced man looking for his true love that he never truly found in the first place.

4. OBSERVE your surroundings—When I was with my best friends I don't think I listened too well. As a matter of fact I know I didn't. They were telling me that I was getting lambasted by this girl while we dating. I didn't want to notice. Why? I think I was going entirely too fast. That should be the part of you that needs to slow down. You're able to observe more keenly. If you want to know how things are going in your relationship, check the facial expressions on your closest friend's face. I can tell you that if it looks brutal, take it as that. Walk around like a hit man looking for his next target. The little things that are overlooked in the beginning will become painful mementos if you chose to marry the problem. Just be alert and don't let love or the fear of not having it blind you from finding a true and lasting relationship.

5. Finally, Test the WATER—True love can be found rather easily. However, a soul mate is about as hard to find as a needle in a haystack. When you're jumping into a relationship, don't just jump in. Think of it as a mountain stream in the middle of Cherokee, North Carolina. The

water is so cold up there even in the summertime that you have to ease your way into it. Feet first, then up to your knees, then the waist, and then you just have built up enough confidence to jump in for complete enjoyment. You know you're in this thing for good when dive in from waist deep and get your hair wet. Knowing that you tested the water three different times; Feet, knee, waist and you're now ready to live the good life. It's the same with a relationship . . . test the water three different times while following the previous four steps.

By following these suggestions, you'll be able to pursue the perfect mate. You may even eliminate the possibility of divorce. It's not a full proof method. But it does protect the individual from incurring endless ridicule from someone who is trying to get out of their current situation. Think of it this way, you just may end up finding the love of your life while thinking you've lost the capacity to love forever. And never again will you have to wonder, or even ask yourself that rhetorical question, "Can this really be love?"

7.

The List

THIS TIME OF MY LIFE COULDN'T END FAST ENOUGH. I WAS CERTAIN that it couldn't and wouldn't happen again. At least that's why I came up with my own shallow version of a cheat sheet. If I'd been through the hot place and survived, someone else could as well. I guess you could call it my giving back to society. But what actually is this list? It's a creative manifest of qualities that I'd look for in a woman. I thought I'd resolve some of the expeditiousness that I'd have during the early stages of a relationship. By grabbing a pen and paper I gave myself the opportunity to gauge what I actually wanted more. Was it beauty? Because no one wants to marry an ugly person do they? How about intelligence? I don't think anyone yearns for someone who they can't relate to intellectually, right? I have to be honest though. When I started this list it was pretty basic. You know in a shallow . . . basic kind of way.

Two items I wrote first was that the woman I desired had to be pretty. Someone that's pleasant to look at was a top priority. Superficial at best, I knew that she had to be beautiful. The funny thing about that was I actually didn't see myself as handsome. So to me, it was like I was trying to get a Princess to marry the frog, before she even kissed him. Please don't misunderstand me. I classified myself on scale of one to ten as a five. Not handsome but not ugly either. And you know me I was okay with occupying the exact middle.

But what I wanted to find was a nine or maybe even a ten. When I look back at this time of my life I feel a little ashamed. The

90

expectations I set for anyone I dated was almost unattainable. It wasn't fair for me to set such a high bar as a measure for a woman. It wasn't just that though. I wrote down even more. Traits that would identify my personal longing, I wanted someone who'd love me for me. However, one thing I discovered is that I should've kept writing. By doing so, it's was almost guaranteed that I would've been increasingly specific.

What happens to you when you only have limited items on your list? You end up grading a woman's worth based upon what she looks like. For the women out there who may be upset with a statement like that, please forgive me. But you have to know that in a small way you do it too. One has to find someone attractive in order for them to develop a love relationship with them. As in the movie Titanic, "It's a mathematical certainty." Imagine sitting across the table from the elephant man on a blind date. Would you at any time after that dinner give him the time of day? No, I don't really think you would. The only reason you'd even check your watch was to see how fast it took to get away from him. So to a degree everyone sets their own personal aspirations when it comes to finding a mate.

Gina left in May of nineteen ninety seven. About two weeks after that I went over to her mother's house to ask her if there was anything I could do to get back together. The divorce issue was still eating at me. Because being a Christian for most of my life I didn't want to divorce. I was torn between what was right and what may've been wrong, but Lord have mercy, I wanted right for me at the moment. I wanted divorce, but I didn't. Maybe it was the fact that I'd lost. I was telling myself that I wanted to save the marriage without having the actual belief to verify what I was actually saying. So one day I drove over to the mother's house. And sitting across from her at the table I asked, "Is there anything I did, or could do to save this marriage?" I was playing with her keys while I waited for her answer, "You are so full of @#$%, you always have been full of it, and all I want from you is my last name back and the three hundred dollars you owe me for the bird."

I started smiling and immediately dropped the keys on the table. Her mother was in the kitchen and turned around to see what was going to happen next. "You know what, you're right. I may be full of it, but I'll have you know . . . this'll be the last time I'll care about the direction of our lives together. Oh! And here is your three hundred dollars," is the last thing I blurted out. Pulling the money out of my wallet I threw it down as I walked out. She looked kind of shocked to hear something so final so she said, "I guess I'll see you later." I smirked like I always do, "Uh! No, you won't."

That was around the thirtieth of May. And from that moment on, I actually thought I was going to be alone for the rest of my life. Which is something I really didn't want, I wanted to be with someone. Just not with her. Being in the state of mind I was in, I wanted to make sure that I had some kind of game plan for the next go around. The list began at that moment. Remember though, I only had four items on the first list. Shallow Chuck before there was a Shallow Hal except I didn't have Tony Robbins to put that mojo thingy on me. I was happy to be going in a different direction than where I was going with Gina. My father and I were traveling more and more, and I didn't have much time for a relationship anyway. But as soon as July arrived I was involved in a list changing event.

Dad and I were home and we needed to get some supper. Like we always did, we closed our eyes and envisioned ourselves driving down the road naming all the restaurants in the process. For the night, Casa Di Pizza beat out all other choices. I wasn't really prepared for what I was about to see. My list that I created was checked off one by one. Check one being the Blond hair, Check two was the Blue Eyes, and Check zero was the girl I saw who was absolutely beautiful. All of the items on my list had been checked.

My father knew her because she was the daughter of a policy holder of his. He told me where they lived. And here I was, being the kind of man who was scared to death to ask anyone anything. I garnered the confidence to drive over to her house and ask her out. Shawna never knew me because she was about five years younger. And like me, she was in the process of a divorce. Finding something that we had in common wasn't hard at all. The more I talked the more I ascertained that she and I would make a good couple.

I was intent on keeping to the list though. And everything had been met with ease. Shawna and I started dating seriously towards the end of July. I have to tell you celebrating my birthday that year became a happier occasion than I'd experienced in all the four years combined with Gina. My father was staying with me at the house one day and it was early morning. The phone rang and I wondered who'd be calling at such an early hour. I picked it up and answered, "Hello." The voice on the other end wasn't familiar so I tried to detect who it was, "Hey, I want to know if I could take you to lunch for your birthday" Still having problems with knowing who I was talking to, "Who is this?" I could hear an obvious hesitation, "This is Ga . . . Gina." I started to chuckle and responded, "Gina who? Gina Jordon? What do you want with taking me to lunch?" Gina sounded like she was trying to hold something back, "I just wanted to take you to lunch, is that okay?" There are times in your life where you can take revenge for some of the things that were done to you or maybe even said to you but it's really best if you just remain silent. So trying to be as nice as I could I retorted, "That's going to be an affirmative no, number one I don't understand you. I don't see or hear from you in two months, then this! Yeah, that'll be a definite no babe. But hey . . . thanks for calling." There was a hint of retribution when I hung up the phone. I felt like I'd gotten her back for all those times she wasn't so nice to me. So, at that moment I wanted to tell Shawna everything that just happened.

Telling her was something I took solace in knowing that I now had someone to share things with, whereas before I had no one. Shawna knew what I was going through because of a similar experience with her ex-husband. Then she asked if I wanted to go back to Gina and I told her, "That's a definite, No!" I think she was thankful to hear such reaffirmation coming from me. That I still wanted to be with her more than anyone else.

There's something about making a list with limited items though. Yes, I found a woman who matched it but it was as if I settled for what I really didn't want in a woman. What do I mean by that? I discovered that there was so much more I wanted but somehow it was left off. Yes, I knew then it was time to go back to the pen and paper.

Brian called on a sunny day in September to ask us, I say us because at the time Shawna and I was a couple, to come to Carowinds for a company picnic. We were excited because this was going to be our first out of town trip together. Driving forty miles north of Columbia on Interstate seventy seven, she asked, "What do you think about tattoos?" Not even thinking about the answer I replied, "I think they're nasty, some people that have them have trouble adjusting to a normal workplace. I don't actually know anyone who has one."

How about when you lift your big ole foot up off the floor and shove it right into your mouth? So much so that your teeth end up landing all over the floor, and it was then where I diagnosed my own foot-to-mouth disease. The way she looked at me was unforgettable. Her face turned blood red as she screamed, "Well, I've got two. And I like them. And I don't appreciate your comment. You're something else you know that?" Without faltering I tried to redeem myself, "However, if you add color to them they can be quite colorful." She wasn't handing out any rapid redemption that day either. So, knowing I'd hurt her I begged for forgiveness and she obliged. She was a Christian so I guess she found it necessary.

I thought maybe our trip would be hampered by what I said. In reality though, she was even nicer to me than she was normally. I guess it was because she wanted to make sure that Brian and Del liked her; which I am happy to say they did. All day long we rode different rides and had a ton of fun. The company paid for everything so we enjoyed it even more. She and I were made to feel like we were employees. Brian's boss even made me look good in front of Shawna because she asked me about my computer experiences with Visual Basic. It turned out to be a wonderful weekend. I was relieved to know that the tattoo thing didn't ruin it. But it did open my eyes to things that were missing off my list. Needing a character refinement, I chose to be more specific when going back to the list.

Shawna was an improvement from the other women I'd gone out with. Beautiful and witty, she did have several faults that I overlooked. Imagine trying to make people laugh and you're girlfriend laughs to support you. That's the way it's supposed to be, right? And there I was, being held out to dry by her shaking her head, "You're so freaking goofy. And please stop, you're not that funny." I let her have this one because of what I said about her tattoos, but now, because of what I experienced. I was attaching new and definitive ideas to my list every day.

Our relationship lasted about eight months which was normal for me. I guess this is the point where both parties find the real "you" character locked within the desire to be in a relationship. After the tattoo thing, I realized that I could continue a good thing with Shawna by just keeping my mouth shut. But there would be occasions where I didn't want to be involved with her romantically, or any other way at that.

We still had a good time together. But some Friday nights she'd want to go bowling with some of her friends from work. Mind you, it wasn't the bowling that was problem. I wasn't very keen on smoking, and Shawna smoked. I wasn't even okay with drinking either but I wanted her to know that I was always the designated driver for my best friends, not hers. I mean it when I tell you that bowling wasn't the problem. It was what they were going to do at the bowling alley. Drinking, smoking, and being radically rambunctious while trying to bowl. Looking back on it, maybe I was just the old fogey sitting there, just wanting to be somewhere else. So needless to say I only went the one time.

It was always eventful when she planned these things and expected me to be there, I wanted nothing of it. She even called me on multiple instances, "Stuck up and arrogant." Then I'd give her the best self-controlled response I could, "Not looking at it like that, I would rather do something else than spending money on something you're going to pee out later." She snickered back, "What about tea? You pee that out too don't you?" Turning my head to side I said, "Yes, you do. But you don't have to wave the smoke out of your eyes to do it." She wasn't looking for a fight so she replied, "I just don't understand why you won't go with me and my friends."

Letting her know that it was mostly the smoke getting in my eyes that kept me out of bowling alleys, I informed her that the fact everyone was there to get inebriated wasn't helping me come to an affirmative decision either. Shawna would smile with those big pearly white teeth of hers and say, "Please?" After which I'd just tell her, "Have a good time, I'll be here if you want to come by afterwards. Oh! If you need a ride home, call me and I'll come and get you. But for you only, I ain't no flipping taxi driver."

Pondering her point of view, I can see how why she said I was arrogant. I thought I was holding firm to my beliefs when to her. It was more like I was attacking hers. The one who is always looking for a winnable situation just found out by staying home that he lost. How did that happen? After all those bowling nights together, Shawna and a man friend of hers got together. Eventually getting together by marriage, and welcoming their first child into the world. What did I learn when this happened?

Had I not been so firm I may've had a different ending to my relationship. But I'd much rather be resting on my laurels than resting on someone else's. However, I was who I was and she was who she was and the rest of the story is history. We broke up for good around February nineteen ninety eight. All through the relationship I wrote down many things but some I felt were unattainable. So I kept the ones I was most comfortable with.

The list already contained attributes that I looked for in a mate. I knew I wanted a pretty woman. Blond hair was a must up until Shawna. I learned that I might be missing something that God had in store for me had I limited him to Blond hair and Blue eyes. Adjusting my list, I chose not to limit myself to a particular color of hair. Walking on the beach one day with your pale complexion girlfriend gives you a new course in life. I noticed that she was getting blisters on her skin from the sun. Superficially, my list began to materialize. I want a woman who could walk down the beach without getting burnt. Number five on the list . . . able to withstand the sunlight.

It sounds so trivial having an item on the list like this but when you can go to the beach and tan in two days without getting burnt, you want to have someone to share this time with. In order for Shawna to enjoy the beach, she'd have to go to tanning salon and get a base tan for about three days. Only then would she be able to withstand the sun.

The list was an intricate part of my development. It's what I defined to myself what I wanted. And let me make myself clear, it was for me, not anyone else. With Shawna, I realized that I didn't want a woman who drank alcohol, smoked, or got burnt while walking the white sand beaches. Something else, I didn't want someone who wanted joint checking accounts after three weeks into a relationship. Here I go again trying to find a woman putting them into categories. This is my list and it is my prerogative to define which characteristics I find more appealing.

Why is the list so important though? Imagine going through life settling for what you can get rather than holding out for the best. It really does work. Sometimes it doesn't seem like it. But getting to a point where we feel like we are pushing God into our time zone. When in reality he operates in all time zones. Had I waited until I completed my list of finding my dream of a woman, I would've saved myself a lot of heartache. Trying to fit one woman into my little box of perfection was hard to do. My mother tells me that I made people feel like crap. Let me just say that wasn't my intention. Disappearing into my own little world I just wouldn't give too much attention to make them think I was interested. To all those girls that may have been affected by my actions I am eternally sorry.

The answer to the question may seem more complex than simple but the list is important to the development of a relationship. After Shawna, I steered clear of anything that wasn't on my list. I wanted to make sure that I measured up to her as well. Not only was I setting the bar higher for her, but for me too. My work ethic wasn't something I was proud of. I thought that if I sold one policy that I'd be finished for the day. Knowing I should've stored up some nuts for the winter, if you will. I didn't want to present someone who had to borrow money from his father to a woman who was expecting me to support her.

Not only did I make a list of what I wanted, but I detailed to myself what I wanted to bring. It sort of follows the Covered

Dish Delight deal. If I was overweight and one of the traits I wanted for my woman was that she be skinny. What kind of man would require something from someone that he didn't require of himself? I considered myself to be a man who was in shape so why couldn't I anticipate a woman who was in shape herself?

This book is all about suggestions so I'll give you a couple. Never show anyone your list. Why wouldn't you? Sacred to you and to you only, it's for your eyes only. Imagine being in a relationship with the love of your life and then they find out that they don't match twenty five percent of your list. On the other hand, picture trying to court someone who is only going out with you for dinner. When they feast their eyes upon that list, they just might run out of the house looking to escape anything that resembles a love relationship. Remember you were the brother they never had. And that is why you should never reveal those intimate thoughts that make up your list. When the time is right, you'll know.

Secondly, be specific in what you define. I was writing things that tickled my fancy. But I wasn't specific. Needless to say, whenever I found myself in a new relationship I'd try and change my list to fit them rather than wait for them to conform to my list. One of the first things I wrote was that I wanted a beautiful woman. What would happen to me if I'd just settled with a woman who was beautiful? Yes, I would have something pleasant to look at but she could also be dumb as dirt.

Thirdly, you need to keep writing, be sure to add those traits you desire. It doesn't have to be to a degree or a percentage point. In other words, make sure that if beauty is what you want, and you also like the fact that she laughs at your jokes. Don't assign percentage points to each item. If you have beauty at seventy five percent and laugh ability at twenty five, there might be a problem. You'll be sitting across the table staring at her with the words, "You're not that funny!" rolling off her lips. If you have laugh ability at seventy five percent and beauty at twenty five, all you're going to get is a woman laughing at everything that's said. Even the waiter asking her what she wants to drink. All the while, she's letting her food roll down her multiple chins only to have what seems to be an Adam's apple hurl it across the table like it was a tennis ball. Whew! There's got to be a balance. Otherwise, things like that will happen with regularity. And somehow I wouldn't think that anyone would want that.

The forth thing is when you finally do arrive at your desired destination, be patient. Sometimes the one that you love may not meet all your standards. They may meet all but one, but you know something? God may not be finished with them yet. My experience is to leave it up to the Lord for him to work it out. If someone doesn't match anything on your list, you need to leave that one alone. God has better things to do than change someone's mind when he has someone else in mind for you.

Being patient allows you to see the forest among the trees. In a previous chapter I told you about my ability to observe my situations from a different perspective. Patience is that vacation. It is the river you are floating down to figure out the complexities of a future relationship. What happens is that you end up riding a magnificent wave right into the white sandy beaches of a wonderful relationship. Learn to wait until your list is complete before making a permanent decision that could haunt you for the rest of your life.

8.

Barrelling Beyond Before

SOMEWHERE TOWARDS THE END OF TWO THOUSAND I HAD AN interesting happenstance. My job allowed me to have Sunday off, and I wanted to start going to church again. I hadn't gone systematically for quite some time. Therefore, I believe my relationship with Christ was suffering. I think solely because I wasn't active anywhere. So doing the only thing I could to sustain my desire to follow him, I found a home within a local independent Baptist church. My sisters graduated High School there. So I found it appealing. I visited with them before but I wasn't actively involved. Up to that point anyway, I hadn't gone anywhere in a while so just to be going somewhere was a step in the right direction. As soon as I walked through the door, I saw a couple of people there with whom I played basketball. I tried to find a seat near them so I wouldn't feel alone. It began to feel considerably more comfortable to be settling in to a God centered life.

Then two weeks went by, I was approached by one of the single adults and was asked, "Have you met my cousin? She saw you and would like to meet you." My flattery was apparent. But my desire to have a girlfriend was not. The job I had was an Operations agent with Delta Airlines. And I was totally happy being able to maximize my flight benefits every week. Not really being tied down to something or someone. My objective was to fly free everywhere in the world that Delta flew. However, my response wasn't registering. I don't think she even heard me. Because she kept on persisting that I should meet her cousin. I told her she needed to fly more so she could understand where I was coming from. Then she assumed that I'd go to Veracruz Mexican restaurant after church and she was right. Because that was the place everyone went. Unbeknownst to me, it is exactly there where she set up an encounter so I wouldn't be surprised. Chomping down on my Speedy Gonzales, rice no beans, and low and behold she walked right up to the table and sat down right next to me. Immediately I looked at the cousin as if to say, "What is this?" Kindness is a virtue that I would test to see if I had a valid argument for being kind. I believe that I was cordial enough to her.

Alise was a pretty young woman to some extent. And I liked the fact that she was a Christian so it was easy to talk to her. But that is where she started telling me about her past. I was blown away by the way she'd tell me that she lost her husband about six months before. With graphic detail mind you. An asphalt loader he was working on was hit by a tractor trailer on the interstate. Tragic to say the least, she was still so young. So that kind of stuff is almost never heard of. But I remained there as a compassionate listener. That is all. Christians are supposed to be compassionate . . . right? But to tell you the truth, these kinds of happenings take me to a place in my mind where I don't want to go. It seemed to me that I should just pacify the cousin, and then get the heck out of there. But being the caring man I was, I chose to ask Alise to a movie. After a couple of months I realized that her husband's death was much more than a death. It was in all actuality, slowly killing her. When someone tells you two weeks before you met them that they were sleeping on the grave of their spouse, what is one to do? Please do not take this wrong, but it would be best to run, and run like the wind. With all the training I had with the Local Emergency Response program, I thought I was prepared to be helpful. And all I really did was fuel the fire that burned deep within her. It became a challenge for me to try and guess which Alise would show up. Personally, I didn't want to continue but something inside of me wouldn't allow me to let go.

We'd be driving down the road and she'd see something that would remind her of her husband. Then all of sudden she'd start crying. I, being the compassionate one tried to ask if there was anything I could do. Maybe even try to change the subject. One instance was where I changed the subject . . . to that of insurance. I thought this to be safe. But was I wrong? It set off emotions that I'd never seen before. Never been one to raise my voice so I didn't want to say one word. I just let her go on and on with this rant. It was kind of hard to take because I saw myself as a perfectionist, and here she was saying that I'd never measure up. Rather than risk not having a ride home, I chose to play the "I must be somewhere else but here" card. Ever heard of this one? I can't say that I made it up. It is just one of those things that when you are involved in an increasingly volatile situation, you basically picture yourself somewhere else.

White Toyota truck driving down the Gordon highway, barbeque in the floorboard, and then in a flash I'm sitting on the sandy shores of Cancun, Mexico. I'd have to go somewhere else in my mind because being there in that truck would've driven me crazy to know that I hadn't perfected anything. As we pulled into her driveway, she said that it'd be best if we didn't see each other anymore. She felt as if she were cheating on her husband. I didn't agree or disagree as her mental state wouldn't have accepted my response anyway. The best thing I did was get in my car and drive away.

From that moment on I referred to her as Crazy Alise. Feeling that I may have failed at my attempt to create a successful relationship, I thought I'd give her time. But in reality, she gave me time. Furthermore, my transition really did go very well. I did not miss the incessant badgering one iota. I tried desperately to understand where she was coming from, I really did. But every time I either said something I shouldn't have or I did something that I shouldn't have. So moving on was the only option I had. And that is when I clarified to myself that I'll never go out on a date with anyone who has had anyone they were close to die. I don't think it would be fair to that person for me to be so different in how I perceived their actions.

Crazy Alise and I had a bad breakup. In the end I said things of which I'm not proud. Now remember that I never experienced or really knew anything about this kind of condition so please forgive me for what I said to her. We were at the cemetery where her husband was buried. She glared at me with tears in her eyes and delicately cried out, "All I want is my husband back!" In a split second not even thinking what was coming out. I told her in my most cynical tone, "Go get him, dig him up, he's right out there." I might as well have shot her between the eyes because that look wasn't something I wanted to see again. If I had ever known before, I knew at that moment that this relationship was over. But it didn't stop there. I continued on, "There are certain things that happen in life that you either have to get over, or it'll get over you. Pick your poison woman. You can either live or die, but it's entirely up to you!" Those that knew any better were taking cover because of all the verbal gunfire being shot around that room. Once again, I was not proud of myself at this moment. There was nothing I could've said to her that would have made it any better. So I did the next best thing to disappearing altogether. I got in my car and drove off those sacred grounds for good. Never to be seen again.

On my way back to North Augusta I drove down the interstate wondering what I could've done differently. I guess I was feeling guilty for saying what I did. But more importantly I wanted to be more compassionate in how I handled a situation like this one. In those times of discovery the Lord speaks to you in a manner that makes you feel like a trumpet is blaring right there beside your ear. Almost to the point of shattering your ear drum. His still small voice uttering, "And we know that God causes everything to work together for the good of those who love God and are called according to his purpose." But how would this apply to something like death? And how would this be applicable to someone who was being browbeaten by their past?

What was he trying to tell me? My conclusion was that if God causes everything to work out for good then eventually it'll work out for good. Even though you may be in the midst of a nightmare, it's not where you'll end up. Take comfort in that fact alone. Unhappy times that occur will not be there forever. How do you know this? Because God is incapable of lying, he must always tell the truth. And if he loves you enough to tell you that everything comes out good. Then guess what? It really does turns out good!

Just to let you know, Crazy Alise did find her wonderland. It doesn't end in a total loss for her. She actually finds love with the man who owned the cemetery where her husband was buried. I have never seen her other than to hear that the children that she wanted to bear were doing well. That is the thing about how our bad situation turned out good for her. This man who would fall in love with Alise knew exactly what it felt like to lose someone close. His wife passed away about six months before her husband. And to me, it was a match made in heaven. I had no clue what these guys were going through. Moping along in my own state of happiness, and I guess I was selfish to an extent. So maybe now, I bet you'd even hear her say, "It's all good!"

To have never seen her since; I've not had an opportunity to apologize for my abhorrent actions. In my ignorance I was unaware of what people go through. However, I knew later what people must go through in order to reach a point where life is worth living again. Deal with your problems as for what they are. An opportunity for incredible personal growth may sound like a constant dripping to someone who has had the love of their lifetime suddenly die. If God didn't call you home, then he still must have a plan for you. If help is needed, then don't draw up into a little ball and wish for your death, ask for help. Why is this so important? Because if you're stuck in that position for long, all you are going to do is roll around as if you were a beach ball going around in circles. There may be someone who wants to be loved, and wants you to love. I keep reverting back to a saying in Meet Joe Black, but keep your options open, lightning could strike.

If Alise would just go down to the cemetery all the time to eat on the bench beside her husband, it wouldn't be a good thing, disastrous in fact. But she didn't. She'd talk to the man who had been where she had been. Seen the same things she saw. Maybe even felt the same things she felt. What ultimately happened is that she left herself open and fell in love with a man not like me, but with a man who actually knew what she was going through. I'd have say with absolute certainty she knows now that everything does works together for the good, so good for her.

Barreling beyond before can mean different things to different people. In fact, there are circumstances that arrive in life and one can either welcome or deny it. My sister Beth was one of those people who welcomed that opportunity. Born almost in an intolerable situation, she lived for five years in what most would characterize as unstable conditions. Her biological mother was someone who didn't take the responsibility of raising a child as a priority. Beth was moved from an unstable to a somewhat stable grandmother's home. The only love she'd feel was from this grandmother. Known as Darlene in those days, she felt safe within this home. There were events happening within those walls that could've taken a child stained by sexual abuse, and given her hope. But it didn't. It never allowed her to garner one ounce of self-worth. However, her decisions made, albeit, later in life, to take those suppressive memories and catapult them into the far depths of her mind. How she do it? Was it an easy process? That would have to be a conclusive, "No" it wasn't an easy process.

I can remember as if it was yesterday. The grass freshly cut with a smell that permeates the air when it's just been mowed. Sweat had just begun to form on my forehead. I was throwing baseballs in the yard, and out of nowhere drove up into the driveway a car with state license plates. Normally a bad thing to see plates of these types drive up into your driveway. But this was a good thing though. As the doors opened, my curiosity was being peaked at its highest level. To the point where the ball being thrown barely scathed my head, I escaped injury to me or anyone else when my glove magically rose to the heavens and snatched it from the clouds.

Two fragile little girls emerged from the back seat. Fear written all over their faces. As if they could speak through their petrified lips, they'd stare in bewilderment. Looking at my mother was this helpless child asking her without ever saying a word, "What in the world is happening to me?" Her sister Jackie was clinging as close to her without being adjoined to her hip. There must've been a million questions. But also, there must've been a million and half emotions. They were captured from a house that would have certainly led them to a life of despair, only to be led to a home full of unconditional love and unlimited personal potential. You could say they were given a second chance at life. Yet, I don't think they knew it at that moment. Accompanied by a social worker, Darlene and Jackie were walking slowly with each step heavier than the last.

In an instant my mother burst out the front door to greet them. Remember now, that both of these girls had been through an emotionally scarring abuse that involved two men. So to see one who they'd be sharing a house, it must've been a terrifying experience. I didn't approach them because I was one of those guys when I was young, that nothing would interrupt my ball playing. Whether I was playing basketball, football, or even baseball; nothing would stop me. Besides, my mother had her hands full when they arrived. She was so excited to be embarking on an adventure with these two girls. The group of them walked into the house to inspect their prospective futures. Still their timid spirits were ever present. The social worker and my mother sat down at the table to discuss details. The girls found comfort within the confines of our couch. Crunched up together between the pillows, I believe that it where they felt most safe. There was so much that was new to my mother then, as well as all of us. You see, before the decision to adopt was made, the entire family had to go through a pre-adoption interview. So yes, we were prepared for the arrival of the girls but not so prepared for how we would handle the emotions that would come up from time to time. One thing though, is that we were all willing. A life changing and life altering state of mind would most definitely be in store.

Up to that point, it was only men in the house, except for my mother of course. And personally, I wasn't at all happy that I'd now have to wear shorts in my room, as well as the rest of the house. With girls now, there'd be no fruit of the looms walking around. So to say that it was an adjustment is an understatement. Truthfully though, to this day I tell you it was worth it.

My father worked as an independent insurance broker. He was gone a lot when I was young. But this particular day he arrived right on time. Finally, when he came walking through the door. Darlene started crying. And when I say crying, I say torrential downpour from those big old cheeky tear ducts. She looked at my dad as if he were the grim reaper coming to take them to that next place. He recognized that she was afraid of him so he quickly positioned himself in his bedroom away from mother and the social worker. He stayed there until he was given approval to come out. My mother was perplexed as to what to do next. So along with the social worker they tried to reintroduce my father as he was asked to come from the room. Needless to say, this introduction went better; both girls began to ease up on the tension they were feeling.

As they removed themselves from their hiding place between the cushions, everyone sat down for a round table discussion except this was a rectangular table. It was really the girls just becoming acquainted with our new family, and their new surroundings. Their faces began to perk up when they found out that they'd have their own bedroom. The only bad thing about them having their own rooms is that they'd have to share a bathroom. From their prospective, everything was getting better by the minute.

I have to be honest, it was a little different having girls in the house. Where you have to be aware of what you wear around the house and what you say. It was hard for someone like me to adjust because I was used to being able to go as I please. And for the first couple of months, every time I'd look at them, it was as if I was the reaper they saw in my dad's eyes. As we moved from day to day, their timid nature began to subside. The smile that was never seen was now becoming a staple of their character. I could see how this would affect most people but now this was making its scheduled arrival into our home. Honestly though, I was kind of still getting used to this change.

How would this event be an opportunity for personal growth? My two sisters now known as Beth and Maggie were given the worst possible future at birth but released into a world of unlimited potential. All they had to do was open their eyes to know that we were a family now. They were now free to pursue dreams they had never known before. Beth was one of those girls who would show everything that was going on inside on her face. So to see her go through the adjustment process, it was rather painful. Why? I believe it was because this was a girl who had been abused by someone around my same age. There was nothing I could do to stop her from looking at me differently. That was until she became a member of that local Independent Baptist Church. She repressed memories that ultimately were tearing her apart. The names Patrick and Leroy still detest her to this day. These guys were doing things to her even as an infant that would turn your stomach. Both people should've been tied up and beaten within an inch of their lives. Maybe even drug down a long dirt road for good measure. But coming from her, forgiveness was not something she understood nor was she handing out at that moment in her life. It would come later.

It wasn't just the sexual abuse that was bothering them. It was the constant emotional and physical abuse they experienced as well. People that were supposed to be protecting her were now taking full advantage of their sinful nature. Her biological mother wasn't any help because she'd leave them only to be further abused. It was not a good situation at all. The state removed them from that terrible position and placed them strategically within their maternal grandmother's protective grasp. Except for the fact that the protection the state sought wasn't being offered in that home. It was once again a playground for the wicked. The uncles were given almost free reign within those walls. It was as if they were taunting both girls. As time would pass, the state stepped in and ultimately closed this relationship connection once and for all. Both girls were then placed into foster care.

In every case that has to deal with sexual abuse, it is extremely difficult to come out of it without any scars. And I am not saying that Beth isn't scarred in some way still today. But what I am saying is that we have to remember that there is one who remains scarred to this day to remind us of our eternal forgiveness. Through years of Southern Gospel preaching it was becoming evident to Beth that she needed something internal to happen. What was eating her alive was the fact that she felt she was being held captive by these memories. By this anger, she was unable to trust men in general terms, or in not so general terms. But God has a way of releasing just the right amount of grace when he knows that we need it. And grace in its abundant nature was relinquished that night with her hind parts parked in a pew.

Forgiveness was never something she thought the uncles or mother deserved. Bitter to the bone, she wasn't about to let these people get into to her "New" life. She'd leave them as they wished in their total depravity. It was best left alone she presumed. Up until that night anyway is when Brother Preacher man spoke about God's forgiveness. I said Brother Preacher man because at this church everyone there was called Brother. You could hear ringing through the congregation, "Brother John! Brother Sam! Brother Zack!" I thought it funny because in a Southern Baptist Church, this just didn't happen. It was always Mister. But whether it was Mister or Brother it didn't matter, what did matter though; was that the word about forgiveness was actually being taught to what she thought to be one person, it was just her. She felt as if everyone left and Brother Preacher man was there talking to her, and to her only. She jumped to her feet and began to run to the Alter. She knew that if she'd forgive as the Lord forgives, she could begin a new life. Where these people who had held her captive within her own mind would no longer have domain over her; she was now protected by the everlasting arms of a forgiving Father.

The moment she dropped to her knees to relinquish those thoughts is the second she realized what true freedom is. It was as if a cancer had been healed. The sky had been cleared of any such cloud that'd hold her motionless. She wasn't able to look at what had happened to her. Because now, she was free. The act of forgiveness is liberating. By giving these people the forgiveness they did not necessarily deserve, she was now free to live a full and completely abundant life.

Beth's before gave her a chance to be taken from the literal depths of hell into a stable satisfying relationship with a family that loved her as heavenly as humanly possible. Why was it so important for her to forgive? She didn't know it at the time but the Bible has explicit instructions to forgive. She was given the word that we should forgive seventy times seven. Which to her meant a lot of forgiving had to take place. She'd begin on that Alter, and would learn even further that she'd apply this teaching to her life for the rest of her life. Given the opportunity to speak to her grandmother, she asked why she wasn't protected. A valid answer was never given. However, Beth is the kind of woman who chose to forgive her grandmother. The blame game was never given consideration. Beth knew then that seventy times seven really does mean seventy times seven.

Where does this all get someone who has barreled beyond before? As for Beth, she navigated through numerous boys to find the man of her dreams. She was honest enough to let him know that this event wouldn't steal, kill, or destroy anything from their current or future relationship. Needless to say, her marriage was the supreme transformation. She was able to look blazingly at the past, pull back the sling shot of life, and shoot everything that happened to her into the great unknown. Beth has just welcomed her own son into this world and is about as happy as a woman can be. She'll continue to live successfully and maintain forgiveness within her own life for the rest of her life.

Her reflection was that she was born again twice. When the Lord told her that she was a new creature in Christ, she believed him. She was born again when she accepted Christ, and she was born again when she accepted the need for her to offer forgiveness. God does speak volumes when someone turns around long enough to listen. And in everything that happened; my sister Beth turned around to listen and truly learned that everything really does turn out good!

9.

The Chutzpah Of Columbia County

THE LIST I DELICATELY DEFINED TOOK DIFFERENT FORMS ALMOST every day. I'd add certain items as soon as I recognized a trait I desired most in a woman. Being a musician, I told myself I wanted to have someone who could sing or play an instrument. If I found what I was looking for, we'd write music together. Remember I was making this list to fit me and I didn't care if it was attainable or not.

So after Shawna, I knew that being in a relationship for me wasn't going to be productive unless I first, got things straight in my head. I mean take the tattoo thing, boy was that tragic? I needed to let people know that these skin arts aren't particularly for me, but for them, they're fine.

From that moment on, my sole purpose was to disappear so I'd be able to define my taste with my travels throughout Europe. The more I traveled overseas I realized I wanted to experience the landmarks with someone by my side. Sitting there at the Coliseum in Rome provides you with a new perspective, where couples are holding hands while pointing towards the Piazzas. It really does make you think there is something more to life than yourself.

I'd just gotten off the plane from Ireland and I wanted to get some software from Best Buy. It wasn't that far from the airport, so I drove on over. Only to pace aisle to aisle trying to figure out the best game to pass my time on the next trip I was planning. Then all of a sudden, a man taps me on the shoulder and asked me if I needed anything. You know these guys? They jump from the appliance department to the software aisle within blinks of an eye. You never know where these guys are coming from. But as he tapped away, I turned around abruptly only to find out that I knew him. Actually, in nineteen ninety seven, I played keyboards in a praise band where he served as youth pastor at a church in downtown Augusta. When he saw that I was me, he was just as surprised. Proceeding to inquire more about what I was doing with my life now, he appeared to have an ulterior motive. I'd find out later in the conversation what that motive actually was.

He said he just started a non-denominational but Southern Baptist affiliated church in Martinez, Georgia. He was amazed that he'd run into me because he needed a keyboardist to lead the music in his church. As I would in all cases, I told him that my interest wasn't to be tied down to a time frame where I had to be somewhere on a specific day. Knowing my passiveness he said, "I didn't say that the job was yours, so it doesn't matter right now, does it? Just come over and play a couple of songs and we'll see if God can use your talents. So when can you come?" Picking up the latest baseball game by Electronic Arts I replied, "Tell you what, I'm going to leave for Rome Saturday and I'll be back Wednesday night, maybe I'll call you at the church and try to set something up." He had a gleam in his eye like he had found the last piece of the puzzle. You could almost tell by the tone of his voice he was excited as he responded back to me, "That sounds like a plan, and I'm going to hold you to it, alright?"

Jumping in the little silver Celica I had at the time, I started to think of how my life had been so sporadic. I hadn't been locked into a church for years. The only church I was getting was on television. With Delta, I had to work so many different shifts that I had no option for Sunday morning service, only pre-recorded service on Channel six. Let us just say that I'll use that for an excuse for right now. And the prospect of performing again was beginning to sound pretty good, at least that's what I was thinking driving down the road.

The fact that I was refining my list was still the most prevalent of all my thoughts. There in the back of my mind I was claiming that the person I'd love would have to be involved in a church. Seeming to be hypocritical, I still chose to write it down anyway. I knew that I'd been involved in church for most of my life so why couldn't I desire this attribute in a woman, right? I was sitting at a red light speeding through all the thoughts in my mind. Questions like what would I do about my pursuit of the perfect woman? And would she be found within the walls of this church? It was then that I decided not to allow the dream of a perfect woman to interfere with my desire to follow my God with service to him through the gift he gave me. Music was easy for me, but I never did anything with it, I just went home to sing and play. Lyrics written with stains of melodies blotted throughout. But let me tell you something, as soon as the light turned green, a quiet peace came over me. I was then hoping I'd do well enough to impress Ken, the pastor. He said he had a drummer and a guitarist in place. All he needed was a keyboard to fill his desire of a full and vibrant praise band.

My trip to Rome was as wonderful as always because it just happens to be one of my favorite cities. I had a friend of mine at the Sheraton Roma that checked me in all the time. A tall beautiful Italian woman named Vanessa who was always incredibly nice. Even though I was forty nine hundred miles from home I always felt like I was at home there at the Roma. Because of my Platinum status, I was awarded the opportunity of checking in upstairs in the Lounge. A place where people who built up points were allowed to eat snacks at night, and breakfast in the morning, it became a magnificent meeting place for a person who wanted to check his mail and get his eat on. Did I mention that this was a great way to save money on eating outside the hotel? My excursions to Rome gave me time to revel in the fact that I was sitting in the very place that some of the Bible was written. It also allocated me the time to add even more items to my ever changing list.

All together I've been to Rome eight times. So I had plenty of time to figure out what moved me as far as my list went. And having Vanessa to polish my Italian was something that started to grow on me too. After the second or third trip, I knew I wanted a woman who could speak multiple languages. She didn't have to be Italian. However, she did have to speak multiple languages.

The flight home was more eventful than I'd wished. The flight to JFK cancelled and all the passengers bound for New York were rerouted over to the Atlanta flight. A bad thing for employees who are trying to fly home to Georgia the day before they are due to go back to work, it looked like I wouldn't make it. The oversell situation was horrendous, from what I can remember, it was like 47 seats oversold. Ultimately though, I made it. Business class too, so it was a bubbly good day for me. Feeling like infinity, it was a longer than usual flight home, normal being ten and half hours but this one took almost twelve. I was eager to get home to be able to go the church to see if the music I was playing was going to work for them at Ken's church.

We landed somewhere close to three o'clock in Atlanta and I left directly from the airport. I didn't want to wait around for the next flight to Augusta so I rented a car. Figuring I'd make it home before the plane did anyway. So it was an easy decision. The church was located about two hours east along Interstate twenty. Driving down the road, I tended to get faster with each mile I drove. After pulling onto Belair Road in Columbia County, I believed it to be the shortest way to get to the church. I pulled in the parking lot in almost record time. Just about a second or two went by and Ken called my phone. He was concerned because he knew I was supposed to show up and he didn't want to hang around if I wasn't coming. My voice was filled with excitement as I toyed with him a bit, "Hey man, it looks like I'm not going to make it. I'm trying to find a parking place." Disappointed with my response he replied, "I waited around, but you say you're not coming." He could hear my voice cracking as if I were laughing and he asked, "What's so funny?" The indication sound of the car door opening was blaring loudly, and I was ready to quell his frustrations, "Ken, I just pulled out front, I'll be in there in a minute. I'm just kidding with you."

Needless to say, I fulfilled the church's requirement for a musician. He found a keyboardist for his dream of a praise and worship team. The title of leader was bestowed upon me from the start. And to this day, I think it was because I was always trying to do songs better than their actual composers. The week before we were to begin the new transition into the world of praise and worship, I was introduced to the congregation. Thinking to myself that this was truly the place to be, it appeared to be a place where I could follow Christ in a way that I'd previously followed him.

Ken's daughter had been visiting other churches in the area. A sixteen year old girl who was searching for her own place in this world I presumed. But hey, I didn't ask any questions. I could tell that Ken wasn't happy about his family not being involved in his church. So one day we are in the hallway and Dona came bouncing through the door with her boyfriend still in the car. As I was introduced as the music man, she seemed impressed enough to ask questions. Ken was beginning to see that there might be a chance of Dona settling for a place in our band. She wasn't the tallest girl but she was stunningly beautiful.

If asked to describe her I'd say she looked like she could pass for a Cherokee Indian, with smoother lines in her face. Both Ken and his daughter could tell I was interested so I asked a question that made me look even worse, "So what are you twenty two, or twenty three?" They started looking at each other and Ken responded, "She's only sixteen!" My eyebrows hit the ceiling as if to paint it with my embarrassment. I was astounded to hear that she was so young when she looked nine or ten years older. But it was what it was. Meaning I played the "I don't care what just happened, I'll just act like it didn't" card. Kind of awkward at first but the more we talked it went away.

Dona surprised us all that following Sunday by showing up at church. With Boyfriend Greg in tow, she even came up on stage and talked to the band a little. Greg was finding comfort in the back row looking on to see where his girlfriend was going. He reminded me of that little dog in the cartoon I used to watch, "Which a way did she go? Which a way did she go?" Following her around like a puppy dog, he was happy just to be with her I guess.

That afternoon, Ken invited me over to his home for swimming and lunch. Perplexed as if I should go, I finally gave in. The meal must I say was fabulous. I never had Green Acre Peas up to that day. And now it's one of my favorite veggies. I thought it was going to be just Ken and his wife, but Dona showed up with her sister. And she seemed to always find a seat next to me, even if Greg was there or not. Here I was an early thirties man being quizzed by a sixteen year old. Every turn I was asked a different question about what I like and what I didn't. Ken noticed that I wasn't comfortable so he asked me to come outside to talk about his vision for the church.

Greg then showed up to take Dona's attention off the music man. But it was evident that the same puppy dog he was chasing around in Dona was found in her running around after me with the same fervor. It didn't seem to bother her that I was almost eighteen years her senior. Ken and I didn't talk about it. I just kind of let it go as if it were a suggestion of infatuation. I was then persuaded by the family to eat dinner with them. Wow! This was exciting to me because I didn't have anything to do on Sunday nights. And now I did.

Trying to eat as fast as I could because I knew it was getting late, and I didn't want to ruin my welcome. Bugging out early was my intention but Dona wanted the family to watch a movie. And guess who she wanted to stay? As if you needed an answer to that question. I did stay. Then about ten o'clock I decided to leave with abruptness but she followed me out. Ken also walked me out and began talking about the prospects of Dona being a part of the praise team. Ken was delighted enough to leave us to discuss the details. What happened was two hours of her letting me know the things she was going through with her mother. Coupled with what she really felt for Greg. I have to be honest I wasn't prepared for such a bombardment of emotion. She was really unhappy with the direction her relationship was going with her mother. And that it was affecting the things she was feeling for Greg. On the golf cart in the garage, she cried more than once. I really didn't know what to do except listen and respond positively. Learning that if someone is in a highly intensive state, don't tell them what to do. Just agree with them if the things they are saying aren't destructive. What I'm saying is that I just sat there and listened to what she had to say.

The thing that was driving her crazy was that her mother was so controlling over her relationship with Greg. She told me at that time, unwanted from me, that she and Greg had consummated their relationship. I didn't say anything. I didn't lift my eyebrows. I tried to show that what I just heard didn't affect me. Truthfully, I have to say that I didn't know what to do except to walk off. But she kept talking so I felt obligated to stay. Her mother kept coming out as if to rescue me but Dona kept going on with the problems she was experiencing.

I left as hurriedly as I had when the movie ended but this time she'd follow me to the car. I jumped in and rolled down the window so she'd know I was serious about my intention to leave. As soon as I drove off, I was relieved to be on my way home because my shift started at four o'clock. Going to work that next morning was exhausting. Guess you could say I was paying the price for the decision I made to stay there at the house.

Tuesday was the night we set aside for practice. Arriving early was something I'd always done, and this wasn't any different. I was the first person there at the church. Unloading the keyboard from the back of a hatchback Celica in quite a feat, so I wanted to have plenty of time. The church had an elaborate sound system that was pretty nice. And I was hearing sounds I'd never heard from my keyboard. Because the system I had at home was nowhere close to what I was hooked up to at the church. Just as I was connecting the power I heard Ken come in and strolling behind him was Dona. I know we talked about it but it wasn't certain if she was coming or not. But I guess this was proof that she was. So I tried to be nice and give her the first choice of which song she wanted to sing.

For the next couple of months we had a wonderful time making music. During July fourth weekend, we prepared a special presentation that included I Pledge Allegiance to The Lamb by Ray Boltz, and God Bless the USA by Lee Greenwood. I also wrote a song for the occasion that illustrated my love for the country. My mother and father, sisters, brother, and Robb's family all showed up to show their support. To me, it was a tremendous success. Dona and I sang a duet that really displayed how talented this girl was. She had almost perfect pitch. So to be singing with her, I would have to say that it was making me sound even better.

Afterwards all of my family went to Red Lobster to eat and guess who shows up? Dona had a friend, and I wish I remembered her name, but she showed up with this friend. Their purpose was to eat with my family, Robb's family and me. The only bad thing about them showing up was the tip was now being added to the ticket. But we let them sit with us anyway. Least we could do, you know? My mother would always talk the horns off a Billy goat and she found it easy to talk with Dona and her friend. However, my mother would tell me after the meal that I needed to do something about her infatuation because it was evident to everyone at the table.

Robb later told me he supported me any way I chose. Although, he was apprehensive about the direction he thought she was going with me. He said, "You need to be careful, man. This girl thinks you hang the moon. And I don't want you getting hurt." Robb was always protecting me either with his brawn or his words. So I retorted, "I'll be careful, you know she's got a boyfriend. So I think I'm safe." I could tell he wanted to say something else. So, I perked my ears towards the sky and waited for his turn, "I'm not worried about you, but you need to see the way she looks at you man." Both of us were walking towards his car and Mandy was putting the kids in their seats. And I tapped Robb on the shoulder, "I kind of see what you're saying but I don't see what you're seeing." All my life I couldn't tell when someone was sweet on me. So to have Robb see things like this was a blessing in disguise.

One night after band practice, Dona was sitting on the floor not wanting to leave. Ken was in his office and all the rest of the band mates were gone for the night. I was changing the words to Take Me Home by John Denver. Then she looked up with those puppy dog eyes and said, "I need your help." Being who I was I told her, "Sure, whatcha need?" She stood up and started crying, and then began pacing towards the wall and back, "I . . . I'd better not tell you." I don't know about you but with me if someone would throw me a bone like that I wanted to know what they were going to say. I asked with great anticipation, "Wha . . . What is it?"

Seeing that she was distraught I wanted to help, sooner rather than later. She then proceeded by requesting, "Can I have some money? I'm going to run away. And I need to get away from that woman in my house. Or else I'm going to kill myself." And never was I one to listen to anyone in such a fragile frame of mind. But somehow she had my attention. I remembered things she told me that night at the house. It was before Dona decided to go to another church. She and her mother had a huge disagreement. One, she said was severe enough for her to bring a shotgun into her suede colored bedroom and lower it as if she'd blow her brains out.

I knew what I did in highly emotional moments so I suggested that she just leave for a couple of days. Somewhere close to home so that she could call her family if she needed to. Her response wasn't as positive as I would've liked, "Look I'm going whether you help me or not. I thought about Texas. Isn't it better if you help me than let me get caught up in a thousand mile trip." Thinking it to be one the craziest hair brained ideas I'd ever heard, I still decided that if she was going to runaway anyway, it'd be best if I could dictate where she went. At least stay somewhere close is what I thought. Dona knew that I had a mountainside cabin in North Georgia close to Cherokee, North Carolina. So asking me was her next move, "Hey, do you still have that place up in the mountains?" My eyebrows were posing the question, "Yes, and what does that have to do with me? It's you that is running away, not me."

"But you could let me stay there, right? It's only about two hours away isn't it?" is what she was beckoning with a soft, almost seductive voice. Shaking my head I felt as if I were being pressured to giving her permission to do what she had set out to do anyway. I finally gave in and said, "Okay, the key is under the mat, you wanta use it, use it, but I've got one request." The tears that ran down her cheeks had dried up by that time and she asked, "Anything, what is it?" Not believing that I was actually jumping into the deep end with this girl I requested, "Take a cell phone and when you're ready, call your dad. He's an important part of my life and I wouldn't want to hurt him even though I know this is going to kill him."

She was as excited as anyone I'd ever seen. It looked as though she had planned this way before I joined the band. And now she had her accomplice. At that time, I was a thirty three year old man who knew better but somehow I let my desire to be in a relationship order my actions whereas I lost my internal logic and took on pure insanity. I went to a bank machine and got hundreds of dollars out for her and told her, "Tomorrow I'll go get you a cell phone, but you got to promise me that you'll call them when you're ready." She started banging around on the drums when she heard me and then retorted somewhat angrily, "Okay, Okay, you've got my word. Look at it this way you may have just saved my life."

And that was something I didn't want to hear. I knew this would forever change my relationship with Ken. This was painful in so many areas. I loved her father. We developed a good pastor-musician relationship that was giving movement to his vision for our church. So to give in to her mission was damaging what we built up so far. Somehow in my utter ignorance I still yielded preferably to her wishes.

Scheming behind closed doors was as foolish as the act of running away itself. But she did it with great precision. The next day she called me from her school and told me, "Love you long time, but I got to tell you what just happened. My mom and I got into it again this morning as well, and my sign language teacher has agreed to keep my clothes in her car until I leave." Always when she'd come up with new details of the plan the apprehension would cover me like a plague. Unsure of my desire to help I asked her, "You went and told her the plan and now she wants to help. So, when are you and crazy going to leave?"

She wasn't exact when, but she was sure that she was leaving. Wishing that I could somehow stop what was inevitable I told her she needed to be careful about whom she told. Her plan was that no one would know and that way when she finally did run away, it'd be left to me knowing the details. But it didn't stop there, before you know it, she told a friend who she wanted to drive, and then her best friend. "Wow, this is scaring me beyond any fear I'd ever had, Dona." exclaiming loudly on the phone. I wasn't taking solace in the fact that I now had multiple accomplices to call my friends either. Going through it just may've been the dumbest thing I'd ever done. From the onset I should've called her father and let him know the whole deal.

But Dona was determined and she wasn't being deterred by anything I had to say. Every Sunday, you could cut the tension between her mother, Dona, and now for some reason, me. After service one day, her mother Kendra came up to me and boldly asked, "You need to come to the church Tuesday night early at around four, so you think you can meet us there?" Not really understanding why she was asking me, I guessed it had something to do with the whole ordeal with Dona. I didn't say too much but gave her my word that I'd be there.

The next day Mark, Dona's brother-in-law, called me and asked me to come over to his house. Her sister heard what her mother was planning to do and Mark wanted to tell me what was going to happen. It was for my protection he said. Mark told me that his mother-in-law was planning to kick me out of the church. And he wanted Biblical principles preserved by having the church handle it rather than the pastor's wife. But Kendra didn't want to hear Mark or her own daughter's wisdom when it came to controlling this particular situation.

When I arrived at Mark's, I was told how to handle Kendra. Mark's wife knew first-hand the things that Dona was going through because she'd gone through a similar experience. But she held out on the side of peace. They were concerned that I didn't take Kendra's actions as a direct representation of the church. I appreciated their warning and left appreciatively with a new purpose.

Anxiety was never an emotion that I had but I believe what I was feeling was about as close to it as you can get. The next night was Tuesday. I knew that Kendra and Ken would be there but as for anyone else, I didn't know. So as I walked in I saw Dona's brother. I was told he'd be there to support his parents. But I didn't understand why he would've come because he wasn't even a member of the church. I couldn't have cared less either way. Almost angrily, I was directed to sit down, guided to a chair placed across the table from Kendra. The things that happened that night I couldn't understand because being a Southern Baptist there were certain procedures that an affiliated church would be expected to handle such a happenstance as mine. "Why was Ken sitting behind his wife at his church? And why is Kendra the one who is chastising me?" I remembered asking myself. Sitting down in a cold metal chair I could feel the temperature rise as soon as I sat down. This woman was serious about the reason she was here. On the other hand, I'd been briefed and was prepared for what she had to say.

She reared back her head and said, "What makes you think that as a thirty four year old man, you can have my daughter who is sixteen as a girlfriend?" I said that I was prepared for what she was going to say but I have to be honest and tell you that I was shocked by this particular question. Knowing that for me to say anything would be the beginning of something bigger than I wanted, I chose to shut up until she finished. "You pervert, you tried to use our good graces to turn her against us, and you sit there saying absolutely nothing. What is wrong with you?" Noticing that this woman was beginning to lose her cool I told her, "Listen, I never wanted anything like this to happen, Ken and I were friends, I loved all of you guys, except for Denny over there, but that's not the point, I never asked Dona for anything, never gave her anything that you guys didn't know about, and here I am being lambasted for what I view to be poor parenting on your part . . . Kendra."

As if the fire I'd set by allowing Dona to manipulate the situation, I just dumped the entire can of gasoline on this one. She was a pale skinned women and the color red began to appear as if what I'd said blew her top. Kendra just about jumped over the table. Denny stood up as if he was going to do something but then I stood up and he sat back down. You could cut the tension in that room with a knife. Ken sat behind his wife like a scared hairless cat. He didn't say too much. And I found that weird because he was the pastor, not his wife. Not taking her serious, she finally calmed down enough to tell me, "Hey! We're going to leave this church immediately, Dona and I will go somewhere else. And you and Ken can decide which way you want to go with this God forsaken place." My head had been bowed down up to that moment. So when I heard her say this, I lifted my head and spoke with authority, "Listen, this has really gotten way out of hand. I think families should worship together, and I'm not a part of your family. I'm the oddball here, not you guys. I'll leave, and you guys can stay here. How's that sound to you people?"

She really didn't know what to say because I'd offered a solution to her problem that she hadn't thought of. Blurting out something she'd heard from a friend, "And why are you going around town telling everyone that you want to marry Dona? I bet you didn't know that we knew Bear, did you?" Talk about being at a loss of words I was there trying to figure out where in the world she heard something like that. Then I remembered.

I had a family friend that I go out to eat with from time to time and I was invited to the Athens Pizzeria in Martinez, Georgia. Darrel was trying to get me to look at a business opportunity and this is what this was. After mostly small talk, Darrel introduced me to a man named Bear, when in reality I knew him somewhat from my days of visiting my family's church. He used to be a member there. I listened for most of the dinner and then, he and I starting talking about things in our own lives. I showed him a picture of Dona that I was given, and told him that this was a girl that had certain traits that I wanted to find in a woman. Then Bear immediately roared from the other side of the table, "Dona Helmsly, what are you doing with that? I've known her since she was a baby." I was afraid that he'd say something that could hurt my relationship with Ken so I told him, "She's in our praise band at the church, but other than that, nothing." Looking at Darrel and pointing to my lips I was signaling for him to keep this a secret.

When I realized that this is what Kendra was talking about I asked her, "Oh! You mean Bear don't you? Why didn't he tell you the truth then? We can call up Darrel right now and ask him what was actually said. But it's irrelevant. You wouldn't believe that either would you?" Her eyes were as red as fire when she heard my sarcasm. Wow, what a hateful woman. "We'd take Bear's word over yours any day, and we want that picture back. He said you were going to marry her so that is what we're going with."

firing back angrily. Shaking my head I stood up and brushed my hands together like Pilate did when he said, "I can no longer be held responsible for this man's blood. His blood is on your hands." She followed me out as I was carrying my keyboard, "When can I expect that picture?" I knew I could be a tremendous pain in the buttocks so I glared back at her and replied, "Hey, I'll tell you what . . . I'll fax it to you!" Then I turned around and walked out never to return again.

A couple of weeks later, I was sitting at Ming Yat's Chinese restaurant in North Augusta when I received the call that she indeed had run away. Mind you, I was there with Robb, my father, and Mark, who was her brother-in-law remember. Mark knew of all the things happening in her home because Dona and her sister were close. And her sister would find out via pillow talk I presume because Mark supported her idea to a point. He wanted her to stay in town though. Her sister told Dona that leaving would make things worse but she'd support her only if she knew where she was going.

Dona left it up to me to decide whether to tell her sister where but I said it really had nothing to do with me, I was just the money. So there we are at the table, and I hung up the phone. I looked at Mark and said, "And so it begins. She just left, man." My father was always a man of wisdom but not so much with an abundance of words. He quickly replied, "You gotta be kiddin me, whatcha going do now boy?" Mark was talking with Robb and turned to say, "Well, this is the day that the Lord has made, huh?" Robb, like I would've done in a different circumstance laughed at my dad. He always copied the way my dad would say if something sounded like it wasn't right, "You gotta be kiddin me? What are you . . . going to do now?"

The color left my face immediately like I had been broadsided with a 2x4. I really never thought she'd do it. But she did, and now, reality was settling in like a bucket of cement on a mid-summer's day. "Wow!" was about the only thing I could mutter. It had to be kind of discreet because Mark knew that she was running away, however only Robb and I knew where she was actually going. Taking up for Robb, he did ask me several times to let the thing go but I still supported Dona. This was the one time I should've listened to my best friend. Hindsight being twenty-twenty, I really . . . really . . . should've heeded his request. But here was the frog with absolutely no hindsight. Just think of it this way, if a frog had hindsight, he'd never bump his butt every time he jumped. Had I just listened to what my friend was telling me, this frog just may have found his lily pad a whole lot sooner.

The next couple of hours were hectic. Her father called several times and asked me if I'd seen either one of them. I really didn't know what he meant . . . the other one? What was the other one? I later found out that she brought her best friend along for the ride. You know the best friend that she told at school. Initially thinking that this might be a good thing I'd later discover that by her tagging along, it would cost me considerable pain. Having to work the next morning I went to bed early. The next thing I know about ten o'clock or so, flashlights are moving around in my back yard like they were looking for something or someone. I heard something at the front door. North Augusta's police were called to come looking for the runaways. And the best friend's parents were accompanying them to search as well. Meeting them on the front porch with a University of Miami jersey and sport shorts on, I chose to let the officers search the inside of the house. If I had to describe my feelings, I'd have to say that I was scared a little.

I never had any brushes with the law other than a minor traffic ticket. So this was all new to me. Then the best friend's parents chimed in, "Where are they? You know you Son of a . . ." I looked at them and told them the same thing I told Ken, "Look guys, I don't know where they are, but if I hear from them I'll call you as soon as I hang up the phone with Ken." The father or maybe the live in boyfriend took a position of force and started huffing and puffing like the big bad wolf, "You don't tell me where they're at, or I will . . ." The officers that were there had just finished searching the house and grabbed him by the arm, "Alright, Okay were finished here. Come on." Pointing towards me, the father threatened me as if he going to beat me up, all five foot six inches of him. And I just started laughing as the officers pulled him away and guided him towards his car.

I walked into my room and noticed I had a missed call, it was Dona who called when all this was going on outside. When I returned her call I told her that by her doing this, she'd opened Pandora's Box within my own little comfort zone. She knew how to say the right thing at the right time just to make a man feel like he was doing the right thing. And with every word that proceeded out of her mouth, it was as smooth as silk. My feelings for Dona had developed into what I believed to be love with reservations. What could I be so reserved about though? The fact that my whole life was held up for ransom and it was like a big game for her. That's when the rain came.

I woke up some five hours later to go to the airport. Paranoid by everything that was happening I chose to stay in operations and not go anywhere else that day. I knew the only people that could come in there were people who had a Security Identification Display Area badge. I knew conclusively, that no one directly related to Dona had one, and I was safe hidden behind those walls. When I got off from work that day I kept looking over my shoulder to see if anyone was following me. I hated feeling this way. I truthfully wanted this to end, and end fast.

When my shift finished, and after closing the door to my Nissan truck I noticed my cell phone had a missed call. What I didn't know was who it was. Strolling through to uncover that it was Detective Brian Janes from the Columbia County Sheriff's Department. This was what I was afraid of, that it'd get this far. Knowing that I had no way out of this, I called him to see what he wanted. "Brian, this is me, and I wanted to know why you're calling." My respect for law enforcement had always been at a high level however with this guy it sounded as though he was trying to demean me. He responded, "Listen, I need you to come out here to the office. We need to talk about what's been taking place. I think you know why." The strength that I thought I had was now gone. So far gone that my fear overtook any confidence I had garnered up to that point. I said, "Hey Brian, I'll come now, how about that?" Informed that it was okay with him and he'd be waiting for me, I drove the thirty or so miles out to Columbia County Sheriff's office.

The Chutzpah began when I walked in the front door asking for Detective Janes. I had only heard about the way they operated from people who had been victimized by Columbia County's schemes, innocent people getting locked up for life because they were tired of so many mistrials. But now, I was experiencing it first-hand. Everything was so new to me I just sat down as he began to set up the interview tape recorder. To tell you the truth, I was glad this thing was actually winding down. Because I was one of those people who didn't like to be caught up in something bad. His interrogations began with, "So you know they've been found right? We located them in a cabin in the mountains of North Georgia, with a rental agreement signed by you." Puckering my lips like I do when I am wondering what is next I replied, "I figured as much." I didn't know what he wanted me to say so then he told me he was on a fact finding mission. Let me tell you something when a detective tells you he or she is on a fact finding mission, what they are really looking for, is a confession. As much as I thought I could hold all of this valuable information in, I sang like a yellow polka dotted canary. "If you tell us what we need to know, I'll personally vouch for you when it counts the most, but you've got to help us out here." he said while rolling around in his chair and playing with the fat rolls in his belly. It seemed as though he was going to pull Little Debbie right out of there, fromunda cheese attached to the locks of her hair.

I kept picking my fingernails knowing ultimately I was finished. I told him everything expecting him to be a man of his word. I quickly replied, "I gave Dona money, a cell phone to call home on when she was ready, and then told them where my cabin was, however I didn't give them a key. And with the best friend I didn't know anything about her until I found out she left with Dona." Then I heard a piercing sound coming from the back corner of his office. Thinking it was a bird I turned to the right to find out it was Brian's partner Detective Hill, a woman who was yelling at me in a high pitched, ear shattering whine, "You're nothing but a pedophile, you sick twisted man, all you people do is look for the easy take."

Instantly I turned back around to Brian and requested, "Can you shut that up? It's about to get on my nerves. She's a woman, and I think she's someone who's objective in this case, so whatever she has to say to me would be biased, so from now on, if you want anything more from me, I'll just talk to you." Brian acted like he was stunned that I'd say this in front of her being an officer and everything. Even stopping the tape from recording what he was about to say to Ms. Hill, "Please, all I'm trying to do is get this thing locked up and I need to know his answers. We'll talk about this later, okay?" She buried her head down in her papers and slithered off like the snake she was. Feeling like Brian and I had an understanding I continued letting him know how everything went down. Dona was nice enough to tell him that I planned the whole thing. Imagine that! I dropped my head in my hands and ran my fingers through my hair and responded, "I don't think she'd do something like that, but I'll take your word for it."

Brian said something at that moment I really should've listened to and just disappeared off the map, "In the beginning we think you played her, but now she is the one who's playing you." Bending my eyebrows towards my nose I was trying to figure out what that meant. Knowing I'd been caught, I wanted to speed up the process in which I'd be punished. I didn't want to wait so I politely asked Brian, "What do I do next? What am I looking at? And when am I going to get the computer back that was under the bed in my cabin?" He started laughing and lifted his hand to point at the picture of his daughter on the wall, "You see this little girl, she is my life, and if I find one ounce of pornography on that computer, I'll lock you so far under the jail, you'll never see the sun again. You got that? The answer you're looking for is when I'm done."

Almost to the point of tears I dropped my keys on his desk, took my index finger and placed it between the loops. I, angrily replied, "I'm not the kind of person you think I am, if you find anything on that computer other than what will either save your life or save your marriage, then I'll give you my truck, my house, and oh yeah! I will even pay the college tuition for that precious little twelve year old you got up there." Sticking a pen in his mouth he reared back and said, "Hey! How did you know she was twelve I didn't tell you that?"

I started laughing then at his insecurities and told him, "Then you need to make sure that you look at your daughter's picture a lot more, her cake is right there with twelve candles on it. I'm not a detective or anything but even I know that if someone has twelve candles, then I am going to go with them being twelve years old."

He didn't like how I said this so he tried to gauge how much I wanted to continue, "Here is the plan, I'm going to finish this up and when I call you, you can come over here and turn yourself in, if you don't, I'll chase you down anywhere you choose to run, you got that." I learned something that day. When a detective is acting like he's your friend, he isn't. He's the clearest picture of the devil himself. Why do I assign this attribute to Brian? He chose to ask me questions that he already knew the answers to. Basically, believing everything the other party was telling him. Towards the end of our conversation that day I felt relieved. Like a humongous weight had been lifted off my shoulders. But I still knew that I'd still have to pay the piper for what I'd done. Walking out of the station he said, "I wish we'd met under different circumstances." Feeling like I had made some impression I responded, "You know what Brian, I really am a good guy caught up in a bad situation." He smiled and said, "Yeah maybe so, but we got a jail full of you guys, and you better keep your phone on anyway, you know?"

Everything calmed down for about a month or so, and then my lawyer called and told me that the plan was for me to turn myself in at eight o'clock in the morning. The charges I was facing were interference with child custody and contributing to the delinquency of a minor. I had already set up a bond so I thought that I'd be free, as my lawyer told me, in a couple of hours. Waiting there in a holding cell, it felt like an eternity. My lawyer didn't even call until about four o'clock. Which at that time I was going crazy. So much so that I was trying to figure out a way that these people could just go away, Mafioso style, if you will. But being a Christian, I was having a hard time forming the thin line between reality and imagination. I sat staring at a white cinder block all day and that will make your mind do strange things. But I knew that I was here because of the choices that I made, so I just sulked in my own pity until I heard the bell ring.

Finally, my lawyer showed up and completed my transition out of jail. You want to talk about a feeling of freedom. I was free at last. And I realized that Brian hadn't done what he told me he was going to do. In not so kind words, he lied to me when he told me he'd help. Without any experience in law enforcement, I started watching court shows. I wanted to unmask new ways of dealing with detectives that don't tell the truth. Throughout the year I found out many things that would give me the confidence to deal with such an unscrupulous detective. I wasn't blaming him for my bad decisions. I was just getting my ducks in order just in case he lied again.

Court dates were set for months in advance and I requested from my lawyers and the judge to be able to travel. And there I was, relegated to the fact that I'd let myself get involved with a girl who had just sold me out for a brand new Mitsubishi Eclipse. I just wanted to disappear, and quickly at that, mainly to the safer confines of Europe. That was my way of judging things objectively remember. But Robb had another plan.

He and I started a candle shop in Gatlinburg, Tennessee and he left to set that up. He asked me to come up there and stay with him, Mandy, and the girls for a couple of days. So I left as fast as I could. What would happen is that I would meet a woman who was from across the pond. I won't say too much about her now because I'll write about her in a later chapter. What I will let you know is that I left the country to visit her in Poland and subsequently my sister Beth went to go dress shopping. Radom, Poland is about five thousand forty two miles from my front door, so I was about as far away from Augusta as I'd ever been. Beth walks into a place where Dona worked and didn't really even notice who she was. Dona came running up to her as if she was the long lost sister and began asking about me. Beth then realized she was about to be thrust into a problem like mine. Because my release from jail was dependent on me not having any contact with any of her family, and this constituted contact. Beth did the best thing she could've done. She high tailed it out of there. Never to return to that side of town again. About three or four days later I was due to return to the states. Beth thought nothing of this because she thought it was innocent. But Dona notified Brian and told him, "He is trying to mess my life up now, by getting his sister to come into the store!" You know how law enforcement is, more charges equals more money. I wasn't off the plane ten minutes and Brian called me to inform me that I was now being charged with aggravated stalking.

Pleased to hear this fresh off my beautiful trip to Poland, I asked him a couple simple questions, "How in the world does someone get charged with something when he is five thousand some odd miles away? Brian, I was with my girlfriend in Radom, Poland. I didn't care what happened in Columbia County. Campeche?" He followed with, "Your sister went into a store where she worked and she said that you sent her in just to see her."

Slamming the phone down so hard that he knew I wasn't happy. How could this happen? How could this family who was calling themselves Christians all over town be so vindictive? Thoughts permeated my mind as fast as they could have. I'd been around ministers all my life but never had I been railroaded by one. Oh! But wait a minute! It was wife who wore the pants in that family. I couldn't believe I was back here at this crap. Turning myself in was becoming an old hat. One I didn't want to wear anymore. I just wanted it to go away. But it seemed to follow me like a disease.

I was tired of it, and it was part of the reason why I left to Poland for a week. The next day I went and turned myself in same time, same place. Eight o'clock sharp expecting that I'd be let go like the last time, I was dead wrong. Brian met me there at the jail and ushered me into a cell this time. I called my lawyer and asked him to meet me there so I could get out quickly. What I got was a handful of empty promises. My lawyer told me I was going to be out as soon as he could get there. I'll have you know that I spent three days in jail for something I didn't think I was guilty of.

Stuck in a place where it would be left up to a judge to let me out. My bond would be set whenever he saw fit and for how much he saw fit. Fasting for three days, I told my prison mates that I'd get out of this place in three days. Not one of them believed me. One of them was in there for the same thing I was accused of, except he had been in there for six months. I told them with conviction, "Don't look at me when I get out, look at the Lord because he's the only way I will get out of here on Wednesday." Just as the words left my lips I heard an inmate yell, "I believe in God too, but there is no !@#$&% way you're getting out of here having to see the Judge you're going to see, he's the one who kept me in here six months." I quickly responded, "Then you'll really know who it was when you don't see me here Wednesday night, right?"

My time in jail was not an event I'd like to remember. I'd much rather forget it. Not much sleep and a whole bunch of fasting and praying. My experience will be engraved in my memory for the rest of my life. Columbia County can take pride in one thing though, a clean jail. I didn't have to worry about dirt or what I perceived previously about an incarceration. And hey, I won't even buy anything in Columbia County to this day. I figured they got enough of my money.

Wednesday morning the breakfast bell rung and all those that had bond hearings were allowed to get theirs first because the hearings started around nine. What irritated me most was the fact that I was locked in chains on my feet, and my hands. Another instance that I couldn't understand, a man charged with petty crimes but yet he was chained as if he had killed eleven people. Didn't make much sense to me but hey, I was happy to finally see daylight. Waiting in a holding cell of sorts for most of the morning, I was called in to appear before the judge. My parents, my sister Beth, and Charlotte was there for emotional support. After the Columbia County assistant District Attorney said her piece and Brian told the judge his piece, my mother and Charlotte pleaded with the judge that I should be let out on my own reconnaissance. Both of them cried while explaining to His Honor how I'd helped people all my life, and this was no different. It seemed as though it was falling on deaf ears. Judge Fleming never lifted his head off the paper he was writing on. I thought he was preoccupied with the morning crosswords. His interest was sure not on me getting out of jail that day.

My lawyer had gone on vacation and he sent a rookie to take his place, and this guy just sat there as the District Attorney was steadily nailing me to a cross. I glared at him for a second and asked, "Are you going to do something about this?" Getting worried about the direction in which I felt we were going, I wanted someone other my mother and friend to stand up and defend me. Mainly the guy I was paying handsomely to get me out of this predicament. He just stood there, waved his finger and did nothing. Meanwhile next to me, Brian was handing the nails to the District Attorney for her to hang me up to dry. Staring at him with my evil eyes I couldn't believe that he kept telling lies again and again to serve notice to me that he was going to win at all cost.

Moving back and forth between my lawyer, Judge Fleming, and the grim reapers; my head felt like it was on a swivel. The only fate I had was slipping away with every word that came out of the District Attorney's mouth. Turning back towards the Judge, interrupting Brian and his Mumbai mistress mid-sentence, I asked the judge, "Your Honor, can I say something here?" Lifting his head long enough for him to peer through the top of his glasses he replied, "Go ahead, but make it quick. I still feel that I don't need to let you out." Feeling like I'd been given a reprieve I continued, "Judge Fleming, Your Honor, I . . . don't need to come here to Columbia County for anything." Brian was becoming increasingly angry with each statement I made. He butted in to tell Judge Fleming, "Your Honor, this man is an extreme flight risk. Plus, his release would put the family in danger." Interrupting Brian once again, I wanted to finish what I was asking the Judge, "Judge, I realize that . . ." The lawyer took his hand at that moment and slapped me on my lapel and told me, "You need to be quiet, don't say anything. He doesn't like it when you do . . ." I don't know what it was about me cutting people off in mid-sentence but I felt like I was being crucified right before my parent's eyes.

I looked at the lawyer and told him, "You're not doing anything to help me, so I'll take it from here." Immediately I turned to

Judge Fleming and said, "Sorry Your Honor, what I was saying was that I don't need to come here, if I need something located here in Columbia County, I promise you I'll drive to Aiken. But please I feel like I'm a good man caught in bad situation. My job at Delta begins this Friday and I . . ."

Cutting me off in mid-sentence I felt like he was giving me some of my own medicine. Perching his pen up to his temple, he elevated his brow as if he hadn't thought of that and then he said, "Hum, Tell you what, Banishment from Columbia County, and twenty five thousand dollar bond." I thought it was a little high but I wanted to drive a literal dagger into Brian's heart for treating me like he did. I could tell he was about as happy as he could be, knowing that there was no way I'd be able to pay that bond. I turned my entire body towards Brian, chains and all, and said, "Your Honor, I'm prepared to pay that now. But where can I pay it? And would it be okay to pay it . . . in hundreds? That's about all I got." Noticing Brian's tobacco stained hands starting to shake and his face turning blood red was unforgettably classic. His anger was so prevalent that he threw his papers together and stormed out of the courtroom, taking his Mumbai mistress with him. At that moment I felt some vindication because I'd just taken on the toughest Judge in Columbia County and lived to tell about it. The only thing I had to do now was to go see my fellow inmates and let them know that God is Good, all the time. And if they knew what was best for them, they'd depend on him with as much blind faith as they witnessed in me. Waving goodbye I really never had any intention of ever seeing that place again. And I have not seen it to this day. I won't even drive by it. Good riddance to everyone I encountered in that God forsaken place.

What does the Chutzpah of Columbia County have anything to do with my development as a man looking for his soul mate? Here I was losing myself in my desire to find love but yet I was blind to the truth. I don't blame them for what I did wrong. I blame them for telling me something that later turned out to be a lie. I wanted the same consideration that he was giving Dona and her family. I knew I'd sacrificed my relationship with Ken for a virtual whim with Dona. That hurt enough to the point where

I remembered what Brian said, "You'll never be a part of any church again when I get finished with you."

Could God use a man who had made the wrong decision in life? The answer is an affirmative, "Yes!" Look at Paul, he made bad decisions with regularity while he was still Saul but God used him in a magnificent way. Would he reward someone who deviated from the plan that he chose for their life? Once again the answer would be "Yes!" Many times the Lord blessed people even though they weren't where he wanted them, yet. The key word there is, "yet." He always sees you where you are, and loves you through it. And eventually you make the right decisions and fall in line as to where God wanted you in the first place. Understand something. You just may have to go through hell and high water in order to achieve the kind of Heaven God intended for you. Being in front of Judge Fleming was a wakeup call to me that ultimate power is in decision. Had I not decided to help Dona in her asinine scheme who knows where my life would've turned out? Maybe I would've been used to build an eight pew church into a full blown powerhouse of worship. But I did help her, and what did I learn from it?

Possibly, I was chasing something that looked like love but didn't have the ability to love back. Columbia County became a bad word for me. I associated everything about this place to that Detective. I don't hate him but I tell you what, if someone needed to use the free minutes on my cell phone to call for an ambulance for him, I'd charge them $18,500 for that call. And for some part to that family, a wife who controlled her husband to a point where his manhood was being challenged by his own daughters. As Christians, they should've handled me in their own way. Not chasing after me like a rabid dog. Kendra wanted my head. She came to Delta and tried to get them to eliminate my free flying position. But Thank God, I built such a tremendous work ethic that my Station Manager just kicked her and Ken out of his office.

I'm not saying I shouldn't have been punished. What I am saying is that when your lawyer tells you he has never seen a pit bull attack a man like Kendra was attacking me, it's pretty bad. He was befuddled at their relentlessness. But one thing for certain I feel like I faced the devil and walked out alive. I didn't want to pursue anything that remotely looked like a church. Remembering her eyes when we were sitting at the church at my dismissal meeting was something ingrained in my mind for years. I did make it through, protected by the loving arms of an Almighty God.

Learning one thing was I needed to be more careful in what I listened to and how I acted upon it. I chose to search for more of a woman than a child who was looking for a way out of her mother's grasp. For about a year I didn't date anyone because I was afraid they'd find out that I'd been thrown in jail for helping a girl out.

The enriching fact of the whole thing is even though I was going through the valley of death I kept adding those items to my list. You should never fall for someone who isn't able to legally sign a contract. That is something I learned the hard way. By keeping my list close to me at all times it was a constant reminder that I was protected by the definitions I was defining for myself. Dona sold me out for a brand new car. And where was I? Left to explain to Insurance companies for the rest of my life why I helped someone who didn't have the ability to help themself. Would I ever find love again even if they found out I spent time in jail? I was okay with traveling again if the answer ended up being, "No!" But I believe the Lord was taking me to a place he knew the answer was an affirmative, "Yes!" God wasn't finished teaching me though. He knew I'd go through two more major relationship decisions in order to reach his calming and peaceful refuge. That process would begin about a year after completion of the Dona effect. And I felt with every fiber of my being that it couldn't come soon enough.

10.

Lincoln Logs . . . Building Something Out Of Nothing

TWO KIDS CONVENIENTLY PLACED UPON THE FAMILY RUG. THERE they were with two gifts opened and ready to build. For Christmas one year, I got an erector set and a set of Lincoln Logs. Those of you that remember these logs remember them well. You were able to build log cabins and millions of other stuff. Constructing houses was about as fun as actually nailing them together with a hammer, however with Lincoln Logs, no glue or nail was needed, just a mind full of imagination and the time to complete it. The erector set I'd use to build moving cars but I'd lose interest quickly. Maybe because what I was building just didn't look that good. A lot of metal connected with screws having no means for an aesthetic overhaul. It amazed me how nothing could become something simply by dumping a bucket of wood on the floor. Throughout my life it seemed like I was always trying to dump that bucket of wood into a relationship. Ultimately knowing that what I was building had nothing to do with what I actually wanted. Essentially, creating something that looked good on the outside but had no substance within . . . virtually building my bridge to nowhere.

I began my new found freedom and felt it to be quite an adventure. Probation allowed me to carry on as if nothing happened. And that's what I did, my flight days with Delta were beginning to build. I believe that if I'd been given credit for my flights I would've probably been a platinum medallion, maybe even a million Miler, which means I flew a lot. Maybe I was doing this to keep my mind from dwelling on the past. Or maybe I was busy adding items that adequately defined my wishes even further. Either way I'd leave the country on Saturday night and return on Wednesday every week, I never got tired of being in the air.

Being in the same place for five years, I had the same ramp supervisor from the time I walked through the door. Bobby D, as we called him was a round plump man who had the best seat in the house, a golf cart. It was so bad that there was a permanent indention in the driver's seat where he'd plant his hind parts all day and every day, Saturday and Sunday's off. When Bobby D was scheduled to work, we knew we'd be a man down. It didn't matter if we had three people scheduled to work, we knew actually it meant we had only two. We did like him for Bobby though, but he'd pick on us like we were his personal servants. When I started I thought his position with the company required him to ride the golf cart back and forth to the ramp because other than that, I saw him do nothing else. We all figured the check he earned was a token gift from Delta Connection.

Bobby tried to get involved in our lives with stories that'd make us feel like he had experienced something similar. But there was a time where his tendencies were driving me crazy. He'd continually badger me over my desire to fly rather than date. I never thought about another man for a second. Nor did I have relations with anyone of the same sex, and never wanted to. The thought of it made me literally sick. Other than being one of the biggest sins in God's eyes, it was reprehensible for me to even be in the same room with a man who was involved sexually with another man. That was thing about Bobby. He was married to a Hawaiian who gave him a hard time at home so I guess he was taking it out on all of us. He always said, "My Crap rolls down your hill." Maybe that gave some reason as to why he picked on us so much.

For three weeks though, he was being tortured by a girl down at the Fixed Based Operations building to see if I was dating anyone. When he found out I was available he asked, "So when are you going to take Savannah out? Beautiful girl and you're not interested, what are you, a faggot?" I retorted instantly but laughingly, "No, I happen to be a straight as an arrow Christian man with no desire to get involved in a relationship right now. I'm happy being happy right now . . . Bobby!" I talked to Savannah many times on the phone but it was always about the trip that I'd just been on. It consisted mostly of small talk because she'd ask me something and I would respond. Not thinking too much about it I was always polite. I just didn't want to get into another relationship where I had to explain myself to anyone.

Bobby kept on with his verbal abuse almost every day. "Testing your homosexuality are you?" was some of the things he'd say. It was making me angry enough but I loved my job so I just turned back and disappeared within my own shell. A turtle of sorts protected by his outer whims except my shell was made of titanium steel with a big Delta Widget painted on the side of it. No matter what he said, I didn't want to do anything to mess my flying benefits up. So I'd come to work and listen to Bobby's incessant badgering until finally I gave in. "Alright, I'll call her but you got to promise you'll never call me a faggot again. That's about to piss me off." I was pleased to hear that he agreed to lay off me for a while but I'd have to go out with Savannah.

About an hour later she called me when Bobby told her that I'd go out with her. She was a pretty girl, blond hair, blue eyes, and a nice full figure. Our conversation consisted mostly of the usual boy girl talk. I wanted to know where she went to church. She wanted to know how in the world I could afford to go on all those trips. Before I continue I will tell you that it is a good thing if you keep your financial dealings to yourself. Needless to say I didn't tell her anything except that I sold life insurance outside of my job at Delta. The plan was for Savannah and me to go to dinner and a movie. I was never one to hold hands on the first date or even kiss. And this one particular date was no exception. A gentlemanly gentleman is how you'd classify how I treated her that night.

She wanted me to go with her to Target the next day so I obliged. I was off for another three days so I had plenty of time. Waiting for her in the Target parking lot felt like an eternity. Finally when the sun fell and I was hiding behind darkened skies she showed up. We perused around the store for an hour or so and went outside to say our goodbyes. Remember now this is the second date so a kiss was optional. We leaned against my truck and talked for awhile. Then out of nowhere, a kiss. Innocent at best, it was a kiss that seemed to last for an hour, sporadically intermingled with small talk.

My relationship with Savannah didn't last long enough to tell you a lot about it. However, I did remember that she had a hard time making a decision. About twenty one when we started dating, she couldn't decide what she wanted more. Was it to be a pilot, or become a student that allowed her an option to fly? Either way I think our relationship was getting in her way. There were good days where I was invited to come over for a family cookout. And when I say family I mean, this girl had seven brothers and sisters. A cookout where some thirty people showed up with hamburgers, hot dogs in arm to supply our small army, it was quite an adventure I'll never forget it. Then, in a second she'd shift from knowing everything to not knowing anything and carrying those emotions with it. But wait there was more.

It was towards the end of our relationship and both of us were trying to find a way out of it. She was trying to go more places to work for fly Ins. Through the years she developed a lot of good friends from Kenosha to Los Angeles. And she missed being there in the middle of it, and I was the thing that was sitting in her way. Her friends were asking her when she'd get her pilot's license and she had no answers. Somewhat embarrassed every time they'd ask, she'd disappear into the shadows trying to hide what she really wanted. I was thirty plus, so I was growing impatient with her indecisiveness. Not that I was ready to throw in the towel but I became more and more irritated with all these people pushing her to make decisions when I thought she needed what everyone needs when they can't decide . . . time.

I knew that if I were to push, I'd be finished in her life. I was new when these guys and girls were not. I listened one day to everything she was saying and then told her, "I love you." Right off the bat she stared at me as if to say, "What did you say?" I started laughing because what I was really trying to do was stop her babbling. Let me say that it worked in two dimensions. She did stop babbling but she also stopped talking. Flat out walked out, she started shifting her eyes around like she didn't know how to take it. I can't say that I really loved her. It was more like . . . like. But I was tired of her not being able to make a decision. From that moment on our relationship changed.

I went from being the guy she called incessantly and leaving Little Debbie's on our counter at work to the guy she'd pass over for her friends at the Florence Fly In. I have to tell you that I was okay with the being passed over bit, but when I had to go get my own Little Debbie's, that was the last straw. I'm really just kidding here but she did go to Florence and what happened there determined the direction that I was going with our relationship.

She said she'd be working, but I thought I just may show up on my way up to Georgetown, South Carolina to see Robb, Mandy, and the girls. Driving my beat up pickup truck for two hours was to me unbearable, so I rented a Pontiac Grand Prix from one of the places at the airport. At least I'd be able to listen to some music on my discs now. I left on a Friday night because I knew that she'd stay the night in a hotel and then work all day Saturday. Hampton Inn was always my choice if a Sheraton wasn't available. When I got there it was somewhere close to eleven. People were still hanging around the pool even though it was late.

Driving around the parking lot I noticed that this was the hotel that she chose so I wanted to park somewhere near her. My room was located on the second floor overlooking my car and right beside the coke machine. I was worried that she'd know I was there. So, all I did was go get a Mountain Dew and a load of candy from the machines. The Braves were playing on the west coast so that meant that I could watch the game until almost one. Some reason though, I couldn't sleep. The internal dialog was running through my mind like the bulls in Pamplona.

Turning over from side to side, I was restless. My biggest concern was what was she doing? And why was I here trying to build something out of nothing? I knew we were finished as a couple, but why couldn't I let go? Then I heard a car door shut. I got up to see who it was and there she was with another man.

She wasn't holding his hand but she was draped all over him like they were the couple that we weren't. I continued to watch them as they were finding their way to their room. I wanted to find out if she was staying with him in his room but a thought came over me, "Why even bother, you're pushing something you don't even want." Just as those words passed my lips, a certain peace came over me like I'd been set free from a bondage that kept me at bay for a couple of months now. I can't say if what I was seeing was cheating on me because we, at that moment were only being held together by a thin piece of thread that any day would've been cut.

I just remember climbing back into bed and sleeping really well because I wasn't worried about it anymore. Guess it was closure that I was looking for in Florence, and that's what I got. I don't actually know if they were in the same room. I really didn't care. The fact was that if I was the man she was telling me I was, she wouldn't have been holding on to him like he was her Siamese twin. This man was an acrobatic wing walker, and I was only someone who worked at the airport. He embodied an avionic adventure while I was best suited for pressurized cabins, mainly with that Delta widget painted on the side. I couldn't blame her for liking this guy. He would have his father fly him up a thousand or so feet. Then he would strap himself to the plane and walk out on the wing. Crazy enough, but quite entertaining, and hey, even I was impressed.

To this day Savannah doesn't know that I spent the night. I didn't want her to know because she may have thought I was checking up on her. I called in sick for Saturday so I could go to this thing. I loved spending the night in hotels. The air conditioners are so cold, and I am one of those people who love ice sticking to the top of my ears in the morning. I woke up just in time for our Continental breakfast. The Fly In was set to start at around ten. Moving the alarm clock around so I could see I noticed that I had an hour to make it before it opened. I told Robb that I was going to stop by to see what was going on. He said he would meet me there.

He and his family met me at the funnel cakes, which is a good place to find me at these kinds of events. And it was there that I told him what I'd seen the night before. Robb in all his wisdom told me, "Listen Coochie man, you don't need that, come on, and we'll go to the beach. You're always into some woman who has an evil demented twin. You don't need to see her or say anything. You just need to come with us." He was right and I knew he was right but that didn't stop me from trying to find her to figure out what we, as a couple, were going to do. Even though I knew we were no longer classified as a couple.

After home boy was done with his wing walker thingy I chose to follow his plane to see where she was working. I felt like she'd be working near him. And rightly so, there she was sitting in a lawn chair as he pulled his plane into a makeshift hanger. He got out, walked over to her, hugged her, and finally nudging her on the lips for a peck or two. When she began to sling her arms around him she saw me walking towards them and immediately turned her pale white skin into a blushing pink shade of rose.

As I made my way up to her she asked, "What're you doing here? Why aren't you at work? I thought I told you I was working and I'd be home tomorrow." Knowing what I'd just seen I could tell she was flustered. Not really knowing what to do or how to explain what had just happened, she just began asking questions. I said to her in a calm sincere resolve, "Robb was coming so his family and I are going to the beach. I felt I'd say Hello while I was passing through. So, I guess it's a hello and it was good to see you. Oh! By the way, where is your badge? I thought you said you were working."

This was a woman who thought I didn't know what I knew. So she told me that she got there about eight that morning, saying that she left from Augusta about five thirty. Which I knew better but I wasn't about to tell her. Also I knew she was in the wing walker's camper for five minutes before she grabbed the lawn chair. Not affecting me at all, I knew it was just a means to the end of our relationship. Wouldn't it have been better had she told me the truth. I don't think she thought I could handle the truth. But contrary to her belief I could handle anything she threw at me including the truth.

I told her that I didn't want to keep her from her work while glancing over to the wing walker who was peeping over to me in his own little way. As I started walking away she said, "I guess I'll see you at home." Shrugging my shoulders I turned back to her and replied, "Maybe . . . Maybe not . . ." I knew then that I wouldn't be putting my time into something that was going nowhere. Arriving about an hour or so later in Georgetown, Robb and I talked about how I keep letting myself get involved with woman who sooner or later, ultimately found other things to keep them busy. Rather than being held in check because I didn't have a successful relationship once again, I chose to enter single Dom with a pen in my hand, and paper on my desk. In other words, I went back to that which made most sense, my ever changing list.

Lincoln County wasn't that far from Columbia County and the way that woman acted towards me wasn't that different either. No, I wasn't sold out for a brand new car. But I was thrown under the bus for a guy who lives on a thin line between life and death. How did I get this far into this thing when I really didn't want to get into it in the first place? Would have I asked her out if it weren't for Bobby? Who knows where I would've ended up? I would've needed more pages in my passport I know that much.

I can't sit here and tell you that Savannah was a bad person. She was only guilty of not being able to make up her mind. Then she'd let frustration control her emotional state for an extended amount of time. I can't blame her for what happened to us. I wasn't patient enough to sit around and wait for her to make a decision. The positive thing about her was that she started making decisions. But those decisions wouldn't include me. And that was okay too.

Something I wouldn't let go was the fact that I'd lost. It was no longer me trying to fall in love. Becoming more about me trying to win, I wasn't happy that I couldn't close the deal with a woman, if you will. When in reality, I should've listened to what I was telling myself in the first place, and not paying attention to anything Bobby said. Who cares if he was insulting me with those off gendered names, this was my decision to take her out not his.

Building on what I thought to be something, I realized it was really absolutely nothing. Going somewhere to nowhere in a couple months, it's like the same two little kids on that rug in the middle of the floor. Pulling on each other coat tails, just long enough to dump Lincoln Logs all over the carpet, and both of them were ready and willing. But what were they going to build? Beginning with the walls, and making them structurally sound. Then it becomes clear that what you set out to build looks nothing like what you have in front of you. Lots of hard work tuning heads but nothing like you planned. Taking your hand as if it were a humongous wrecking crane, you destroy the cabin with extreme force . . . and then you're left with Lincoln Logs everywhere.

What do you do now? You have to start with a plan. Can't build a house without blueprints can you? What makes you think you build a relationship without a plan? Remember the list? That is the blueprint for things you want out of a relationship. Maybe even the things you want to put into it. I added something from my experience with Savannah. I knew conclusively that I desperately needed a woman who could make up her mind. And in short fashion mind you. From then on, I'd file it as a definite necessary attribute. Realizing that Savannah didn't know which direction she wanted to go, how could she know which direction in which she wanted to go with someone else?

Truthfully, you should be sure that both you and the person you are courting are heading in the same direction. Noticing these things early can save you a lot of time. With Savannah, I was trying to build something out of nothing. I should've just scrapped it after dinner and a movie and chalked it up to experience. In essence, demolishing anything I'd built with my Lincoln County Lincoln Logs. Certainly destroying it way before it materialized into a relational farce. Always putting on our happy faces when in reality, we we're just going the motions. Possibly just to satisfy Bobby's cravings, who knows? But I have to give it to her. She helped me make a transition into what would later be deemed the happiest days of my life.

Viewing my happenstances as an opportunity for personal growth, I began using it as a learning experience. Making sure I closely evaluated the direction in which I . . . wanted to go with it. Asking questions that do nothing but stimulate an opportunity, I'd ponder questions like, "How can I learn from it? Or what can I take from this that I can apply it to a decision I'll make in the future?" Savannah was the last American woman I ever dated. I began taking subtle hints from friends who actually dated people in other countries like Hungary, or friends who had German wives; I knew I wanted to be treated like these guys were being treated. I had nothing against American girls but I needed to change my approach because what I was doing with my current dating process wasn't working for me at all. My Roma girl Vanessa was no longer an option because I had no more vacation left for the year. Not being able to spend time with someone puts that relationship on a back burner of sorts. I didn't think she deserved that. So, what was I going to do? And then Robb called.

He'd just moved to Gatlinburg, Tennessee to run our candle shop we had just purchased. Around the fifth of May the phone rang with some good news, "Man, you got to get up here. There are twins up here that have your name written all over them!" Needless to say, with my list in hand I flew to Knoxville and then drove to Gatlinburg. From there I was pleasantly surprised to meet a beautiful girl named Kamila. As easy as it was walking down the strip, it ultimately begins . . . My European Experience!

11.

A Departure From Normality

OUR CANDLE SHOP WAS LOCATED ABOUT TWO OR THREE STORES down from the Hard Rock Café. I thought it to be a perfect location because of all the passing traffic. Therefore, for all intents and purposes, it was an easy investment. Robb, Robb's dad, me and my dad all went in together with equal amounts. Robb's investment would consist of running the store. We needed someone to open at ten o'clock and close whenever the people stopped walking by our door. Robb would fill that need.

The first day I arrived there at the store it had just rained. I knew that a mountain river moved fast but the river located behind our store had risen up almost to our window sill. I was afraid that one of the girls would get swept away so I asked Robb if I could take them to get some ice cream.

That was the thing about being in a vacation hotspot; there were places to eat everywhere. I was surprised that we didn't sell out of candles every day. If our business was dependent on the actual number of people that passed through the door, we would've been fine. But as in all enterprises, there are many variables that determine a business' success.

There was an old timey photograph store two doors down from us that was part of the summer work exchange program. For those of you that don't know what this is I'll tell you. Every May or so, college students will leave their respective International Universities and come to the United States to work. Our government provides them with a visa that allows them to work and gives them a culture emulsion experience that they'll never forget. Throughout the summer, they're given an opportunity to earn enough money to live for an entire year in their own countries. To me it's one of the nicest things that our country can do for these guys.

Walking down the sidewalk with Robb's girls, I looked inside the store only to have someone following me with her eyes as I passed by. Robb hadn't told me yet where the twins were so when I saw two people that looked exactly alike, I knew that this just might be the place. I tripped over my own feet, turned back to her, and just smiled. She was smiling as well. But when she saw me look back she quickly turned around to talk to her sister. I called Robb on the cell phone, "Hey Man, I think I just saw the twins. Are they in that old timey photo place?" He answered, "Coo . . . chie man, whatcha think?" Puckering my lips like I always do, "Nice, I think she was looking at me as well." He was curious as to which one was looking, I answered him as if I knew, "You know . . . the one with the brown hair, and brown eyes." Robb retorted, "But they look exactly the same." I started chuckling, "Yeah, they do. And that's why I'll say it's the one in front, leaning on the door. Go outside and check her out, she's the one."

After finishing my ice cream with Robb's kids, we went to the aquarium. In Gatlinburg, it's one of the biggest attractions there. So for the afternoon, I took them there. I could see the girl at the photo place from the top of the hill. She was still leaning against the door. Maybe she was waiting for me, maybe she wasn't, but as soon as I got out of the Aquarium, I figured she'd be gone for the day.

I didn't try to rush through because the girls had never been to an aquarium so I really wanted them to enjoy it. I chose to let them gauge our pace rather than limiting them to a restrictive time frame. So after a couple of hours, all of them were exhausted and wanting to go back to the store. We headed that way. The rain was long gone and it'd become fairly warm. You know for someone who didn't have kids to suddenly having three to take care of was quite an adjustment. Something I wasn't used to, and let me tell you, it took everything I had to stay with them.

They weren't wild or anything, it was just that all three of them had their own direction in which they wanted to go.

Like a teacher assembles all of her students together, I quickly rang in all the girls. I sort of had an ulterior motive. Actually, I wanted to see if the girl at the shop was still there. Full steam ahead towards the candle shop, I turned the corner and just about ran into her leaning on the door. She looked up and smiled again. I smiled and spoke bashfully, "Well, hello." I thought I scared her because she ran so fast back into the photo place. But my purpose at that moment was only to bring the girls back to Mandy and find out what we were eating for supper.

As soon as Robb saw me come in, he was helping someone and motioned for me to stay there. When the person completed her purchase, Robb thanked her and then turned to me and said, "Well, did ya ask her?" Shrugging my shoulders and pointing towards my chest, "You know me, it was just hello." Robb said when I told him that, "You gotta be kiddin me, whatami going to do with you? Just talk to her, man." Standing up from my slump I stood there with confidence and ready for battle, "okay I will, I'll be back in a moment."

Walking out I acted like I tripped on the threshold, both he and Mandy laughed and then Mandy motioned with her hands towards the photo place, "Go get her." I felt like I'd just been shot out of one of those cages that hold the horses at the Kentucky Derby. My heart was racing because I had no idea what I was going to say. But I did it, walking the two doors down seemingly felt like it was the beginning of forever. She was at the door looking the other way as I started moving towards her. Turning back towards the candle shop, she saw me coming, and walked back into the photo place. I approached the door, and saw her sitting on a fence post looking like a Hollywood prop while smiling, she said, "Hello, would you like to take picture with me?" When I heard this I was stunned because every time I walked by she would run away as if I'd done something wrong. When I heard what she was asking, "Why yes, I would like to take a picture with you." Glancing back at her sister, she started laughing, "I mean here, not with me." Already nervous I wanted to get this thing over with so I blurted out, "Listen I don't know if you've noticed but I've been walking by this place all day trying to get up enough courage to come in here and ask you out. What is stopping you from going out to eat with me when you get off?"

Confused, she kept trying to get her sister to help her get out of a situation that she didn't feel so comfortable with. "Please, I have boyfriend. I can't go out with you. He wouldn't like it." responding in a quiet but stern voice. Taking my hand and placing it on her shoulder I continued, "But you have to eat don't you? That's all I'm asking, just join me for dinner." I could tell that she wasn't sure what she wanted to do so I let off the dinner thing. I knew the twins were from another country but had no idea where so I asked, "Where are you ladies from?"

Her sister came over to join in, "We from Polska." Knowing what that meant because of travels around Germany I said, "Poland, how about that? I've been to the Czech Republic, Germany and Austria but never to Poland, but from what I know, isn't it cold there?" She went to help someone and turned back to me and asked, "Where you from?" I told her I lived in a small town outside of Augusta, Georgia and from there I was interested how someone from Poland would make the trip all the way here to Gatlinburg, Tennessee. We must've talked on and off for about an hour. Never once did she bend on going to dinner though. Intermittently, I'd keep asking. But it didn't matter. She then asked me, "Hey Chak, would you like to see our pictures?" That is how Polish people say Chuck so I responded nicely, "Yes I would. Where are they?" She pulled out an envelope and then showed them to me. I have to say I was really impressed. I'd been sitting there talking to both of them for a little more than an hour and I didn't even know their names. So I said, "Wait a minute before I tell you what I think about these pictures I need to know who I'm looking at. What are your names?"

Blushingly she said, "My name Kamila, and this my sister Sylvia. And this is our friend Margaret. She is behind me and Sylvia on the motorcycle." To be so shy she was showing me pictures that were incredibly provocative. Not too many people here in the states would take pictures of themselves in fishnet and skimpy tops for a laugh. But these girls did. And I was the first one to see these pictures outside of those staying with them at the hotel. Lifting my eyebrows I said, "Unbelievable! This is amazing, you girls are quite photogenic. And now that I've seen your pictures, what are y'all doing tonight?" Sylvia kept nudging Kamila to tell me, "We have to go to Wal-Mart. We not go to dinner because we need girl things." Not really knowing what Sylvia was getting ready to ask her to do so I asked them, "How are you guys getting there?"

Sylvia hit Kamila on the arm again, "Tell him. He is nice guy." There I was waiting for an answer and Kamila was just about to tell me when Margaret interrupted, "Hey can I go?" Always someone who loved company I told her, "Of course, but how are you guys getting there?" Not wanting to ask, Kamila said, "We are riding bus, and it takes two hours to make short trip. We no be back for a while." My head bending to the side I whispered, "Hey, you see the car up there on the hill? That'll get you there in about ten minutes . . . tops. I can take you guys and then bring you back home when you're finished."

All of them started jumping around as if they had just won the lottery then Kamila looked at me and said, "But hey, it is not date. Okay?" Smiling back at her, I told her, "Okay no date, Just Wal-Mart. And that's fine with me." Jumping in the car I noticed that Robb and Mandy were long gone. I guess they figured that I was more preoccupied than to decide where they were going to eat, which rightly so, I was.

Nonetheless, I was happy to be sitting beside the same girl I'd thought about all day. But I wanted to know more than the name of her boyfriend. I wanted to know everything she felt comfortable enough to share with me. We stayed in Wal-Mart for another hour or so, and then she asked me which department that she could find a compact disk player. She missed her own country's music and needed something to play it on.

She and I walked from aisle to aisle searching for the perfect player, and then a song came on the radio by Maroon 5 called *She Will Be Loved.* Both of us started singing and dancing right there in the middle of Wal-Mart. People were staring at us while we were making complete fools of ourselves, some of them laughing uncontrollably at how we were so footloose and fancy free in the middle of a major department store. That's when Sylvia and Margaret came from the underwear department carrying conversation appetizers.

Sylvia brought a lingerie outfit for Kamila to try on and was trying to get me to make a comment on what I actually thought about it. I wasn't about to comment on something that I knew had repercussions. They were trying to get Kamila embarrassed by showing what she wore to bed. But I didn't bite. I just turned around to find a camera that Kamila wanted. I discovered that night that Europeans have no problem talking about things of a sexual nature. Where in the states, we hide behind our walls of insecurities only to venture out when we think our doors are locked. It isn't a bad thing to be so open it was just making me a little uncomfortable about the things that I was being asked by people that I'd just met. But remember, it was me, the quiet little American in a room full of Polish girls.

Leaving the store that night I felt like a man who had three girlfriends. All of them were latching on to me singing their tunes as loud as they could. I had come a long way from the time I spent with Dona and her family. I didn't know where I was going with this but I knew it had nothing to do with Columbia County. And that part made me feel like a brand new man.

I opened the door for all girls but gave special attention to Kamila. I closed her door with two hands so she'd feel that I was partial to her. Not even two miles down the road I was looking in the rear view mirror at Sylvia when she tapped Kamila on the shoulder, "Hey let's go to Applebee's, we could get a couple of beers. That way Chak doesn't have to go home and you can talk." Liking this idea I shook my head in agreement. Kamila then replied, "But don't we have something to do?" Margaret spoke wittingly, "You can call him when you get home. We are hungry."

About the time I was turning into the parking lot, the rain came down torrentially. And pointing towards the back window I said, "Okay listen, I've got an umbrella back there but my only request is that Kamila has the middle. Don't worry about me. I'll walk in the rain." Taking both of her hands Sylvia was moving her sister's shoulders, "You see, I told you."

Applebee's was a blast. I wasn't one to drink so I just watched them drink while I was sipping on my virgin Piña Colada. I knew that Europeans drank a lot but I had no idea that their tolerance was as high as it was. As small a girl as Kamila was, she would out drink Marty who had enough room in his stomach for a small Korean family. But we talked about everything that night, and she never got drunk. Not even tipsy, she'd ask me about my family as I would find out about hers. Honestly though. I was worn out and ready to sleep. But I still wanted to hang out there. Lucky enough, Applebee's was closing so I asked them, "Did you all need a ride home?" As they said, "Yes" I unlocked the car so we could leave. I thought that I'd fall asleep at the wheel because I didn't actually know where they were staying. If it was in the mountains like Robb and Mandy it would be almost two o'clock before I got to sleep. I was staying at the Hampton Inn that night and how blessed do you think I was to have them staying in a hotel right behind me.

Dropping them off was my plan but Kamila wanted me to come up to see their room. At this time I couldn't drive without my eyes wanting to close so what made me think I was prepared to climb stairs. But I did what any man would do in my circumstance, I went upstairs. Remember now, this was two thirty in the morning and guess what we walk into? A hotel room full of Russians, Slovakians, Hungarians and the rest of her Polish pals who were here for the summer sitting around drinking. I stayed for about twenty or so minutes and told her I'd see her tomorrow, hopefully. But I figured something out that night. All of those guys from those other countries could drink like a fish, and go without sleep for what seemed to be days. They must've been on cocaine or something like it to stay up that long.

The next day would be the beginning of a relationship that I never really got a grip on. What does that mean? Remember when I said she had a boyfriend? She did have one. He loved her very much and was picked out by her father. Being in the Polish military was a badge of honor that provided them with an income that was definite and prosperous. Whereas other professions in Poland weren't as sure with regards to receiving a salary. All of my travels before led me to places that were blessed monetarily so I really had no inkling that a country so close to Germany would be as non-profitable as it was. Her father was making about eight hundred dollars a month which over there was an awesome salary. When she told me that her boyfriend was in the same area of military service that her father served, I took it as maybe she wanted something different. That difference, I thought, could be me.

Throughout June, July, August, and September I was in Gatlinburg from Saturday to Wednesday afternoon. Every night we'd have dinner, go walking around, and just talk about plans for our respective worlds. She'd make me feel as though I was the only one there even if we were in the midst of a thousand people. We had a wonderful time but then she told me that in September, she'd be leaving back to Roddick. Making sure that she really never lost him here in the states, she told me that she did forget about him many times when we were together.

We went to Dollywood one day, and she was supposed to be home in order to receive a call from him, but she wasn't. If I had to blame it on anyone, it would have to be Sylvia. I felt like she wanted Kamila to fall in love with me, not with him. I had no reservations with that but I didn't want to push her into feeling something that she didn't want to feel.

But here it was, four months of getting to know Poland's best girl, and I wasn't ready to give up. She called me and asked for me to take them to Atlanta for their flight home, so I did. Personal day you know? At work, I would've been fired had they known what I was doing when I was supposed to be there. But I thought this would be the last time I'd see the girls. I knew that Kamila and Sylvia were going, but Margaret wanted to ride too. And I had no problem with that.

I took four forty one all the way down, at least to Athens anyway. I wanted to show Kamila the river in Cherokee. We had talked about going kayaking down it many times but every time we set out it began to rain. Taking her by The Oconoluftee I could tell she wanted to get out but we really didn't have enough time. She also wanted to see the casino. So I took her by Harrah's and drove around the parking lot. It was as if she didn't want to leave. But she knew she had too. Even Sylvia was crying in the back seat not because she knew that her man was waiting for her in Poland, but rather it was that she was torn between here and there. Margaret was okay with whatever.

It didn't take long to drive through the mountains after we left Cherokee. They were so impressed with the trees. Being green in the middle of September would never happen in their country. What she was trying to tell me was that their winters were earlier than ours.

Warsaw, to them was a big city but when we hit the city limits of Atlanta, their necks bowed straight up the skyline. The Westin downtown was the building that Kamila said, "I'd be willing to give up my flight home to see the inside of that" Turning the radio down so I could tell her something I replied, "I promise you now that if you ever come back, I'll take you to eat on the top floor. You see those lights spinning around up there, that's where the restaurant is." All of them said almost in unison, "That would be great. I can't wait"

Dropping them off on the North end of the airport, I went on to park. I had my badge with me so I could walk them to their gate. The only bad thing about this flight was that she was flying Lufthansa and not Delta. Other than that I was looking forward to seeing them off. But I wasn't prepared for what I'd do. When she was about to go board her plane I hugged her and started crying. Thinking that I wouldn't see her again because I knew she was due to marry Roddick. I was just happy to have had the time I did with her. As she hugged me back she kissed me on the cheek. I started to tear up then but I held out until she boarded. Really, I don't know why I was crying. I guess it was Sylvia because she was crying too. Kamila was leaving to go see someone else right? And I was going home to see an empty house. Maybe that's why.

Going through the motions everyday thereafter, I chose to email her about once a week. She would email me about a week after I sent her one. Feeling like I had no control over the direction of my love life I made a commitment to go see her. One day in November I flew to Warsaw to see them except they didn't know I was coming. I got stuck in Munich because I was flying on Lufthansa Express. Blessed beyond my wildest dreams, I got a tremendous break. The agent working the gate saw my badge and asked me, "What department are you in? Can you jump seat? We are full other than that." Knowing that I had reservations at the Warsaw Westin and I'd be charged for it anyway if I didn't show up so I shook my head and said, "Operations, and of course many times." I knew full well that it was illegal in the United States for an Operations agent to ride jump seat. I was led to the middle seat in the cockpit of a CR7, which is a seventy seat regional jet.

That to me was worth every second that I waited for everybody else to board the plane not knowing if I was going to get on or not. We talked about the distinguishable differences in Lufthansa and Delta. I think they thought I was a pilot, so I played the part. I knew a lot about the RJ because we had just acquired them as well except ours were having software issues. Nonetheless, it was the first and last time I had ever flown in the front of an airplane. Talk about a different perspective. Those guys were flying that bird by just changing knobs rather than touching the yoke. About two or three hundred feet from the runway in Warsaw, they finally grabbed the yoke to land it. It was truly amazing. Had I been through this when I was younger I know for sure that I would've been a pilot.

I had no idea how or even if I'd contact Kamila. Yes, I did want to see her but not if Roddick was anywhere around. After checking in as fast I could, I drove down to Radom, Poland. About eight o'clock that night I started driving around just to take in what her town looked like. I really didn't know if I was going to call her or not.

Then a still small voice came over me and said, "What in the world are you doing here? You know full well that she's in love with someone else and here you are driving around this crazy town." The same voice that told me to go to Radom, was now telling me to go back to the hotel. And honestly, I was thinking it best to just fly back home the next day.

Not really knowing what to do next, I emailed her when I got back. At that time, I didn't expect her to call or anything, but I was pleasantly surprised at what actually happened. When I woke up the next morning I noticed that my red light on the phone was flashing. I called downstairs to check my messages, and smiled when I found out that it was Kamila. She had just left Radom on the train and was on her way to Warsaw. Saying that it'd take about an hour or so, I jumped up to take a shower real quick. And as soon as I walked out of the bathroom, I got a phone call from the concierge telling me that I had a Ms. Sczepanska waiting for me in the lobby, and was it okay to let her come up.

After telling them it was okay I waited for her to come to my room. Conveniently located on the top floor, she was impressed at how nice my room was. I felt as though she was happy to see me. However, I didn't know for sure, but she did want to take me around the city. So, I took that as a positive step. The only thing I was concerned about was her being home for Roddick's call. I wanted to make sure that she made her train at four o'clock.

We walked around most of downtown Warsaw. In fact, I noticed a place where Stephen Seagal filmed a movie of his. There was a town square where a scene involved an older man sitting on a park bench. I wanted to be sure I sat there sort of imagining myself in the film. Kamila had no idea what I was doing. Through her broken English she was trying to get me to explain what I was doing. She started to understand where I was coming from once I told her about the movie. We walked all day even taking in lunch at a local restaurant. I tried some regional cuisine but I have to tell you that it wasn't something I found tasty. I think it needed a lot of seasoning because it was extremely bland. You have to know that I didn't have Polish food up to that moment. But when there aren't any American places to eat you have to find something you can to keep down. Otherwise, you'll be paying good money to clean the regurgitated carpet in your hotel. Mostly though, it was okay. At three o'clock I asked her, "Don't you need to catch a train?" She turned back towards me with an expression that I'll never forget. One that tells me, "I need to go, but I don't really want to go."

Kamila was unsure which way the train station was and she was asking me. Laughingly, "This is your country, and your town, I was going to ask you but hey, we can ask someone who does know." She started shaking her head in agreement. We stopped the first person we saw and were unsuccessful. Then the next one and luckily she told us, "You have to go through those trees, and it is just on the other side of those big buildings over there." while she was pointing towards a park. There we were in a full run through a most certain rain. Mist had already begun to fall. Running down the stairs, she turned back to say goodbye and came up to me, kissed me, and then said, "We can't do this again. I've got Roddick and I . . ." Pointing towards her train I took my finger as if to say, "Go . . . Go . . . But here, take the wine . . ." Handing her the bottle I got as local welcoming gift from the Westin. She took it and ran to catch her train.

Thinking that it would be last time I'd see her I started to tear up. Confident that she'd caught her train I left the station and tried to find my hotel. Let me tell you something, my hotel was a whole lot easier to find than that train station. It just so happened to be a couple of blocks over. Once I walked through my door I jumped in my bed because I was freezing. The rain had been so cold that my clothes were wet. Totally exhausted from the day's activities I felt like I wanted to take a nap. With that thought came almost instantly the concierge downstairs. He was asking me if I needed anything. Then he asked me, "Mr. Merci, Ms. Sczepanska is here again, do you want me to give her a key to your room. You can imagine me sitting there wondering why she was back and then realizing that she must've missed her only train home. I was actually smiling because I felt God had given me at least another hour or two with her while I drove her home.

For sure, she'd miss Roddick's call. I just hoped that I wouldn't be the one she would blame. When she came in, as timid as she was, she didn't really want to ask me for anything. I knew that she needed a ride home so I asked, "So you need a ride home, huh?" Knowing that she missed the only train that went to Radom, I could tell she didn't want to ask but she just started shaking her head as if to say, "Yes." I think she was afraid of what Roddick was going to think if she wasn't there when he called. She was faithful enough to tell him about me, but to what extent he knew I didn't know.

I rented a Toyota Tercel because their bigger car rates were crazy high. At seven hundred dollars for a Tercel, I'd hate to see what their rates were for a Taurus or something like that. You know what though? I only needed four wheels, an engine, and preferably a heater. So I was good. Kamila wanted to drive to Radom but she didn't have a license. So I was scared that she would wreck and cause me massive problems with the Polish Insurance company that I had on that car. Driving South, through many small towns I noticed that it wasn't that much different than our smaller towns. Barns in open fields, newly manicured pastures, and cows were mostly prevalent along the road. They weren't even tied up in open fields.

Kamila was like a scared little girl who was trying to hide her feelings. She was so confused and really didn't know how to relate it to me. She directed me towards her house but told me to park short because she didn't want anyone in her family to see her. Sylvia knew that she was coming to see me, as well as her sister Anya, but no one else knew. We sat in a parking lot in a military base where she lived. Sylvia walked down to meet us, hugged me, and asked if I could come with them to the officer's club. Certain that I was leaving in the morning, I said, "No." But Kamila turned to me and requested, "Please!"

This was the thing with her. I could never tell when she was serious. One day she wanted me to be there with her, then the next she was shipping me out on the next FedEx truck. Needless to say, I went and watched them drink and talk about things that were happening in their lives. Sylvia was engaged to a pilot so he and I talked about some of the sorties that he was flying. He seemed to be a nice guy and when he found out I worked for an airline, he wanted to find out more about the aircraft we flew. The night was full of excitement. Still I don't know how these guys over there drink so much without getting drunk. But it is what it is. As I was preparing to leave that night, Kamila told me, "You can't come back here. If Roddick finds out that you were here, you might be in trouble. I'm going to marry him, eventually. So please, can you for me?"

It didn't take long to find out that I needed to help her get her life back. By my leaving it would free her mind up so that

Roddick wouldn't feel so insecure about what she was doing with me. There was always something therapeutic about flying home from an International country. Maybe it was the meal in Business Elite, I don't know. But what I did know was that I was ready to leave my Polish experience in the past.

Arriving back in the United States, I wanted to forget her but I found it pretty difficult. For Christmas, I sent Kamila and Sylvia's family a box full of gifts. Anya and her girl, I even sent a basketball because Anya's girl had just taken up this wonderful sport. Which I found out later that it was a good day for them. Their mother and father never had such a good Christmas like that. Gifts were given based upon information I obtained when I was there in Radom. And meeting her father, I knew he loved fishing, so my gift to him was a tackle box slam full of equipment. From what Kamila said, he started crying when he opened his gift.

For two months I didn't hear from them and then one day she emailed me to see how I was doing. Immediately, I wrote her back to let her know that I was excited to have heard from her. We traded letters for about a week then nothing. I was okay with that because I felt myself getting emotionally involved again so I wanted to let it go.

As dumb a move I'd ever done, I took off for a couple of days and left for Poland again. She was telling me that she had to go to Krakow and wasn't happy about having to go alone. I went to Margaret's house when I got to Radom. She called the girls over so she could surprise them. When Kamila came in, she saw me and started crying. I didn't know how to take it. Was she crying because I was there and she wasn't happy about it? Or was it that she was actually glad I was there? Either way I was there and if she wanted me to, I'd take her to Krakow. I'll have you know that she wasn't happy, but the more we talked, the better it got.

When Margaret and Sylvia found out that I was going, they asked if they could go as well. I said, "Sure . . . if you want, that'd be great." Kamila was going to stay at a dorm there but now we had three more people. It just so happened, that Margaret's boyfriend was there in college. I noticed a Sheraton on the banks of the Wisla River there in Krakow. Touring the city was an adventure itself but you have to know that these girls I was with had never stayed in a hotel like this. And I wanted to make sure they weren't disappointed. So I did what any man would do, I booked it.

What later followed was their arrival into a five star hotel. I checked in and they were prepared to go stay at the college somehow. That is when I handed Kamila the keys to their room. Her eyebrows lifted as she said, "What is this? We can't stay here. We don't have money." I looked at her and said, "Hey, I don't either, we can just use the points. But hey I'm right next door to you guys. So after you guys get cleaned up, you can meet me down here for supper."

Their necks bent upward towards the ceiling they couldn't believe that they were in a place this nice. Laughing, and talking all the way up the elevator, they couldn't believe that they were having this much fun. The next day after our free breakfast, they thanked me and wanted to be my personal tour guide to the city of Krakow. Even Margaret's boyfriend showed up, so for the rest of the day I felt like I was integrated into a slice of Polish culture.

Upon returning to Radom, Kamila and I had the same conversation we had when I left the first time except this time it was more intense. We sat outside her father's house and she was telling, "Chak, you don't need to love me, I will tell again. I'm marrying Roddick, he loves me . . . You need to go home and not come back . . . You need to find someone else to love." I knew that she was right but I didn't want to hear what she was saying. I interrupted her and replied, "Kamila, what if I don't want to love someone else? What if I want to love you?"

She sat there in a dumbfounded state and then responded, "But you can't, you will find . . . Chak . . . if I didn't have Roddick I would've fallen in love with you a long time ago but I do have him, and when you find someone to love, she will love you like you love her." Guessing that I wasn't getting anywhere close to where I wanted I retorted, "Okay, I don't think I will but I'll give you my word I won't come back here. I promise." Both of us with tears running down our cheeks I walked her to her door and let her know I wasn't coming back. She closed the door and that was the last time I saw Radom. I honestly, never went back. I did think about her from time to time. But I wouldn't let my thought determine my flight plan for the weekends. So I guess you could say that I was okay with being single again. Then I thought about it. I was actually single the whole time I spent with Kamila. She had Roddick from the beginning and I had nothing. Had I not been so confident when I met her, I would've heard her say that she was happy with him. But I didn't, I actually thought that my American way of romance would stop her from loving him. I was wrong in the beginning and wrong in the end. On my way home this time I realized that no matter how many times she told me I was the best man she'd ever met, I was still the man who was standing between her definition of happiness and what she truly wanted in her life.

The truth was that she wasn't going to leave Poland to come to the United States, and I wasn't going to leave the United States to live anywhere. So what I had done for months now was prolonging the inevitable. Kamila was now free in Poland to patch any damage I may've done by showing up. Roddick knew that he loved her and that Kamila was having doubts. You know what? She, in the end, felt that her love for him was worth a whole lot more than having some dude from America trying to sweep her off her feet. I just wanted her to be happy.

The following May, my nephew Brad and I went to Gatlinburg and went by that same old timey photo place. Kamila and Sylvia weren't there but her manager was. She met me before so she ran out to talk to me, "Have you seen the twins?" Not knowing that they were in the states I said, "No, I had no idea they were even here." She then replied, "Yeah they are, and they're up at Baskin Robbins. Go up there. I'm sure they'd be happy to see you."

I asked Brad, "Do you want some ice cream?" He knew what I was actually asking but hey, he was up for anything much less, some frozen refreshment. After getting the go ahead from him we walked in and waited for the girls to see us. Both of them were preoccupied serving customers who were trying to cool down from the blistering May sun. Once Kamila saw me she was surprised and excited. After choosing my ice cream, I went to pay, and Kamila pointing to a booth in front of the store said, "I'll pay for these. You can sit over there in the corner" Brad and I sat down and I remember him telling me, "She still likes you man. Whatcha going to do? Are we staying here or going back to Cherokee?" Digging my spoon in my ice cream cup and placing it in my mouth I replied, "You think so? You know she looks kind of different. Not as pretty somehow. But hey, we'll wait and see what happens."

When Kamila finished her duties and was taking a break, she walked over and sat down right next to me. I introduced her to Brad and told her this was my nephew that goes kayaking with me all the time. She remembered him from our conversations and it looked as though she was happy to meet him. She asked me, "How long have you been here?" I was intent on answering her but I almost stuttered when I responded, "Ah . . . um . . . Brad and I were headed to Cherokee and he wanted to come up to Gatlinburg so see the girls walking around the strip. What about you? I didn't know you guys were coming this year. I thought you'd be married by now."

She was unsure how to answer but she did her best, "Roddick is in Virginia training with your military, he is supposed to come here and take me to Florida. But how are you?" I kept looking at Brad to see if he was ready to go because I knew I was. Then I asked, "You want me to stick around and wait for you guys to get off from here?" That look of uncertainty was all the answer I needed. She said after taking a bite of my ice cream, "We get off at twelve tonight, and we're staying at the same hotel."

Having finished his ice cream, Brad asked me, "Hey man, are we going to walk around or what?" I think he was trying to help me make a decision that he knew I wasn't ready to make. So we left without telling the twins, "No" or "Yes." Giving Brad the opportunity to walk up and down the strip I told him I wanted an ice cold drink they had down at the Aquarium. He agreed that it'd be an awesome thing to do because the car was parked right across the street. Then he spun around and posed a question, "So, we're staying here tonight?" I thought about what he was asking and said, "I'll tell you later." About two minutes after that

I motioned towards the car with the key remote to unlock it. Brad was wondering what we're doing. He met a couple of ladies and was ready to either stay or go. Like I said, he was game for anything.

We climbed in the car and started driving south towards Cherokee. I wanted to stop by and see Margaret. She was always nice to me, even letting me stay with them a couple of nights while I was in Poland. The least I could do was stop by and say, "Hello." Once we left the restaurant where Margaret worked, Brad didn't know what we were going to do so he asked me again, "You going to tell me what we're doing?" I didn't want to keep him from meeting any ladies in Gatlinburg or Cherokee so I gave him my decision, "We're going back to Cherokee. If we can get back early enough we'll hit the river. Is that alright with you, or did you want to stay?"

He wasn't disappointed with my decision at all. He just wanted to know something. Then his inquisitive nature was peeking interest as to why we weren't staying for Kamila. I said, "We aren't staying. I know I told her we were but she doesn't look like the same person. She was skinny before, but now she looks like she's been on crack since I left Poland. Plus, I don't think it's fair for me to drag her into a place where I don't think she wants to go. So I guess we will just leave this one here in Gatlinburg and chalk it up to experience."

Brad, I think was actually relived that we wouldn't be waiting around to watch people drink for a couple of hours anyway. But he was interested in why I didn't want to stay. So he prodded even further, "But I thought you liked her. You sure you want to go." Rolling down my window so that I could breathe in that wonderful mountain air I replied, "Brad, maybe you'll understand one day. But there comes a time when you have to cut your losses and move ahead. That's what I'm doing. But look at it this way. Now we'll have two more days on the river."

That was the last time I saw or heard from Kamila. And to tell you the truth, I prayed for her nothing but the best. I didn't want to get involved with someone who really had no intention of getting involved with me. For almost a year, I'd been chasing love in a foreign land but what I received from that pursuit was to me, much more gratifying.

As I always did in the past, I went back to my list to add something. I knew that I enjoyed my life with Kamila. Even though she never said she loved me. I felt loved because of the way she treated me. Don't get me wrong, I didn't add an item to my list that the woman I wanted had to be from a different country because I thought American woman were inferior. I added it because with Kamila, I felt I was being treated the way that I always wanted to be treated.

The ironic thing about it was that, back in the trivial part of my brain, I knew that my life could never be what I wanted when the woman who I was choosing was not choosing me. That was the reality. But it didn't stop there. I remember things about Kamila that I didn't necessarily like. I remember thinking, "Like the girl but didn't like the girl's habits." I knew that Eastern European's drank but to the extent that they drank I really had no idea. I didn't drink and I didn't want my woman to drink. I'm talking about alcohol. And these Polish people can flat out drink. That was okay for them, but I didn't so much care for it. So I added that particular trait to my list.

I never blamed anyone for a bad situation. And I'm not saying that being with Kamila was a bad situation. But what I am saying is that I learned how to communicate effectively with a woman from a foreign country. I didn't know it then but it would lead me to different places where my experience would help me make better decisions in that pursuit.

From there, I started venturing out into other countries like the Ukraine, Hungary, and even Russia. My mission was strategically defined. So much so that I knew I'd never again date an American woman. I knew definitively what I was looking for in a woman. Departing from each airport I knew that my departure from normality had also taken flight. Just like an airplane would lift off the ground, my desire to find an International woman would also be taking off towards those global skies.

Having been so bruised mentally from the normal relationships I had in the United States, I recognized that I needed something else. Maybe I needed to fly away like I always did to change my perspective. Maybe not, but until Kamila, I never acknowledged it. So I'm thankful to have been given the ticket to board the plane that would eventually take me to the love of my life. In essence, the non-relationship with my friend from Radom, Poland would be guaranteeing my eventual departure from normality and my surefire arrival upon abnormality.

12.

A Russian Bride Without Being Anywhere Close To Russia

AFTER MY ADVENTURE WITH KAMILA I KNEW LIFE AS I KNEW IT had changed. I knew conclusively that I didn't want to delve into an American way of dating. The norm was for an American man to find an American woman. Court for a while and when they would feel comfortable about the magnitude of their love, they would marry. Yes, I had friends who were involved with International women but for me, I never dove into that type of relational involvement.

Where and how would I begin were the questions banging around the inside of my mind? The International women that I knew were headed home in a couple of months. And that was the thing about those college students who come over here for the summer. Their primary focus is on the money. When they left their respective countries their minds are not on pursuing love, it is centered on the amount of American dollars they can exchange for their own currencies. I learned that the hard way. But honestly, I can't say it was painful because when you get involved with someone you know definitely has a boyfriend, you can't blame what happens on anyone but yourself.

Most men would want the love of their life to be present and accounted for, right? With the summer work program girls, their presence was only guaranteed for about five months. After that, you'd better be working for a major airline who allows you to fly free if you desire any success in that relationship. If I were to pursue a woman who never had an intention of moving to the United States, then what gives me the assurance that the relationship would materialize into anything but a long distance love affair? What do most men and women want most out of the love of their life? I believe it is time. That's because if you're present and accounted for, time is the most precious gift a man can give.

Think about it this way. God gave his most precious gift in his son Jesus. His purpose was to save the entire world from a most certain death. In essence, he gave us time to live our lives through Christ himself. Anyone who has a relationship with him knows he's omnipresent, and forever accounted for. Taking a page out of his book of life and applying it to my own. I realized that I needed to go back and analyze certain aspects of my own personal development. Then as I always did when I learned something new, I added the item to my list. Making sure the woman in which I would bestow my time would also bestow upon me the same. In other words, she would almost definitely have to live in the United States. Or I could move to her country which I really didn't want to do. You see, I believed foreign countries were nice to visit but there is something altogether different about living there, something almost socialist about them. Miniature soviets, as I saw them.

Even though she never knew it, I believe Kamila helped me carve out the path I was headed with my love life. One being the way she treated me like I wanted to be treated. Therefore, I knew that anyone I dated had to at least measure up to that level of willing thoughtfulness. It sounds like an impossible task but I didn't expect something out of someone if I wasn't willing to offer it myself.

I remember when we were driving down the road towards Lublin, Poland and Kamila asked me, "I know you and I are not couple but say we are, would you move to Poland for me?" We talked about many things on that trip including what our thoughts were on premarital sex, but I still, was surprised to hear her ask me this particular question. Taking my time I passively responded, "What do you mean? What about you, would you move to the States or would it be that I'd move here?" She was a smart woman so she could tell that I didn't really want to answer her directly or indirectly. Somehow, it was like she already knew what my response would be, but she asked anyway.

"You know what I mean. Would you move here for me?" she replied. The expression on my face answered the question way before I could even open my mouth, "Of course, that's if we're a couple, right? What about you?" I thought maybe she'd give me a run of the mill answer like the one I was feeding her. But she was honest. And by that honesty, I knew what I desired most in a relationship would never be found there in Poland. She said, "I would never move anywhere, I want to teach here at Politechna Radomska. My life is here, and always will be."

That's when I decided I was tired of putting so much of me into something I felt was a proverbial dead horse. I was tired of trying to move the immovable. Think of being present and accounted for as being the water that supplies a flower with the necessary amount of nourishment. What happens to the flower when water no longer serves as nourishment because its source has run bone dry? Obviously it ceases to flourish and eventually dies as its petals become withered and broken.

I can't say this enough. Never settle for this type of mal-nourishment. You deserve better than to have love dry up within the depths of your soul. Just because the love of your life decided they'd much rather be somewhere else. It doesn't mean that you need to give up on the relationship you're dreaming of. Kamila was settled within her own borders. And I knew she'd never be present or accounted for in a relationship with anyone outside of Poland. So knowing that, I took it to mean that I should find someone else who needed me to be there for them as they would be there for me. As always, I applied what I learned and it provided me with the direction I needed to go.

But how would I find someone who was different than Kamila? She'd have to possess attributes I was searching for, right? I was intent on not settling for the elegance of an International romance, but rather I'd be going full steam ahead towards my own definition of International stylishness. From there I was comfortable trying to determine which area of the world I would be most satisfied with. But where does one go for the questions that seem to have no answers? I knew where . . . but I was relieved when I heard someone cry out from the other side of the room, "Google it!"

At work we had an internet connection that was available to us for company use only. They were very explicit about their network being used for anything but approved sites. Priding myself on being a model employee, I wasn't about to push them into firing me because I decided to use their network to create my domestic profile on an International site. We were allowed to use Google, but were discouraged from surfing the net. But you know what? I somehow found a way to find these sites without cookies being saved. Yes, they could have caught me had they been looking for me, but no, I was never caught. I then, in the search bar, would type, "Russian Bride" and then wait for a response.

Let me tell you if you're looking for something having Google as your guide, you'd better be prepared for an overwhelming experience. Just as soon as I typed those words in, I was bombarded with a plethora of sites that were the so called, "Russian Bride" sites. The first thing I did was create a personal profile, which would be accompanied by pictures. It was one requirement most of the International sites had for those of us searching for Mrs. Right. So, led by determination and grit I dove into a whole new world.

It was convenient the way I was allowed to sort the women that I wanted to see. And what it provided me was a way to sift through what I didn't find so appealing. Women were eliminated by simply checking a box. I didn't want an older woman because I was an older man and I wanted my children to have at least one young parent. It was as easy as checking the age checkbox eighteen through twenty five. Most of those sites would also let you sort based upon hair color, weight, height, or even which country you felt most comfortable with.

Providing introductions to women from Latvia to Kazakhstan, it was their intention to give you as much to choose from as they possibly could. Once your profile is approved, you're given the freedom to browse through thousands of girls at your leisure. And I did just that. I was amazed at how stunningly beautiful these women were. Their bodies looked as curvaceous as an Enzo Ferrari. It seemed these girls were spending most of their time either at the gym or at the internet café to see who was writing them. Flipping through each profile I noticed that most of them looked like they needed something to eat. I liked skinny but some of them were almost anorexic. Yes, we had beautiful women here in the states but none of them were looking for someone like me. At least that is what I thought, anyway. Those that knew me knew that I was a shallow man and a woman's beauty was the motivating factor in finding a mate. So being able to browse around the world without ever stepping on a plane was working for me. The only problem was that I was searching more and more at work. That was it. Of course I never got in trouble even when my Station Manager knew what I was doing.

The plan would work like this. I'd send letters to women I liked, and then if they liked what they saw in my profile, they'd respond accordingly. This was absolute liberation for me because I was somewhat introverted in real life. But in this International cyber world I had an alter ego. I was eliminating my fear of rejection simply by being able to write rather than speak. They give you the opportunity to call them on the phone but I was afraid that I'd create an even larger language barrier. Simply by me not understanding what they were trying to say. I knew that I was safe just sticking with the letters.

There was a drawback though. Most International dating sites have a fee that you pay when you either receive or send a letter. Minimal at most, it averaged about six dollars for each letter. I was a member of many of these sites so it was getting pretty expensive. Your response time would range from one to three days depending on their interest, I guess. The option was there to send flowers. I have to say that I never sent flowers to anyone outside of the United States. It was an adventure living in this world for a while. But remember, it was getting expensive. I guess I was spending close to three hundred dollars a month just to communicate to a woman who would pretty much just answer questions. That's when I decided that I needed to concentrate on limiting membership to two sites. Think about how much money you'd spend if you had women in five different countries and you're shelling out six dollars for each one every two days. I can tell you that you'd better be making some serious dough just to keep up.

I narrowed it down to a couple of International dating sites. One that was located in Maine who to me had the most to offer. Their selection of women spanned the globe it seemed more than others. However, I did go to the other sites to browse but never to communicate. I'd get letters from women there but I wouldn't answer. Maybe I was being passive, not really giving them a chance, but I just wanted to be able to communicate with some of them without losing the ability to pay for it. The way I looked at it was, I'd rather have a lot of a little than a little of a lot.

With this site in Maine, I found someone who was extremely attractive and a couple more that were just as beautiful. But two of them I'd write every day. Elena and Anna were their names. Settling for these two I'd log in to their site, wanting to see if they responded. Most of the time I'd receive Elena's letter as soon as I got to work, and would read Anna's when I got to the office in North Augusta. You know how you hear that sound, "You've got Mail!" on America Online. When I opened my letter I didn't hear anything but my internal dialog screaming at the top of its lungs, "Hey Man, you really do have mail!"

Rather amusing to me because sometimes I'd express myself to my work mates in ways that it would make them laugh. I had four friends there who are like sisters to me so I would let them read it and see what they had to say. Finding it laughable because Becca, Kim, Tracie, and Neecy would always say what do these International girls have that we don't have? I responded, "For one, they speak a foreign language. But you know what? The woman I'm looking for has part of you Becca, the unmarried part, part of Kim, part Neecy, and even a little Tracie mixed in." What I was trying to tell them was that I needed parts of them in order to define the love of my life. Neecy, in particular, would analyze each woman and say what about her she liked, giving me insight that I might've missed otherwise.

Elena had black hair and brown eyes and lived in Odessa, Ukraine. Located on the Black Sea it was the place where most of the Ukraine would spend their summer vacation. Anna was also from a small town on the outskirts of Odessa. I told them that while I found it pleasurable to receive their letter, I would rather meet her face to face. "We could write for many months yet never know where we're headed." I wrote. After contemplating several options, she asked me, "So, when are you coming to Odessa?"

A question you should never ask a single man who is looking for a reason to leave the country to find love. So immediately, I started planning the when. Except I had one problem, we weren't allowed to take vacation during Master's week in Augusta. So guess what? I had to wait for another ten days before I could leave. I then told Anna that I was planning to come to Odessa and I never heard from her again. To me, I was intrigued by Anna's actions because at the time we'd been communicating back and forth for about three months. And then, "Bam!" when she found out I was coming to Odessa. But Elena was different she was actually planning what we'd do when I got there.

In Augusta, during the Master's, Delta brings the big jets in to accommodate passengers. So on the Monday I was scheduled to leave, I got to fly on a 767 out of Augusta which was a treat to me. Something else I didn't understand about my Station Manager then, he was aware that I was leaving the day Master's ended but he was mad that I was leaving at ten. His anger forced me to stay through that flight and wait for the noon. Those two hours would create a massive headache. I knew that if I wanted to meet the flight in Kiev, I needed to get on that flight at ten. What do I do now? I had no way of contacting Elena to tell her my dilemma. At that moment I knew that maybe it would've been a good thing to have known her number. But I didn't so I just climbed into my seat trying to beat flight times that I knew were ahead of me.

I wasn't mad with my Station Manager for holding me there, I was always happy to get those big jets in and out of Augusta as fast as I could. Excited would best characterize where my head was then. I just wished that I could've snapped my fingers and traveled to the Ukraine through some kind of spaceship because it was a long . . . long trip. Augusta to Atlanta, Atlanta to New York, New York to Paris, Paris to Kiev would wear anyone down even one who was used to flying every week, even someone like me. Arriving in Kiev I saw that the flight to Odessa was still there so I ran through Customs and went to the domestic terminal. Which in Kiev was a lot like Augusta in the first week of April, nonetheless I had to run as fast as I could with suitcase in tow.

Throwing open the doors I noticed that the sign changed from boarding to departed. Knowing that the next flight wasn't going to leave until tomorrow I was perplexed as to what to do. Odessa was about two hundred miles from Kiev. My hotel would surely charge my credit card if I didn't show up. The questions ran through my mind faster than I could ever run from terminal to terminal, so what was I going to do? Always priding myself on being intuitive I started looking for a taxi driver who could speak English.

After realizing that he'd have to drive me to Odessa he knew he could stick it to me. He said in broken English, "I take you, two hundred ninety five American." My ticket to Odessa on Ukrainian Airlines was only a hundred dollars so I thought this was outrageous. But guess what? When you have Elena in the back of your head yelling, "Am I not important enough to meet me there tonight?" Funny thing was that she wasn't even there and I heard her in Kiev. I responded, "How about you do it for two hundred?" Having the smell of Vodka on his lapel I have to tell you I was worried a little bit. But with his cigarette stained fingernails he lifted his hand and said, "Two hundred ninety, I no go for less." Growing impatient as time was passing and knowing that I only had five days off and I didn't want to waste them in Kiev. Needless to say, I handed him the money and said, "But I'll have you know, I need to be in Odessa tonight."

Elena had planned for us to meet in the town square next to the water fountain there in Odessa. Except it looked like I'd be about two hours late. The drive down to Odessa from Kiev was a lot like Poland. Lots and lots of land being cultivated for harvest, it seemed like a peaceful place to be. Even as anxious as I was to be there in Odessa, I just knew that Elena would wait for me.

I informed the taxi driver that I wanted to go the Hotel Mozart first. Then if he'd wait for me while I checked in, he could take me to the town square where I supposed to meet Elena.

After giving him a ten dollar tip, he was happy to take me down to the square. I have to tell you that I had just traveled thousands of miles, worn slap out, but just knew she'd be there. As we drove around the circle I scanned over each person to realize that Elena wasn't there. I couldn't believe it. The water fountain had no one within twenty feet of it. The only thing I was thinking was, "Where was she?"

How could this happen? Now, what would I do? Why would she do this to me? I shrugged my shoulders and said, "Well, I guess these girls really aren't any different than what I've dated. But hey, maybe I'll just see her tomorrow, right? She knows where I'm staying, so she can call me there." I just motioned to the driver to take me back to the hotel. That night, I have to tell you, I slept better than I had for a long time. I felt like I had been up for three days. I'd pray about it and then drift off in my own little dreamland express.

The next morning I woke up early raring to go. I wanted to let Elena know that I was here, but how in the world could I find her? The night before I sent her a letter to let her know that I was there but maybe I just missed her. But I got nothing. Frantically, I spent most of the morning walking around the city wondering what to do. And friend, there aren't any Chick-fil-A's in the Ukraine for a nice warm breakfast. And at nine o'clock in the morning you want something more than a lukewarm cup of Borscht. I was at a loss of ideas as to where my next move was, but then surprisingly, I saw an American Business Center.

The center was where I could send packages to the United States. At least that is what the name implies, right? I wasn't only wrong, I was dead wrong. The only problem I was facing was they weren't open until ten that morning. The wait lasted a little more than an hour. But the surprise I felt when I walked in lasted longer than that. But what was it though?

As soon as the door closed behind me I noticed the American Business Center was a place to conduct business, but it was predominately an International Dating Center for Ukrainian women. How about that? There were pictures and profiles everywhere. Yeah, I knew what this place was, and I didn't think that they could help me find Elena. After discussing my dilemma, I asked them, "What do you guys suggest?" And their response provided me with something I hadn't thought of, "Why don't you send a courier to her house and let her know that way." Wow! I really hadn't thought of that. Pulling out my wallet, I paid them forty four dollars to send it and told them how to contact me at the Hotel Mozart.

They weren't finished though. Giving me a welcoming package that included a surplus of available Ukrainian women, they suggested that since I was here, I might as well go out with one of their girls. Satisfied with what we were doing with Elena I wanted to give the courier a chance to return with either a positive or negative message. Not having much to do except walking around Odessa, I was told to come back about three or so. I took in the city and was looking for places to eat. Just in case Elena showed up I'd be ready.

Exhausted from it all I showed up at the Business Center just as requested. Their reply was, "Have some good news and some bad news, which one do you want first?" Being one who likes to get the inevitable over with I said, "How about the bad." To tell you the truth I was prepared for what I heard. The courier went to Elena's house and there was no one there. When I asked if they left the note he replied, "No one living there, I ask nee bor." Looking at the manager girl I asked, "If that was the bad news, what could be so good about her standing me up."

If someone has traveled seven thousand miles and wants to meet you, the least you could do is show up. But she didn't even live where she told me she lived. So I waited patiently for the good news. The owner of the Business Center arrived, and he was actually an American who was married to the manager girl who happened to be Ukrainian. His wife told him what happened to me and he said he knew exactly how I felt. In fact, the exact same thing happened to him when he first started searching for an International woman. It was his job to be the bearer of the good news. He looked at me, then handed me an envelope containing five pictures of Ukrainian women. And offered me a proposition, "There are five women in there who are looking for a well groomed man like yourself. It usually cost eighty dollars for an introduction session but since you've already paid the forty four for the courier, I'll be willing to set this up for another forty. Pondering over it for a while I decided I really didn't have anything to lose. So I handed him the forty dollars and waited for a girl who was also named Elena. He called her as soon as he was sure that I'd be going. She must've been sitting by the phone because she was there at the office in no time at all. It was really good for me because I was getting hungry. And I'll have you know that when you're in a foreign country, spaghetti is always . . . the safest meal. You really have to be a complete moron to mess that up.

We walked downtown Odessa to an Italian eatery and talked a little. When I say a little, that means very little. She was a nice woman but communicating with her in person was difficult. My limited Ukrainian, I imagine, was just as difficult for her to understand my English. There was a time where I felt like a fish out of water. It was almost painful. But I endured it for the rest of the evening. Telling her that it was a pleasure to have met her and when I got home I would like to call her. Knowing that neither one of us had any such intention, I'd just drop her off at the Business Center and make plans for flying out of there with my tail tucked between my legs.

Now I had to go back to the place where I work and let all the people know what happened. The embarrassment of it all is to have gone so far to find my true love but yet fall so short of finding anything but mere disappointment. My work mates except for Becca, Kim, Neecy, and Tracie were mocking me for going in the first place, now when they found out what happened; I'd be the brunt of not one, but all of their jokes. I didn't mind because to some extent I think I deserved it.

Here I was shelling out six dollars a letter to someone who I don't think even existed. Maybe she was taken out of a magazine and was being used as bait for an American idiot looking for his Juliet. I don't know why she didn't show up. But I can remember what homeboy said at the Business Center when he told me that he'd been there before, "Listen man, this market is full of disappointments. I can tell you that most of those sites you were showing me are nothing but a bunch of Russian Mafia, men mind you, sitting at a desk with a bottle of Vodka, stealing every dollar you send them. They'll drag you along by giving only generalizations for as long as they can." Shocked by what he told me I can't say that I believed him. But as soon as I heard these words it finally made sense. These girls, both Elena and Anna would never directly answer a question. Especially one that had anything to do with Jesus, it was like they were scared to say anything other than they believed in God. That being an item on my list I found most appealing. I needed a woman who could share things with me, including her relationship with Christ, not one who just said, "I believe in god." I wanted someone who always looked at God with a capital G.

The only consolation I had was I'd be in Paris by four o'clock and spend the rest of the morning there. In France, the pastries are heavenly. I just wanted to get to a Sheraton as fast as I could. Even though I was as far from home, I felt like I'd be home . . . when I was jumping in the bed there. I guess I wanted to pass the night away so I'd sit there and enjoy that wonderful breakfast. For that particular trip I looked at it as a reward for the torment I endured in Odessa.

Imagine a man flying thousands of miles to find the woman of his dreams, and once he gets there to meet her. She stands him up in the middle of an unfamiliar town while he is left staring at a water fountain praying, "Lord Jesus, what's wrong with me? All she had to do was wait an hour or two." When you pray something like that, you've got to know that you're going to get an answer. Sometimes you're hiding behind your own grief but remember something, you're going to get that answer. For me, it was usually a still soft voice comforting me while I was looking outside an aircraft window at thirty five thousand feet.

You see I was finished entirely with the town of Odessa, Ukraine. I took the taxi to the airport making sure I made the flight at eleven o'clock. The only thing I wanted at that time was to connect in Kiev. I knew I'd better make that flight. Flying standby though was never guaranteed, but I'll have you know I did make it. So after a long layover, I was going to arrive in Paris right at midnight. I couldn't understand why Ukrainian Airlines had some pretty wacked out flight schedules. Delta always flew West in the daytime, so this was new to me. Boarding the plane in Kiev I was tired but really couldn't sleep because I was thinking about everything that had just happened. I gazed out the window and was struck with God's awesome beauty and that's when I heard his calming voice. "Son, you may feel like you're a small speck in a vast expansive world. But I want you to look out there in the midst of all those stars, I have the brightest of them all set aside for you, but I'm not finished with her yet. And remember something; I may not be finished with you either. So let's keep talking and I'm sure the woman you're searching for . . . just may find you."

And that's how it was as peace came over me like everything was going to be okay. Somehow, someway I knew it. But I still arrived in North Augusta with a new mission. Get rid of all the profiles on those International Dating sites. I didn't want to talk the Russian Mafia anymore. It seemed like every girl I talked with for the past six months really was a man. Every time I'd get a letter from someone who was interested in me, I just imagined a fat little Russian dude in a rundown school building sitting in a dilapidated desk smoking a pack full of cigarettes. All the while sipping his Vodka, as he send as much provocative pictures as he could or maybe an enticing letter just to provoke me into writing another letter to a woman named Olga, or Oksana, or yes, even Elena. And that image alone was enough to keep me from returning their mail. However, I had an idea of how I'd deal with this apparent disappointment. Knowing that whatever happened, Becca, Kim, Neecy, and Tracie would always try to make me feel better. I'd just go back to work and let the others bash me for a while I guess because, I deserved it. The idea though was to go back through all the women I ever dated seriously and inscribe what I thought would be the end result had I stayed with them. Then I started thinking it wouldn't be productive for me and decided against doing anything like it. To me, I think mostly it was a way of getting my mind off trying to find a Russian Bride . . . without actually being anything close to a Russian.

13.

Looking For Love
In All The Wrong Places

TASHKENT UZBEKISTAN IS ABOUT SEVEN THOUSAND EIGHT HUNDRED eighty eight miles away from Augusta. Almost all the way to China, it's the largest city in Uzbekistan. As population goes, Tashkent has about two and half million people living there and their dominant religion is Islam. In fact, it's about eighty eight percent Muslim. A peaceful nation mostly that has more to offer than just silk. Known for this soft commodity for over a thousand years, the Silk Road served as a major trade route between China and its European partners for most of that time.

Up until nineteen ninety one, Uzbekistan was held under the grasp of the Soviet Union. And after becoming an independent country, Uzbeks were finally given reason to celebrate. Certain constraints were now unconstrained through independence to provide freedom to pursue what is best for the people. Even though there were still marriages arranged by the parents, it's now acceptable for someone to find a mate based solely upon their own desire, not the desire of a mother or father. It doesn't matter where you go in this world, there's always going to be people chasing love. As much as I hate to say it, some will never find it because they're being thrust into an undesired relationship by their parents.

One example you may've noticed was a documentary on Uzbekistan by the Travel Channel. Anthony Bourdain documented his trip there by following a couple who was getting married.

Dressed in traditional European garb, it was evident that these two people wanted to be somewhere else other than where they were headed as a married couple. The woman looked miserable. As if she was resolved to being placed in a powerless situation. I believe that when you're involved in a life changing event like marriage, you should have a smile a mile wide permanently ingrained within the lines of your face.

Many women and men look for love there as they would here in the states. Except for one difference, men expect the women to be something that most of the time they really don't want to be. During this chapter we'll learn about an Uzbek girl who goes from date to date trying to determine what she desires most in the man of her dreams. We'll call her Shahlo.

She was seventeen and half years old when she began noticing there was more to life than being with her girlfriends at the college. Her degree came from the Oriental College there in central Tashkent, and upon graduating she realized that she just might be the last of her class to get married. It seemed like everyone she knew was either getting married or having children. Shahlo wanted love and she didn't want to settle for anything less.

Around two thousand three, Shahlo dated with regularity. When a nice man would ask her to join him for dinner, she took that as an opportunity to try and find her Prince Charming. That was the thing. Here she was being led to believe that these guys were going to have something that she'd find attractive, and that is truly all she wanted.

Shahlo was a modern Muslim woman who set out to find love. Her primary desire was that she'd find someone of similar faith. But what she found was that these guys weren't giving her what she wanted or needed. I guess it is part of their culture that a man from this part of the world would require a woman to walk behind him. All Shahlo was doing was dating only . . . maybe for discovery. Wanting to find out what she wanted in a man, she found that there were men who were better suited as a friend than a lover. And some who weren't even capable of leaving their mother's overprotective embrace.

One person in particular was named Ruslan. He loved Shahlo sincerely only to be given the title of best man friend. He was of mixed origin. Father being Russian and his mother being from Azerbaijan, she thought he was a good listener. Comforting Shahlo whenever, and he was always there if she needed him. One day she was upset at an incident that happened at work where her manager was insinuating that she was doing something wrong, and he was there in minutes. Making sure she had a shoulder to cry on should she need it. Ruslan never made any sexual advances so Shahlo felt safe when she was with him. During lunch one day she even joked, "Hey Ruslan, who knows? If I don't find what I'm looking for by the time I turn twenty eight, then you and I could get married." He was amused to an extent but I can imagine that he felt like I did when those girls would tell me, "You're the brother I never had." A kiss of death of sorts, but he was happy just being her friend. He wished ultimately though that maybe one day it would happen as the joke implied. But for now he'd be there for her in any capacity she saw fit.

I know exactly how he felt. I'd been the wisher at the well throwing all the quarters I had only to realize that love the way that God intended didn't have to be forced. That was the thing about Ruslan and Shahlo. She never felt rushed into a relationship with him. Basically trusting him with every innate detail she shared. Never once did he betray her. And as life would have it, they just continued on as friends. I'll have you know that they remain close to this day.

Then there was Otabek. A stumpy Uzbek man who felt he was King and any woman he dated would be his Lady. Shahlo learned that being with him really did require her to make constant adjustments. Not only that but she wasn't allowed to say anything or even be herself when she was around him. Somehow she was just going through the motions, and then acted as if she was happy. When in reality she was the poster child for a perpetual state of misery. Ruslan's friendship never had trust issues. However, with Otabek, she knew that she'd rather keep things to herself than share anything with him and face certain scorn.

Its not that she was afraid of him, in fact, she felt comfortable on the pedestal that Otabek placed her. Remember now that Shahlo was looking for love and love like this she wanted nothing of. Passionately imprisoned by her own desire, she just wanted to be loved as she could love someone else. And while she was in a relationship, it wasn't where she wanted to be. Otabek did nothing for her. He never even told her that he loved her. Sometimes even being compared to Ruslan, there was no way he could measure up to how she was treated by her friend. There was numerous times when you could almost hear her scream all the way over here in the United States, "What if I meet someone nice? And I'm stuck here with this guy." It wasn't that he made her feel mistreated, he was just scared. Fearful of any negative reaction that Shahlo would give, he played it safe by not being available except when it was convenient for him. And you remember what happens when someone isn't present and accounted for, right?

Knowing that he wouldn't end it, Shahlo chose to call a relational truce. Neither one of them wanted to be blamed for an unsuccessful endeavor. Therefore, through Shahlo's initiation, the relationship found a mutual end allowing both to pursue other people.

It seemed like the best thing in the world to happen to her. She dated more and more. In fact, Shahlo counted eighty different dates with eighty different people in a little over a year. Her motive was that there must be someone out there and through it all, she'd find him. After college Shahlo was at home and she received a call from her mother who was at work, "Shahlo, can you bring the umbrella up here to the office? It's starting to rain and I do not want to get wet tonight when I walk home." She wasn't expecting to meet anyone there at the office building. She was only going to see her mother.

A thirty four year old Turkish Uzbek man name Mahmud stared at Shahlo from the third floor window. Her mother was on the second floor and that is where she was headed. But Mahmud flew out of his own office and met Shahlo at the stairwell. He kept staring at her as if he liked what he saw. It was two thousand three and Shahlo was happily single. Back in the back part of her mind she was interested. But being the classy woman she was, she'd never say anything that made her seem so desperate. Noticing that he was going out of his way to speak to her, she ran into her mother's office. That day she'd only exchange, "Hello's!"

Around the same time the following week Shahlo was beckoned once more to her mother's work. It's not important why. But what is important is that Mahmud seemed to be waiting patiently for Shahlo's return. Knowing full well that she'd visit someone on the second floor, he positioned himself in a way where a collision was imminent. Just like he planned, Shahlo ran right into him. Having his head down he knew he wanted to say something but the only thing he could render was, "Hello!" The next thing you know they were sitting there for close to an hour talking about the idiosyncrasies of life.

From October two thousand three to December the same year, they were taking their relationship to new levels. Muhmud was Muslim as was Shahlo still and I can't say for certain but it was his custom for her to walk behind him. Shahlo was totally stressed out because her mother wanted for her daughter to stay with this guy no matter how bad she was treated. Why would she want something like that? Mahmud made a lot of money at least by Uzbek standards. And by driving a brand new Hyundai, he presented an image that Shahlo's mother wanted for her daughter. Not so much from Shahlo's desire because she wanted so much more. Fed up with the way it seemed that he didn't want to be with her. Or show her off as his girlfriend. She felt as if she were a third class passenger sitting in the back seat of a first class car. Dating began to wear upon her like a dilapidated soccer jersey. In other words, it just wasn't looking that good to Shahlo anymore.

She wanted love so she concentrated on finding someone nice. Men were asking her out to dinner almost every week. Still after taking them up on their invitation she'd be disappointed at how it all turned out. Never really getting serious with anyone after Mahmud she suddenly found herself in a place where he was actually looking like the best option. Everyone else seemed to be either too young or just incredibly immature. So in two thousand four, she and Mahmud started dating again. For the first couple of weeks, it was great. She was even reserved to the fact that she may even marry him. But he never changed. It actually got worse. Remember that he didn't want her to be with him unless he wanted to be with her. And only then, and that she felt was pathetic. "I'm not his love slave!" she'd tell her mother.

Oh and then the mother would tell her, "What do you want? This man makes money." Frustrated by what her mother was saying Shahlo responded, "I want love! I want someone to love me! Not feel like I am supposed to please him without ever being pleased myself. I mean, Mom, you found Dad." Shahlo's mother was a widow at the tender age of thirty. So she knew exactly what it meant to struggle financially. She wanted what Mahmud had to offer, which was freedom from the endless worries of having nothing at all. Her mother wanted more than bread and water three or four days a week.

Muhmud was the way out and her mother knew it. But that didn't make Shahlo feel any better because she was getting fed up with the entire dating process. This guy was getting so complacent that he wouldn't even drop Shahlo off at her house. He would drive up to the nearest Subway station so that she could get home. By herself mind you. It didn't matter if it was raining or not. That is who Muhmud was, an Ook Shawnee, which in Cherokee translates to, "Donkey whole in the ground." It got to the point where Shahlo asked herself every day, "What I am doing here? There is got to be something better."

Even though she felt trapped she knew that the end was near. The self-worth that she had was just a little more than non-existent. He was all about himself and for the most part it was her mother that pushed her to continue. One night after Shahlo came home from work, she and her mother had a fight. Thoroughly exhausted because she'd been there all day covering two shifts, and the only thing she wanted to do was sleep. Now she had to stay up and fight with her mom. "What a day?" she whispered to herself.

Her mom said, "You say you want love but love like that doesn't exist. You're not going to find it. You need money, and this man's got it." Rubbing her index finger and thumb together symbolizing what she felt was more important than love, she kept insisting, "Let's imagine that you find a man who doesn't have money but gives you all the love in the world. He loves you so much but he can't support you in any way. And one day you'll leave him because you're are tired of being naked. Not having any clothes, and starving to death. Daughter, you need money first!"

Immediately following this tirade, "Then I will work and I will take care of him. It doesn't matter if he is not working, as long as he loves me and treats me right." The mother retorted, "Who needs a man who doesn't take care of his woman?" Knowing that this had no end Shahlo ended it with, "Mom, you know what. I will find a man, who loves me and works to take care of me, and I will work and we will help each other."

Shahlo started walking away and then her mother fired one last shot, "Forget about that, love like that doesn't exist. Only money exists. And if you knew what was best you'd find that first." Somehow she got a full night's sleep because her mother wore her out even more than she already was.

The next day was a brand new day for Shahlo. Being the first week of January two thousand five she was going to break it off with Mahmud for good. No more testing to see if she'd get a cell phone from him. Never again would she feel that she had to do things to satisfy him before he'd even think about doing things to please her. As she left the house that day, she told her mother, "Today is a new day, and I'm going to find the perfect man."

In amazement her mother asked, "How you going to do that? Why don't you go to the agency Nigora went to?" Shahlo never thought about doing something like this so she said, "It's not dangerous?" Her mother sensed that Shahlo was headed out for the day so she told her about a friend's daughter. Nigora was feeling the same cultural pressure that Shahlo was feeling. And she went to a Russian dating agency. Her purpose was revenue driven. She didn't want a man for love, Nigora wanted to have a man for money. And guess what? She met a man from England that fit the bill. He was a diamond broker that traveled many times to Africa so she knew that he must make loads of cash. The agency helped Nigora sink her teeth so far into this man he must have had puncture wounds in his back. Nonetheless, they got married. And she had her cash. I mean she had her man. From there Shahlo knew she'd at least give it a try.

Interested beyond measure she asked her mother, "Can you call Nigora's mother and ask her what agency she went to? I have to go get my salary at Dedeman and when I get back and maybe we can go together."

So there you have it, an Uzbek woman successfully navigating through controlling and manipulative men to discover there may be better options outside her own country. She was primed and ready. Knowing conclusively that she'd been looking for love in all the wrong places, she'd allow herself now to delve into a new and intuitive means of relational development. And finally gaining confidence in the direction in which she was headed. Don't get me wrong, she had no idea that she'd even find someone to love her. Shahlo didn't feel all that beautiful but she knew this just might be the last chance to find love the way that God intended. And that she felt was worth any risk she might face.

14.

A Cup Of Instant Instanbul, Please

TASHKENT IS A BIG METROPOLITAN CITY THAT IS SPREAD OUT SO getting places without a car can be quite painful. She'd have to start off by subway and travel for about twenty minutes. Stopping eight times before she'd actually get to a bus station where she'd have to ride a boiling hot bus for another ten minutes. Upon reaching her destination, Shahlo pushed through an overcrowded bus to walk across several busy streets just to get to the agency's apartment building. It must've been miserable because she was covered in sweat and she still had to walk up three flights of stairs. Finally, she felt relieved as she knocked on a metallic iron door geared up to meet a woman named Alla who ran the Julienna Russian agency.

When the door opened Alla said, "Hello, how are you, I've been waiting for you." Perturbed by the time it took to get there Shahlo replies, "I'm sorry, I was lost." Closing the door behind her she was asked if she wanted to sit down. As she moved through the apartment she sat down at a table to go over what this particular agency actually does for her. Alla was kind enough to ask, "Would you like something to drink?" As much as Shahlo wanted something she answered, "No, no thank you. I'm sorry I kept you waiting." There were two women sitting at the table where Shahlo was sitting. And as soon as Alla walked over to join them, these two girls were introduced as her daughter Julienna and a friend named Tursunoy.

They placed an application on the table for Shahlo to fill out. It had spaces for everything that was needed to create a valid and desirable profile. Getting right down to what religion she was, this application defined every trait she had, and even spaces for what she wanted from her prospective man. Alla was surprised by Shahlo's desire to have a Christian man. She knew she was Muslim and she couldn't figure out why this girl would want a Christian. She did the only thing that made sense to her as she asked Shahlo, "Why would you do something like that?" This was the first time she even contemplated dating someone outside the Islamic faith so she really didn't know how to answer but she tried anyway, "I want to be heard. With a Muslim man, if I'd ask him something, he'd tell me to shut up because I'm a woman. I want a fifty-fifty relationship where my opinion can actually be heard and I don't want to share my man. And I heard that Christian men are more faithful to their women." Alla said sarcastically, "Are you sure about that? What about a Catholic?" Shahlo immediately followed with, "It doesn't matter, just as long as he isn't Muslim. I don't care, but I'd like more a Christian than I would Catholic."

Agreeing with the direction in which Shahlo wanted to go, Alla said, "Okay, we'll put that in your profile and see what happens." A feeling of exciting anticipation was seething from Shahlo's skin because she knew that this was the beginning of something spectacularly wonderful. But wait, there was more. Alla continued by asking, "There are two kinds of men, men with money and men without. So, what kind of man do you want?" Without even taking a breath Shahlo replied, "My mother and I just had this same conversation this week and I told her I wanted a man who would love me and it wasn't important for him to have any money." Alla seemed confused because she didn't understand why because most of the women in her agency were looking for a man who had substantial means. In fact, it was then that she told Shahlo, "Listen, I don't have any ugly women here. One of the requirements you must have in your profile is that you must be beautiful . . . which you are. And being that, you really need to find a man with money." Listening to Julienna and Alla transform what she wanted into what they actually wanted for her she reminded them, "I need a man who is going to love me. If he's poor it doesn't matter. However, I think he has to at least afford the necessities."

The profile complete so she thought. And now Shahlo was ready to receive letters from men all over the world. That's when Alla requested more than just a simple application. Every profile wouldn't be adequate without pictures. Therefore, Alla proceeded to tell her client she had to bring some from a local Photographer. Shahlo brought them just as prescribed but wasn't prepared for what followed, "I've been flipping through these and you need something more if you want to meet a man through this agency. I don't know how much Nigora told you but you need to show more." Not following where Alla was trying to take her, Shahlo asked, "Show more what? I didn't even talk to Nigora. I asked her mother and she told me this was a good place to come."

Walking over to her desk and pulling a photo album out of a drawer Alla said, "Let me show you something. You see how these girls are bending down in a fishnet shirt? It's much more revealing than the pictures you brought in? You've got to show more of your stomach." Shahlo wasn't going to go this route because she was a classy woman and being provocative was something she didn't think she was even capable of. So she retorted, "These girls are wearing underwear with a see through shirt wrapped around them, and you can almost see up their uh huh's. I'm not going to do that. I'll take my chances with just being me." Alla knew what it took to get men to look at her women so she tries to persuade Shahlo, "If you come here looking for a man, you're not going to if you don't show your body. Most girls show their bodies because men want to see it to make sure they aren't going to date someone who looks nothing like the picture in their profile." Still Shahlo wasn't happy about having to take more pictures that would reveal so much of her body so she tells Alla, "I'll go but just use these for right now. I just think these girls are too open." Both Alla and Shahlo agreed that it'd work for them. Now it was time to discuss prices.

Julienna brings a sheet over to the table only to lay it down in front of Alla and Shahlo. Seeing what it is, she asks, "So this is it, this is what I'm going to pay for each letter." Julienna points to a column and says, "When you receive a letter you have to pay ten cents for us to print it off. And then over in this column is what you'd pay when you send a letter.

Still pretty excited, so it didn't matter what it was, she just wanted to get started. The very next day she got fifty letters from men all over the world just like she wanted. Remember now, she had to pay ten cents for each one so she shelled out five dollars. In Tashkent, that was a fortune for one day. She saw it as an investment in her future. What she found out was that she'd pay right at a dollar and fifty cents for those letters she chose to send.

When I say a fortune, Shahlo worked as a health club administrator at Dedeman Resort Hotels, and her earnings was nowhere close to a fortune. Most salaries in Uzbekistan averaged around sixty dollars a month. But because she was an administrator, she was clearing eighty. The only conciliation was that she had tips which could be used for these letters. She felt her salary had to be used to help her mother support the family. What a woman, using her hard earned money to take care of her mother, brother, and sister. She'd work sometimes seventy hours a week and her salary wouldn't be used for anything she wanted. As soon as she got home it would be given to her mom. The kids had to eat you know. When you sit around and calculate what it'd take to effectively communicate with someone from another country, it does let you know how much this woman wanted to find a man that would love her as much as she'd love him.

She went through the same process the next day, train, bus, and all, and found out that she was quite popular. Shahlo could've had her pick from all these men who were writing her. But she chose to correspond with a man named Riley from Vancouver, British Columbia. This was the fifth of May in two thousand five and she was about as excited as she'd ever been. Finally after all she'd been through, there was a man with whom she could frequently communicate and develop a relationship that would possibly lead to marriage. Remember now, that this was only one out of fifty, so she'd still have to thumb through the others and find the ones that moved her romantically. Alla would make Shahlo pay for all letters, and it didn't matter if she just wanted to limit it to a few. She'd have to pay for those letters too. She considered it a small price to pay for the idealistic outcome she desired.

So here was Riley. His first letter to Shahlo was simply amazing. So much so that it altered her perception of this Agency dating thing. They began a day by day conversation where they would talk about everything from the climate in Uzbekistan to what it would be like if she'd be able to meet his nephews and nieces. Shahlo would rush home from Dedeman, change her clothes and hop the Subway to Alla's house. You know something? This Alla must've loved Shahlo. Because to me, it looks as though Shahlo was the cash cow for her agency. Yes, there were other girls but none were getting the responses that she was getting. Maybe some were getting twenty or so letters, and unfortunately some were lucky to get five. Nonetheless, Shahlo was happy to be able to correspond with Riley.

One day she got a letter from Riley and he was asking her about the visa process for travel to Uzbekistan. After researching what it'd take, Shahlo informed him that it was easier if there was an invitation letter. She'd be more than happy to oblige so that he could see her beautiful country. That was the plan and then something happened. She didn't know how but suddenly Riley stopped writing or even calling after about a month. There were all sorts of questions running through her mind. Like where did he go? Or why would he write me, getting my hopes up and then leave me hanging without as much as a goodbye Thank you very much? When she got to the agency one day she asked Alla, "What do you think is wrong with Riley? He hasn't called or written me in a week or so." Shahlo was puzzled by Alla's reaction. She was shrugging her shoulders and not looking her in the eyes when she answered, "Well, I don't know. He must have found a Ukrainian girl."

From that moment on, Shahlo didn't trust Alla. Knowing that she was paying a lot of money to find a man and it seemed that every time she'd get close, somehow the man would stop writing. "What is this woman doing? Did she say something to Riley where he wouldn't write me?" she whispered to herself. Wondering that maybe she said something that would make him look elsewhere for an International woman. Riley was the same man who talked of really starting to like her so why would he just take off? It was killing her but she just took it as experience and started writing other men. She knew that she couldn't beat herself up and let this one man ruin her pursuit of the perfect man. So she headed back to the agency and said, "Hey, this is Riley's loss, not mine!"

Then there was Matthew from Australia. She was writing him to find out his interest and he was a rugged man who loved being in the woods. Shahlo was a clean woman who couldn't picture herself skinning a deer in the middle of the forest while her man was picking grit out of his teeth with a piece of bark. Somehow she also envisioned her life with this man and it didn't look pretty. Don't get her wrong she was going to be happy either way. But she'd rather find a man who appreciated her as a classy sophisticated woman. Matthew's time was short and he knew it. So after two weeks Shahlo let him down easy, "You're a nice man, but you're not my type. I think you would be suited better with a woman who loves to hunt and fish rather than someone like me who likes to be in the home." Matthew being the burly man from down under locked it up inside and actually took her advice. I'll have you know that he eventually found love with a woman from Uzbekistan. He even thanked Shahlo later because this particular woman was a hunter just like himself and he felt it was a perfect match. When Shahlo discovered Matthew was happy, she was relieved because she thought she had actually hurt his feelings. But now, she knew that he was indeed, thankfully happy.

Letters were coming in everyday and Shahlo couldn't find adequate time to read them all so she had them screened for the qualities she desired most in a man. Alla selected a letter from a guy named Phillip. He was from London and seemed to be interested in the possibility of coming to Uzbekistan because he wanted to meet Shahlo. In his first letter he told her, "You're the most attractive person I have ever corresponded with." Thinking this was going to be a good one, she stopped writing so much to the other guys. There were two more but after a while they stopped writing as well. All she had to do now was concentrate on Phillip. She was comfortable with the direction that they seemed to be going. He was asking, "I'm not writing anyone else, so are you?" Knowing that whatever she said she might be held responsible she replied, "No, I'm happy with where we seem to be headed, so no I'm not writing anyone else."

She expected Phillip to jump into a more progressive relationship but he didn't. He was content with just sending and receiving letters. So she made the first step, "Hey, are we going to write forever?" Phillip knew where she was going with this question so he felt free enough to ask, "No we aren't. Actually I was going to see if you wanted to meet. But I have to go on a business meeting first." Shahlo wanted to know where the man who she'd been writing for two months was going so she asked, "Where do you need to go?" Phillip was hesitant on giving her a truthful answer and she could tell by his response, "Our Company does business in the Ukraine, and I'll be there three weeks, so I'll write you when I get back." Timid by nature Shahlo just wished him the best and then patiently waited for his return. Although, she'd still go to the agency to see who was writing. Her purpose was still to find someone with whom she could love. And just because Phillip had left didn't mean she had to stop looking. Shahlo goes to the agency and the first thing she does is tell Alla, "Phillip has left for the Ukraine, so I need to find other men." It was something that all along Alla had been trying to get Shahlo to do. "Check out more options, you don't need to settle with just one. You have more letters than anyone here so write more to them."

Knowing that Alla had ulterior motives by suggesting this, Shahlo replied, "Okay, just pick a few out you think I'll like and I'll try." But you know something? The letters came in multitudes and she knew that she still had to pay for them no matter how many of them she read. The tips were huge at this time in her life. She felt that she wouldn't be able to communicate with the men that Alla picked. Somehow though, God allowed people to see how kind and genuine this woman was, and led them to tip more than normal. Needless to say they were impressed with the health club administrator at the Dedeman Resort Hotel. To this day Shahlo says that she would've never been able to communicate as much as she did without those tips. Calling it her, "Lifeblood for love" because she knew without it she would've never been able to find anything resembling love much less love itself.

She didn't hear from Phillip for three weeks so she'd correspond with others from various parts of the world. This time though she had more interest from men here in the United States. Flipping through a thousand letters, Shahlo picked five that tickled her fancy. One of those five was a thirty something year old man who was fed up with woman in his own country. No, he didn't judge all women based upon his bad experiences. But yes, he did make decisions that would lead him to a relationship outside his own comfortable surroundings. But something stopped Shahlo from writing first. I guess she was unsure that this man who was dressed in a tuxedo would even respond. Alla was looking over her shoulder and said, "Listen! Why wouldn't he? You are beautiful woman! I tell you this. We'll write him and see what happens." Shahlo wasn't convinced that this man would write because she didn't think that she was pretty enough. Even after Alla told her she should drop her fear at the door and write this man, Shahlo responded, "He looks too good. He will never write. His profile is too handsome."

Needless to say she took Alla's advice and let her write this man. And not even two days later Shahlo was pleasantly surprised to receive a letter from a man in yes, this little ole town of North Augusta, South Carolina. She was asking herself while basking in her excitement, "How amazing is it that I could correspond with someone in Atlanta, home of Coca Cola?" I introduced myself using my informal name so she would feel comfortable. "My name is Chuck Mercier and I will be thirty six years old in a little more than twenty days. I am a Christian man with lots of hobbies but I will hold off from letting you know any of them until I know you want to hear them."

So there I went, I'd just received and responded to a woman that I thought was a fat little Russian Mafia dude. To be honest with you, you have to remember. When I got back from the Ukraine I pulled my profiles off all international sites. At least that is what I thought anyway. Because somehow Shahlo sent a letter to my personal email account with the Microsoft Network, and I didn't understand how. But nonetheless, I got it and was entirely skeptical. What did I do? Well, for the first couple of letters I pictured this bottle of Russian Vodka sitting on the corner of a desk in a smoke filled room while a little unshaven mujchina with pudgy fingers was typing away on an outdated computer. With an image like that running through my mind how was I going to be seriously talking to her if indeed, she was real. Don't get me wrong. The picture I received from this girl was astonishingly beautiful. Breathtaking in fact, I couldn't believe that a woman like this needed to find a man in her own country, much less through a place like the World Wide Web.

I did something I thought was rather unorthodox. If this was the Russian Mafia trying to bleed out six dollars a letter like those dudes in the Ukraine, well then I'd try to craft my letters in a way that I'd talk to both this beautiful woman and that fat little Russian dude. I feel that the name of Jesus is the most powerful name in the entire world so I'd ask Shahlo about what she thought about him. At first, she'd answer that she thought he was the creator but would elaborate more on what her mother thought of him. You see, Muslims believe that Jesus is a prophet. But stop short of declaring him the Son of God. When I started my correspondence with this woman from Uzbekistan I had no idea where this place was. So I did what I think anyone would have done, I Google it. Judging from her clothes I could tell that she may have been Muslim by religion but she didn't follow the custom of covering her hair. So I continued on with wanting to know what she felt about Jesus.

This was the first time in all my writing to women in foreign countries that the questions I asked would be answered directly. My problem with the women I had corresponded with in the Ukraine or in Russia would be that if I asked a question. Only generalizations would be given. To me, it was frustrating because I wanted to know more about the woman just in case I felt I wanted to carry my relationship further.

There was one woman I was writing in Lutsk, Ukraine where I wanted to test her knowledge of her own town. Just to see if she was really from where she said she was from, I asked her if she'd ever been to the Orphanage there in Lutsk. She responded by telling me that this was a sad place to visit so even though she'd been there, she didn't want to go back. Even going so far as telling me it was a place that was so close to her apartment that she could walk to it. When I told her that there were no Orphanages in Lutsk, and actually it was about hundred miles away in Lviv she never even acknowledged that I was calling her bluff. I knew that it'd be last time I'd be writing her. "Just answer the flipping question woman!" I remembered saying to myself.

That is why my skepticism was so well preserved because I was just asking questions to communicate truthfully with a woman who had mailed me a letter first. I didn't take it out on Shahlo when she wrote. Because to my surprise, she was answering questions with absolutes, and I could tell that she was ready for a relationship with a man who was just as honest as she was. Therefore, when she received my letters, she began more and more letting her attention go to answering mine only. The others letters were only paid for because that was the fulfillment of her pledge to the Agency. Alla worried that Shahlo was investing so much time into one man that it'd ultimately kill her Agency. Some even said she was the cow that Alla had always dreamed of. I have to say I didn't mind, because that one man was me.

After about three weeks of writing, Shahlo and I decided to try communicating outside the Agency. She'd go to the internet café and write me with her personal Yahoo account. I would then correspond with her via Microsoft Network. That was the plan and I have to say that it worked to perfection. We started writing at the Agency on June twenty ninth two thousand five and here it was almost the middle of July. We were headed to the place where we'd always dreamed of, except that neither of us had physically met. We'd only talked on the internet.

So one day in the last week of July I made a suggestion that we should meet in Athens, Greece. From the progression of our correspondence I was sure Shahlo would say, "Yes!" But when I suggested that we meet there, she told me, "We do not have Greece Embassy." Immediately I started thinking about what she did have. I asked her, "So what embassy do you guys have?" When she said Turkey I was torn because I'd heard things about

Istanbul that were good and bad from the flight attendant friends I had at Delta. Yet, I told her, "Okay, you go and see where the embassy is tomorrow. And what I'll do is see what I'll have to do to get there." The next day I received all the information about the embassy. She was afraid that I wouldn't write her anymore when she told me that she couldn't afford the plane ticket so she was quite hesitant on telling me. But I pulled it out of her by telling her that I realized with their economy the way it was, I would go and send her money for the airline ticket. She was ecstatic. I couldn't see her but I could almost tell that she was going absolutely crazy.

Seven hundred dollars and seven days later we were ready for our rendezvous with destiny. The only thing stopping us was my sister Beth's wedding. She was getting married on September seventeenth. And as soon as I found out that Shahlo received her ticket from Turkish Airlines, I wanted to leave then. But I gave my word to my sister that I'd play for her wedding. So that's what I did. Immediately following the reception, I drove to Atlanta and spent the night at the Westin at the airport. Knowing that my flight was leaving New York at five the next day I'd do all I could to not miss it. The way I looked at it. This would be the beginning of something revolutionary. I was going to meet what I thought to be the woman of my dreams. And there wasn't anything that would keep me from making that flight. As much as I had flown this was actually the first time I had flown into John F. Kennedy. So I wasn't sure where I'd have to go to catch an international flight. I would just have to ask where to go, when I got there. The only problem was that I only had forty two minutes before the flight to Istanbul was scheduled to depart. Knowing that, I would have to do things quickly.

Running out the boarding gate I realized that I was ten minutes early. Equipped with that blessing I chose to search out the gate myself. You know men, if they don't have to ask, they won't. And it just so happened I ended up in the International terminal with my plane scheduled to depart out of the domestic side. You want talk about frustration, I'd just come from that side and now, time was getting short. Remember I had fifty two minutes and now I was down to twenty five. Which means Delta would've already started to board, and possibly even clearing all the stand bys. Here I was covered in sweat because I was running to and fro many times over. Then I saw the gate agent lift the microphone up to announce final call, I handed her my seat request with relief that I was now finally aboard the Dreamland Express.

I arrived in Turkey a day before Shahlo was scheduled to arrive. So I went and slept most of the day at the Hilton and then had a wonderful Turkish dinner at the hotel restaurant. I don't know if you have ever been to Turkey but if you like olives, you'll like Turkey. It seemed like they used olives for everything. The buffet was a little pricey but once I started eating I knew why. It was absolutely heavenly. There were sandwich meats that reminded me a lot of Germany. When you hadn't eaten all day, it was a perfect way to send you off into a most satisfying slumber.

I was about as excited as I'd ever been because somehow I knew this woman would show up. I didn't believe that I'd be left at the fountain in the middle of town with nothing but an ounce of pride left. This was it. All I had to do was go to sleep and she'd be there at nine o'clock the next day. It was hard to get to sleep that night because I knew the next day could absolutely change my life.

Morning came not soon enough as the sun broke through the curtains in my room, and I ran around my room getting things just right for the flight to Izmir today. Shower, shave, and smell good stuff was all I needed. Running down the hall to the elevator I couldn't wait to get to the airport. The taxi had already been summoned by the front desk so that was one thing I didn't have to prepare for.

Just in case you haven't taken a taxi in Istanbul, my driver thought he was Mario Andretti. He was driving in heavy traffic at dangerously high speeds. I prayed up just in case his brakes weren't as good as he seemed to think they were. I believe it was his sole purpose to drive as fast as he could and then see how close he could get to the car in front of him without crashing. If I hadn't prayed up I think I would've had to change my drawers. Arriving safely even after his frantic driving, He dropped me off at the domestic side of the airport and this is where I was supposed to meet Shahlo. I handed him the fare plus a tip with a comment, "You shouldn't be driving here in Turkey. You should be a race car driver in the United States. They get paid a lot more than this." He just smiled and responded politely, "Shank you! I do eet!" Waving to him, I just about tripped over the curb to walk into the terminal. Soldiers with machine guns were standing there in full military gear chuckling a bit. But I didn't mind, I just wanted to go and wait for her to show up. Part of me expected her not to show but I proceeded as if she would. Even at one point getting up to check the flight from Tashkent to Istanbul to see if she had boarded, and guess what? She did. How did I know because in the states Federal law dictates that no names shall be given out for any purpose? This was Turkey, and not the United States. Remember?

It's hard to explain the emotions I had going through my mind at that moment when I heard she was on the plane and she'd be arriving any second. Like a kid in a candy store with a handful of money. I was happy beyond happy; and scared a little bit too. We had only written each other so what was communication going to be like when we were face to face? I change seats numerous times trying to find the best viewpoint for those entering from the International terminal. Even walking down the long hallway just to see if I could meet her closer to her gate, but she wasn't there.

I then found a comfortable place to wait. "Please hurry!" I was asking myself. Then as if the clouds disappeared and gave rhyme to every reason I ever had, Shahlo came around the corner looking like a Princess who had left her castle to find her Prince. And not to say that I was the Prince, I was just a man who was sitting in the back part of the room waiting for his, "Juliet." My index finger was placed on my cheek while my thumb held my head up securing it under my chin.

Then she spoke in a way that it seemed to me I was hearing all the angels in Heaven singing. In Shahlo's pictures she was beautiful. But when you're looking at her face to face, it was even harder to catch your breath. Standing up, I proceeded over to her and started smiling. And immediately she recognized that I was the same person she'd been writing to for the past two and half months. This was it. The woman I'd been searching for, but wait a minute. Could she speak English like she said she could or was that something we'd have to work around? Then she spoke, "I can . . . not . . . b lieve you are here. I can . . . not . . . b lieve I am here. This is good!"

I grabbed her by the hands and embraced her to place a kiss gently on her forehead. Telling her, "I am so happy to be here, and I wish you knew how long it took me to get here." Both of us knew each other intimately by our correspondence but we would have to learn each other's idiosyncrasies. Which to me would be a pleasure, and I knew she felt the same way. This trip wasn't finished. She just arrived, and we still had to fly down to Izmir. So I grabbed our bags and we left for the gate. I could sit here and tell you that this woman was the woman of my dreams, and we lived happily ever after. But I'd be stopping way short of where I wanted to take you guys.

There was much more. In an instant, my cup of Istanbul coffee would then be served not for one, but happily for two. What could possibly make this trip to Izmir any better than my adventure to the European capital of Turkey? At the time I didn't know but ready for anything. From there, Shahlo and I flew Turkish Air down to Izmir and my purpose would be to change the interpersonal definitions that she and I had previously defined in our letters. Think of it as the first tablespoon of a loving relationship within our collective cups of instant Istanbul.

15.

The Emphasis On Ephesus

IZMIR IS A TOWN SOUTH TO SOUTHWEST OF ISTANBUL, TURKEY. When we were flying in, it looked a lot like you were flying into Los Angeles, vectoring in from the Palm Springs side of LA. There were barren mountainsides covered in a dry desert brush. You could see sand being blown across major roadways. I even wondered sitting there in my own little comfort zone whether it'd be a good idea to be driving through these little baby tornados. I knew that Çeşme, the town we were going to was located along the Aegean Sea. But the thing I didn't know was how long and how easy it'd be to get there.

I just wanted to land and land quickly. Perpetually looking at Shahlo and she didn't even turn around. So I was left to wonder if she was even thinking about our trip, "I should've asked if I could sit beside her." I kept saying to myself. Then it was as if I could hear those same words dancing off the follicles of her hair, "Why didn't he sit next to me? He brings me all the way here and sits two rows back. Why isn't he going to talk to me?"

Have you ever been in a situation where you didn't know what to do? You just go with the flow. Sitting where you're told to sit, and do what you're directed to do. I did just that. Without much thought I just found my seat and sat down. I mean this was a Turkish airline, and I was flying in a discounted seat. So I didn't want to cause any trouble. Even though I should've paid more attention to Shahlo because if I had, I would've sat next to her and been what she expected of me in the first place. But

I was then as I was before, totally oblivious to everything and everyone around me.

Deplaning was an adventure in itself. Shahlo was given a seat in front of me and I had all the bags with me. The challenge was going to be how I'd carry all these bags off the plane. I lifted my hand toward her and pointed towards the front of the plane. Speaking softly I said, "Meet me out at the gate, I'll get the bags." Remember that Shahlo knew English but the things we say in slang may or may not be understood by someone from another country. She stared at me and started shaking her head in agreement and then responded, "I will."

You know how it is when you're deplaning? There are those people who have no sense of urgency. And the only thing you want to do is get off the freaking plane. Then there was the older passenger who has been told to wait for wheelchair assistance. I was behind the woman who didn't think it was pertinent to move in a progressive manner. I didn't speak Turkish so I just told her, "Did you know there isn't anyone in front of you? You can actually go now." I was intensely frustrated by her absence of awareness that there were other people besides her on the plane. Taking my hand and if to shoo her to move, I imagined she felt as if I actually pushed her physically.

Finally she started moving. All I wanted was to see Shahlo again and talk, because I'd been waiting for these moments for the better half of my adult life. The woman who refused to move creamed the old woman waiting for the wheelchair square on the top of the head. For those of you that have been to Europe, you know those Saran covered suitcases that everyone carries. Well, one of the big ones hit her. And my smile was not that I was laughing at an older woman getting hit; it was that this crazy woman had taken a bag that would've been checked in the United States on the plane. Her disregard for anyone sitting in an aisle seat was repulsive. She didn't even turn around to say she was sorry. "Please just let me off this plane!" I prayed.

When I walked through the door of the jet way, Shahlo was standing there waiting for me. Wondering what happen she asked, "What took you so long?" I didn't know if I should tell her because I didn't want to portray my impatience so close to the beginning of our relationship. So I just nodded and responded, "An older woman was hit in the head by a falling bag, and I wanted to make sure she was okay." How's that for taking a bad incident on the plane and turning it into a transformational situation in the gatehouse? She thought this man she met was the man she had searched for. Saying to herself, "Wow, he even helps the elderly." The reality was that I did ask her if she was okay but that isn't what kept me. It was the crazy woman with a bag that was big enough to carry her smallest child.

I then held Shahlo's hand and walked proudly through the Izmir airport. I couldn't wait to get to the Taxi. I stood there wondering how far we were from the Sheraton in Çeşme, just knowing the driver would know. After claiming our other bags, we were greeted by multiple drivers that were trying to entice us to choose them for our transportation needs. They were lined up outside the Terminal and I tried to find a Mercedes, so when the driver asked, I'd shake my head, "Yes!"

This was a van so there was plenty of room. When our driver loaded the bags in the back I asked him, "How much to get me to the Sheraton in Çeşme?" He didn't seem to understand me so I asked again, "Sheraton, Çeşme, how much is it?" Then the light went off in his head as if what I was asking finally made sense, "Ahh . . . One humdred doll hairs . . . Five tee minutes."

I looked at Shahlo and said to her, "Good enough, if you're ready, we'll go." Holding her hand for about forty nine of those fifty minutes, I kept glancing over to smile. She was more beautiful than any picture she'd ever sent me. And now I'd be there with her for another eight days. As if I didn't have something to look forward to, I was continuously happy.

As we drove up to our hotel it looked like a castle placed conveniently on the ocean sands. Driving down the hill, you could obviously tell that this was a Sheraton. There were nice Turkish homes built around it, and the hotel was extremely nice. I had a magnificent surprise planned for Shahlo when she got checked in to her room. So I was ready to get checked in as well.

I can't say that I had every detail planned but most of the places I wanted to visit were pretty much set in stone. It'd be two days before we'd go to Ephesus and that is where I planned the most unforgettable moment thus far in our relationship, probably in my life up to this time. Everything else that happened after that would either define our future together or deny it.

We walked into the hotel lobby after tipping our driver. He didn't say too much except to help us carry our bags. Baggage clerks were conveniently standing with a luggage cart. Therefore, they knew that our cabbie needed help. So, our bags were carried up to our rooms without us having to do anything. Even though Shahlo worked in a resort hotel she seemed amazed by the place where we were going to stay for the next six days. As I was busy checking in, she was moving in circles glancing at the fountain in the middle of the lobby. Maybe Dedeman was a nice hotel, but it seemed this Sheraton was a step above where she worked. From the expression on her face, I was glad I picked this particular hotel. And somehow, I think she was too.

I gave her the key to her room, and I took the key to mine. Timidly, she glided over those marble floors trying to peek outside the windows. She asked me, "Are we on the sea? I've never been to sea. My country has no ocean, and this is beautiful." Placing my hand gently upon her back and massaging the curvature of her spine with my fingernails I responded, "Yes we are, I believe that's the Aegean Sea." It seemed like she absorbed everything. The hotel, the ocean, even the beach, she walked around as if she were a child who discovered these things for the first time. And we hadn't even reached our rooms yet. When I wrote about out trip to Turkey, I sent her a picture of her hotel room. That is the only thing she had to go on. So to actually see it was a captivating treat.

But when the baggage clerk opened her door and she bent down to see where she'd sleep for the next five days, she almost started crying. She smiled then lifted her hands and placed them over her face and then cried out, "I have flat screen television in my room? King size bed, and a couch?" I loved it, I felt like I had done something right. She was completely and unequivocally ecstatic about this new adventure. I knew that she had been on a plane for about six hours so I suggested, "Okay my lady, if you want, you can go use the bath room. And when you're finished, I'll let you sleep for a couple of hours. Then we'll go eat at the restaurant downstairs." The first day she really didn't say too much except for, "Yes, okay, and Ebi." I didn't know what that meant until later, she'd tell me that Ebi means "Wow!" in Uzbek. Needless to say, when she saw the hotel, "Ebi!" Then when she saw her room, "Ebi!" And hey, I was getting used to this word because it provided all the confirmation I needed to let me know that I was doing something good.

I woke Shahlo up around six that evening because truthfully I was starving to death. She looked just as beautiful when she woke up as when she went to sleep. I thought to myself, "This could be good. She wakes up like she goes to bed. Shouldn't take her long to get ready?" Remember I was hungry, but I didn't want her to see the impatient "ready to eat at six o'clock" hungry man that I was trying hard to hold down inside me. The only thing I had to eat that day was the breakfast bar at the Hilton in Istanbul. And that was as at six that morning. A man my size needed to eat and eat soon.

Taking pictures of us going down the hall, even taking some walking into the elevator, and both of us were unbelievably happy. As the door of the elevator flew open, we turned to the right and found the hostess stand at the restaurant. I said, "Hello, that'll be for two please, non-smoking!" My eyebrows drew southward gazing peripherally as I asked Shahlo, "Oh! By the way, you don't need to sit in smoking do you?" She responded, "No, non-smoking is good." Through our correspondence she did tell me that she didn't smoke but I wanted to make sure that she was okay with our sitting in a non-smoking section. We were led to a table close to the window. If you'd look to the right or the left you'd be taking in some of the most beautiful shoreline in the world. Comparing it to a place I'd been before, I'd have to say it's a close resemblance to the Morning Star beach in Saint Thomas, Virgin Islands. Just absolutely stunning, the sand, the ocean, the girl, everything about it, and oh, did I mention that even the buffet was wonderful? Feeling as though I'd been given a reprieve from the Lord himself, I just sat there thanking him for every second. It was exceedingly surreal.

After the meal we returned to Shahlo's room and watched Shrek. She'd never seen it and was asking what her surprise was because I hadn't given it to her when we checked in. I made her think that the movies I brought were her surprise. So as I set up the movie, I turned quickly to kiss her, and then I said, "Oh! This isn't your surprise by the way." She was stunned by the kiss I think, but then she said, "Well, What is it then?"

I had the staff place our luggage that I had in her room on the luggage rack. She started wondering what was in my bag. So putting down the DVD cover on the television I zipped the bag open and told her, "Listen, don't take this personal but I remember you telling me that you didn't have a lot to Bring here, so I wanted to make sure you were taken care of, I got you a couple of things."

First I handed her some pajamas. Then a warm up suit just in case she needed to work out. Then some smell good stuff. And after all that I wanted her to have a Los Angeles Lakers shirt because I had one and hey, we could match. She was pleased beyond measure. Placing her hands over her face seemed to be the thing she did when she felt embarrassed. She then asked me, "Why did you buy me all this? I love it! This is the best day of my life." I wanted you to have everything you needed to have an amazing vacation here in Turkey. I replied softly, "This is just the beginning, you told me in our letters that you didn't have much to Bring. So my sister and I went shopping to make sure that indeed you did have it." Her appreciation was so overwhelming that I even started crying. Seeing those tears roll down her cheeks I felt like I had found the sensitive woman I'd searched for. It was an amazing moment, one that I'll remember for the rest of my life.

The next day we toured the area around the hotel. Downtown Çeşme was set up like a fortress. There were cannons lined up protecting the harbor. Beautiful flowers were draped over castle walls, and there were tiny shops that were filled with everything from Tea pots to key chains. I wanted to make sure she had money to buy her family something, so I tried to find a bank machine. When I did, I had no idea what monetary system there was in Turkey so I just handed her a hundred dollar bill. "You can buy your mother something if you want." I said to her while placing the bill in the palm of her hand. We ended up buying a Tea pot for her, and my mother.

A nice Turkish man was obliged to help us. And when he invited us to buy more, we obliged him. From what I expected of a predominately Muslim country, I really didn't expect people to be so friendly. He wouldn't take "No" for an answer for us joining him for tea. He made both of us sit while he went and made some Apple tea for us. It was pretty neat. I wanted to buy more from him just to show him how much we appreciated the time we spent with him. And you know something? He didn't even charge us for the Tea.

Shahlo and I walked around the bay admiring the sailboats that were tied there. One of them was quite impressive. Almost like a pirate ship it had huge sails hoisted to the heavens. I told Shahlo, "I bet that's an expensive ride, I wish we could take a cruise and have dinner in the middle of the ocean." She looked at me as if she knew exactly what I was talking about and responded accordingly, "I can't swim too well. I think I'd be afraid to leave land." After telling her that I'd be there to save her, the fear seemed to subside substantially. Even so much as to tell me, "I feel safe with you already." But I have to be honest with you. That made me feel as though I were a Knight and I was now strong enough and capable enough to protect my Princess. It was bizarre to me that we were as close to the ocean as we could get and there weren't any shrimp. Shahlo had never eaten seafood and I wanted to see her facial expressions when she ate it for the first time. I guess I'd have to wait for that one though.

For the rest of the afternoon we perused the back end of the city. There were camera shops, an outdoor café, and a plethora of T-shirt gift places. I guess I wore my "American" clothes that day because every time I went by a store with the door open, someone would try and pull me in. They were telling me, "Buy here, discount for American!" For the sake of time, we'd make quick runs through just to satisfy them. We chose a couple magnets from various places, because in a way I almost felt guilty. When I say quick runs, I mean quick, because it doesn't take me long once the sun starts going down to get incredibly hungry. With thirty minutes of daylight left, all I wanted to do was get back to the hotel and eat. For tomorrow was going to be the day of all days. Whereas I'd be putting an extreme emphasis in Ephesus, maybe even portraying that the best of life was yet to come.

For tonight though, it'd be just me and my lady having a nice dinner and a movie. I brought a lot of movies. And I thought that once the movie ended, it'd be a good time for us to discuss our future. When we got back to the hotel, I thought we were going to eat at the hotel restaurant but Shahlo wanted to order room service. I guess she felt exhausted because we hiked around the city for what seemed like a hundred miles, and all she wanted to do was sit down and enjoy our time together. She turned to me in her room and said, "We have busy day tomorrow don't we? Can we just stay in here and order in?" Understanding full well where she was going with her question I responded, "Of course, but I have two questions for you. What movie do you want to watch? And what do you want to order?" We had a wonderful evening watching Ever After with Drew Barrymore and sharing a nice meal together.

Later that night I retreated to my room and as soon as I laid my head on the pillow, I knew for certain I'd be dreaming of that buffet. I couldn't wait to wake up the next morning for two reasons. One, I'd be able to see the woman of my dreams sitting across the table from me, and secondly I'd perch myself as close to the buffet table as I could get.

Upon waking up around seven the next morning, I knocked on Shahlo's door to see if she was ready for breakfast and she told me, "just a couple more minutes." Man I was starving to death, and I knew I had to stockpile because we were headed to Ephesus. I didn't know anything about this place but from what I saw driving in, it didn't look like there would be anywhere to eat. I told her to eat as much as she could because I didn't think there were many options for lunch.

She asked me, "Why are we going to Ephesus?" I knew exactly why but I wanted her to think something totally different so I responded, "Well, you know who Paul is?" She looked at me inquisitively and replied, "No, I do not, who is Paul?" The smile on my face wasn't that I was laughing at her. But rather it was that she was so childlike and really wanted to know. As for me, I really wanted her to know so I answered, "Paul wrote almost half the Bible's New Testament. One of those books is Ephesians. And it's about the people from the same town we're going to today. In fact, lots of history!"

She seemed to get it but I can't say she exuded any excitement. I was about to jump out of my skin trying to get to this place. Think of it this way, I'd been reading the Bible pretty regularly since the eighth grade and now I'd be walking the same ground as did some of the greatest men in faith of all time. Events and places that transpired within those pages would be laid out in vivid lifelike form. She and I would live what I'd read. And throughout different stages of our personal tour I could educate her as to what Paul was trying to tell the Ephesian people.

Our taxi dropped us off at the top of the hill and you could tell that there was somewhat of a valley below. So I took Shahlo's hand and led her through. I observed then that she'd become more immersed into this culture the further along we went. She'd smile as if she wanted to ask a question but was afraid that I'd think she was stupid. Turning around rather abruptly I asked her, "Are you excited?" And just as she was about to answer she stood on a rock that wasn't firmly planted. Blurting out as she started to fall, "Help!" And me, knowing that I wasn't that far in front of her caught her in my protective embrace, "Whoa, there my Lady, are you alright? You can't hurt yourself now . . . we still have six more days on the trip." It was amusing for one reason. No longer had I got those words out of my mouth when I smacked a huge cornerstone with the bottom part of my shin, and then I started falling face first but I did something altogether different to try and recover.

I tripped over one rock then kicked another, and finally came to a secure place while standing there holding on to whatever pride I had left. Shahlo was thinking I was doing it on purpose as she mentioned, "Are you trying to make me laugh? If so, you are doing a good job of it." My grin told her that I was okay with looking like a complete fool while acting out Chevy Chase in one of his movies. Fumbling around just to catch her laughing was worth even if I wasn't really acting. I was jumping up and twisting around to look at her reaching out to help me. I just held on for dear life and didn't let her go, making sure that she and I were extremely careful walking through those rocks.

Before I go any further getting into what actually was the Emphasis on Ephesus. Let me provide some insight as to why I would choose this city over any other to create such a tremendous romantic impact. My whole life I tried to live as a Godly man even though I had fallen many times. So decisions that were made began with me asking myself this question, "Is this something that would please the Lord? "When Shahlo and I were corresponding quite frequently and we started planning a place to meet. I thought about Corinth, Greece and kindly suggested Athens. She seemed thrilled. However, that excitement was short lived because she grew extremely disappointed with having to tell me that Tashkent didn't have a Grecian Embassy. As soon as I read those words, I started thinking about places that Delta flew direct. Either out of Atlanta or New York, I just wanted to meet her, didn't matter where, so I asked about Turkey.

The next day I was pleased to find out from Shahlo that indeed, there was a Turkish Embassy in Uzbekistan. My decision for Turkey was based entirely on a previous Bible study. I didn't tell her at that time my reasons for going there. But I did let her know that my being a Christian, it was a place I felt I'd learn more about my own life. Fortunately, she was game for anything.

The theatre there in Ephesus was symbolic for an event that started out violent then after hours of negotiations turned extremely peaceful. All while the Apostle Paul had found refuge elsewhere. I wanted to see that. I wanted to give her a once in a lifetime experience of an ancient Biblical city.

In chapter five of Ephesians, Paul was explicit in illustrating to us that love today should be as love was then. He said that we should love our wives as Christ loved his bride, that bride being his church. And through these words, he bestowed on us a wonderful gift for those of us trying to discover new meanings of love in our own lives.

So why would I go this far and not tell you what the emphasis was? First of all, I wanted you to understand that I was finally in prime position to be decisive about a relationship for the first time in my life. Only when I began planning my trip to Ephesus did I get the point where what I was looking for in love, finally coincided with what I really wanted in love.

There we were on what I thought to be the most important day of our extended vacation. Day three of an eight day adventure, Shahlo was beginning to doubt my intentions for bringing her to Turkey. It seemed as though I wasn't serious about my relationship with her. But I was and I was careful not to let my biggest surprise out of the bag. As we passed numerous mentions of history I could tell she was enjoying every minute.

There still was some apprehension, maybe even some nervousness as to where we might be headed in our future. I could sense this and I knew that today she'd have the answer she desired most by the end of the day. And no, I couldn't hear her saying, "Why would he bring me to Turkey just for fun?" But I could tell she wanted more than what she was getting. Just about the time we passed the Temple, I turned to my left and found a Pomegranate tree and told Shahlo, "You see that tree? I eat those things all the time. And this is the first time I've seen where they actually come from. It's simply amazing!"

Confusion is the state in which I could clearly say defined the look on her face when I told her this. You know what though? She still smiled making me feel better about what I'd just said. Then the Olive trees we saw on the right, I'd never seen trees like this so when someone told me that Olives were grown there, my belief would flow far from their truth. Now though, I was actually witnessing first hand that indeed there were olives right there on a tree. Imagine the Ephesian people have the delicacy of pomegranates and olives hanging right outside their own windows. It must have been a wonderful thing.

I just wanted to pull a handful of either of them down but I thought maybe I'd make a fool of myself with the woman of my dreams. And imagine if I got arrested in a foreign country for having complete ignorance of the law. How much do you think she'd love me then? In reality, I didn't know if I'd break the law, but I sure didn't want to take that chance either. Last thing I needed was for my new girlfriend to bail me out of a Turkish prison. What an impression that'd make on the mom back home, huh? Guess what though? Nothing dreadful happened so by the grace if God, we were good.

Steering clear of anything that would ultimately cause this day to be ruined I knew then that I could now see the theatre in full view. It was situated towards the end of the city so its magnitude was hidden. But the closer you got, you could tell that this place probably sat close to twenty five thousand people. It was huge. Shahlo was wondering why most its foundation was still intact while most of Ephesus was in ruins. The only thing I could tell her was that I thought it must have been the focal point of the city. Therefore, it must have been preserved more than the rest of it. That's when I took Shahlo's hand and led her to the furthest right hand corner in the highest part of the theatre.

In relevant terms, it's probably about three or four rows from the top of a high school football stadium. Pretty high up so you could see the entire theatre, and for the most part, the entire valley surrounding Ephesus. It was beautiful. The wind felt there was a lot cooler than what we felt while navigating those rocks below. And then as I sat there I'd tell her of the biblical story of how Paul was being persecuted for his teachings right there in the theatre.

His friends were trying to persuade him to flee this very event because in a way, "The Natives were getting restless." The locals there were angry at Paul for ruining their business. The merchants were selling different statues of the Goddess Artemis and here was a man preaching to multitudes of people that following a man named Jesus meant doing away with such business. In essence, he was destroying the livelihood that most of the Ephesian venders were enjoying. So they became increasingly angry, and a riot developed within the confines of the theatre. Violent people were trying to convince others to take matters into their own hands but peace would prevail. I told Shahlo that this event began with extreme hostility, but ended with an agreement for prosperity.

She really had no idea what I was going to do, and it even seemed that she didn't understand what I was trying to say.

That's when I decided to make my move. She would know now what the Emphasis on Ephesus really was. So, then I stood up, leaned towards her and began talking, "You know everything that happened here was written about as a vicious situation that turned peaceful. And I don't know if you've ever had volatile events in your life but I want to promise you that I'll do everything in my power to ensure that we shall pursue peaceful situations in our own lives for the absolute rest of our lives."

Shahlo turned her head slightly as if she had something to say but I had to stop her. I knew that if I hesitated and stopped talking, everything I was about to say wasn't going to come out the way I wanted. So I continued, "Shahlo, what I'm saying is that I wanted to know if you'd be my wife and spend the rest of your life with me?"

As soon as she heard the words come out of my mouth, she noticed the ring that I was taking out of my pocket. Then she said, "Is that diamond?" I responded with an inquisitive nature, "Yes it is, and truly, there's nothing else I'd want for you. But babe, I haven't heard a yes yet." I really didn't think she was trying to be rude but she interrupted me mid-sentence, "Please do not take what I said about the diamond wrong, but I've never seen one. Because it's hard to find someone who has diamond in Uzbekistan, and now I have one, and oh . . . yes! I would love to be your wife, oh my goodness . . . but I have to tell you something okay? Don't think badly of me though. Will you?"

I didn't know what to think at that moment. Was she going to tell me something I didn't want to hear? Maybe something she did wrong and she wanted me to know right up front? In the short amount of time that transpired after the proposal I really didn't know how to take it. But I let her finish. I prodded her to tell me, "So what is it?" And she was ready to talk and get it clean. She proceeded, "I was going to ask you if you didn't ask me to marry you. I was here the first day and you didn't ask me, the second day went by and no request for marriage. Nothing, so I told my mother that I was going to ask you if you didn't ask me before we left."

I have to tell you that here was this absolutely beautiful woman telling me that she was going to ask me to marry her.

When in reality she could've married anyone she chose. But she picked me, even before I picked her. Which to me means that everything I was searching for in a woman I'd finally found. It was a perfect match perfectly made in Heaven.

From there, our trip took us around Turkey and Istanbul. The most disheartening moment came when I had to say goodbye to her at the airport for her flight home. I knew I'd see her again but we both sat there crying. As if we missed each other already and we hadn't even left yet. This was a time in my life that I shall treasure for the rest of my life. Those moments were engrained in the depths of my soul. And it all started with an Emphasis on Ephesus. However, now and forever more, we'd begin our personal pursuit towards our own little fairy tale.

16.

My Own Little Fairy Tale
For A Million Dollars, Alex!

BY THE TIME **I** HIT THE SIXTH GRADE **I** KNEW **I** WANTED TO MAKE a million dollars. To me, it was just another way of achieving status. Where no one could ever make fun of me based upon what I didn't have. It's amazing how I told myself I wanted to be something more so early in life. But I did just that. Making a million dollars was an end to a means for me. Even though I was mowing lawns to hide what I thought of my outer appearance, I still had inhibitions about what was going on in my inner world.

You'd have to understand the town I lived in. Maybe even the church I was going to. Everyone, it seemed, had money so the only way I thought I'd fit in, would be to make more than they did.

I was ridiculed almost daily because of my desire to make a million dollars. My fellow students were telling me, "You'll never make it, you're crazy. Do you know how hard it is for someone to make that kind of money?" Clearly I heard them but I wouldn't let what they said stop me from thinking I was positively headed in the right direction. My thoughts were, "Hey if they're ready to think small then let them think it. I flat out won't do it." Nevertheless, I'd wonder how in the world, "Am I going to make it?" Oh, the pressure I must've felt, possibly unbearable. Imagine an eighth grader thinking he's got only fourteen years to make it, or he wasn't going to measure up in his own mind.

To me, it seemed classrooms were only there for me to have time enough to think through what it'd take to fulfill those monetary aspirations. Don't get me wrong, I did alright but the mediocrity that most saw in me was nothing more than me planning my personal escape from my own sense of mediocrity. But where was I going to go when I felt so comfortable in my surroundings? I mean hey, North Augusta was safe.

The answer would be found in what most people thought of my persistent ideas. Most times, people didn't encourage, they'd discourage me from truly finding success. Whether it's by my own definition, or theirs, they were inherently brutal. So yes, I'd hide my thoughts from most until I met Robb. I'd never had a friend who'd think the same way I did. Those pipe dreams that everyone else thought were impossible were a sounding board for my new best friend.

In the late eighties, Robb's father left Texas, selling their multimillion dollar ranch. So he'd already seen that it could be done. Robb knew that and that's why I think he listened to me. I'd be alone for five and half years dabbling on my little napkins. And now I had someone who'd take note without telling me it was impossible.

I can't say that my friendship with Robb was built solely on our ability to share ideas but it surely did help. He was the only one, and I'm including my parents who wouldn't laugh at some of the thoughts I'd be throwing around. To this day, he's still the only one who'll listen to the idea all the way through before judging its success.

Why the million dollar dream though? Maybe it was the fact that I tried my hand at organized football and knew that I'd never be the one whose father was paying for the Monday night meals, so ultimately, I wouldn't be the one starting. What experiences do you think I would've had if it weren't for Coach Long? What if I hadn't earned the money for those clothes, then where do you think my self-esteem would've ended up? I don't really know, and when I look back on it, in my opinion, I don't think it would've mattered anyway.

Like I said, the million dollars was an end to a means. I looked around and observed what was happening to the guys around me. If I wanted the cheerleader kind of beauty, then I'd have to redefine my monetary projections. Because the one thing I found common in all of these guys was their positions in a status quo. Money to these people was the answer to the women they dated. Maybe they looked like they were supposed to be in GQ and that's the reason they had their choice of female companionship. But that wasn't it, because some of them looked like they could pass for the front cover of the newest volume of Dog & Pony world magazine. It had to be the money that women saw. What else could it be? The girls were nice enough to talk to me but never in my wildest dreams would I ever be given an opportunity to go out on a date with them. Guess you could say that I was way out of a poor man's league. And you know what? It wasn't just me thinking this way about these girls; sadly, it was about two thirds, shoot maybe even five eighths of the entire school. I kept thinking if I was ever going to have a beautiful woman, a nice car, or whatever I saw in these guys, I'd have to MAKE THE MILLION DOLLARS.

That's why I chose to pursue the monetary means of justification. Because I thought I'd only be worthy of such beauty if I had an open hand full of cash. Maybe the talking I was doing to be nice would manifest into something more of what I thought I wanted in a woman. Oh! Did I mention that I was a tad bit shallow back then too? You'd think I'd grow out of it, wouldn't you?

But after high school, the pursuit never changed, although my urgency did. Remember now that I only had some eight years left on my twenty eight year plan. So as I started dating college girls, I wondered if I was giving up too much in thinking time. Because I'm a firm believer that a woman needs attention and here I was staring into space while she blabbers on about something that happened in her class that day. I had to decide then what I wanted more? Was it the money or the girl?

If I get the girl, would I need the million to make her happy? It was a lot to think about while supposedly trying to pass Southern Studies. All the while finding out the woman you're courting has the hottie notties for someone else. I always found comfort in knowing that if I'd just make the money, all of these women would love me. I want to be sure to tell you that this wasn't the case at all. There had to me more and I knew it.

I asked myself, "Do I want a woman who loves me just for money? And how would I know?" Incredibly painful thinking it'd be too late and I'd be crucified within my own captive desire for beauty, yet, die knowing that if not for the money, she'd be gone. Whew! What a way for a man to live.

The truth is that I wanted the million dollars more, because it was the cash that solved more problems to me. I could live without the girl but what would happen if I gave up on a plan that was recalled more times in my mind than my own name?

I still had a massive problem with the monkey of mediocrity proverbially sitting on my back though. So what could I do to thump him off his relative high horse? The best thing a man can do when he's faced with these questions is be objective. And ask yourself another question, "Has anyone ever earned a million dollars while being the absolute picture of mediocrity?"

No, No, and No they have not. The point is that I didn't see myself as being mediocre. I saw myself as implementing a plan. And all I was doing was changing a variable here and there to reach my goal. And if something wasn't working, I'd change it.

I'd later find out that this was called the Ultimate Success Formula as defined by Anthony Robbins. But I was using it as shield for what others were calling mediocrity. So the picture of it began to fade more and more with every intuitive idea that found its place upon my napkin. Robb has always been the mirror that I'd role play with to see if what I was saying actually made sense. But what about circumstances and how that may stop my pursuit stone cold? How would I handle something like that?

I believe that it's a blessing from the Lord. When I was seventeen I'd be given a sister that moved past her yesterdays, and then some years later, I'd be provided time with a widowed middle aged woman who after her horrid experience with Mr. Good Luck Chuck here, found comfort with a man who turned out to be the man of her dreams. I learned that these two people were dealt some pretty intense happenstances and then moved past what they thought to be, imminent death situations. If they could do it, then I knew I could. So I wasn't going to let dreadful things change the direction in which I wanted to go. I'd utilize it as an immediate fuel source for the rocket I'd fly towards my definition of success.

Would all of my inner dialog overwhelm me? Would I lose focus on what I desired most, or would I make a decision to change what I thought about the pursuit? As Delta became my primary employer, my thoughts began sinking in, that I may need something else besides my desire to be rich.

When you have a concierge ask you if you'd like to go on a dinner cruise for two, and then witness him totally change his demeanor when you tell him you want a table for one, it makes one want something more than the money it'd take to tip this man. It was at that moment that I knew there was something more to life than planning to make a million dollars. Even if I had a million at that time, I think I'd still be telling you that I wanted a woman to enjoy a nice dinner cruise upon the Vltava River. Imagine sitting across the table from a suitcase full of money. Everyone staring at you, what would they say then? Probably you'd be getting some of the same looks I got from that concierge. As if to say, "Would you look at that man with the table setting on the other side of the table there? What's wrong with him? Why didn't they just remove the setting?" Maybe you'd hear this, maybe you wouldn't. But either way, you can decide you'd be much happier if you'd just be clear and honest with yourself.

Since this is my fairy tale, I'll write it as I choose. The way I want. I keep telling you there is ultimate power in decision. And I'm not saying that you have to decide right away. Just know the difference in ignoring a woman because you've got your head so far up a million dollar baby that you smell like a poop that makes your eyes water. It might be the one you're courting who turns out to be the person helping you find those million reasons. Who knows until you try, right?

Through marriage, I may have found my reasoning. However, I was giving up on my fairy tale because no, I hadn't found monetary satisfaction, nor had I found happiness. But why didn't

I? I think in part because I forced it. I ran into something because of my fear rather than letting it come to me.

It's the same concept of waiting for your pitches in baseball. What happens when you swing too soon? You strike out. What happens when you swing late? You once again, strike out. So what I'm saying here is that you don't have to force it. A home run in life will surely come your way. I can almost guarantee it.

In the movie Meet Joe Black, there was a question posed by the character Susan Parrish, "What are we going to do now?" And Joe looks over to her and responds, "It'll come to us." My point is that when you decide which direction you're headed, just let it come to you. And if it doesn't fit, please, please don't force it, no matter who tells you different.

Most people view being arrested a bad thing, but to me it gave me the chance to make new life changing decisions. Ultimately, I think it was a good thing. I don't blame anyone because it was my fault I let my desire to find love get clouded by bad judgment. Learning that if I'd just let God show me his ultimate will, I won't find myself looking for excuses when there isn't any. I believe it was this event that clarified where I wanted to find love. Possibly, it was then where I'd print my tickets certifying my departure from normality.

But as if stupidity needed refuge, I'd try again. I'd let someone else's insults make decisions for me. How insane was that? But remember something though, I cannot and will not blame Bobby for something I did. Savannah was nice enough, but I think it was my relationship with her that solidified my desire to find an international flair. I couldn't imagine that if I was designing my own fairy tale it'd change with the wind. And boy, with Savannah, let me just say that the wind changed almost daily. So much so you'd need a wind sock. Imagine trying to land on that cross wind runway! Whew! So, even in make believe, there needs to be decisiveness.

From what I'd heard of international relationships, it was a good thing. But until I actually jumped into it, I never knew how cold or hot the water was. Kamila answered many of the questions I contemplated previously. But let me tell you something, if you're looking for a fairy tale. Make sure you're fairy tale doesn't have a boyfriend. I think I wasted a lot of time cultivating something when I should've just respected her and moved on to another.

It didn't matter if I'd been to Poland, the Ukraine, or even Russia the results were the same. My fairy tale was nothing more than a couple of interesting stories. And had I been just a little more stubborn, I may have missed out on the best million dollar investment I could ever make.

Not until I reached Shahlo did I realize that making a million dollars would do nothing for my own little fairy tale. I'd been left in the middle of Odessa, Ukraine and I was finished trying to find love with an international flair. Then I received her letter with a hint of wonder. You see, when I got home from the Ukraine I'd taken all of my profiles off the web and here I get a letter to my personal Microsoft account. To this day I don't know how it happened. My MSN account was nowhere to be found within any of my profiles.

I chose to think that God was pulling those strings my way. It's the same as when he created Adam. There he was sleeping, taking in everything that he was given, and then God sees he needs something else. I have to say that Adam was like me sitting in one of Delta's Business Class seats. Maybe he was on his Business Class rock or something like it. Maybe even thinking that life just can't get any better than where he was at right at that moment. When he least expects it, God presents Eve and immediately Adam responds, "Eureka!" Which means in today's language, "Wow!" He knew it was God who moved things out of the way to bring him the love of a lifetime. So how does that relate to me and Shahlo?

I knew then that my life is nothing like a game of Jeopardy. I didn't need a man named Alex dictating my fairy tale. I needed a man who knows all the answers rather than one having those little white cards in his hand. His name is more to a man than he'll ever need in a woman. His name is Jesus. I chose to let go before and I picked it back up. You know the saying, "Let go and let God?" That was me. We'll just call it my "Belt Loop" philosophy. It's where you'll go and lay something down at the Altar, and then as soon as you walk away, you realize that you've tied it to your belt loop. Dragging it behind you, and guess what? Knowing that it's still there, you refuse to let Christ handle it.

We are so busy letting Alex answer our questions that we forget he still has to refer back to the cards for the answer. The last thing I tried with my pursuit of a dream was just let God lead where he felt I was best suited. Whether it was Rome, or even Austria, I was okay with being single if that's where he saw me. But you know what? I found my Juliet. Shahlo navigated through endless doubt to find her Romeo. And what do you think I said when God presented her to me? Yep, you guessed it, "Eureka!"

Same Adam, Same Chuck, I'd find my fairy tale laid out before my eyes only after I let God cut the rope I'd attached to my belt loop.

And when you find the one he's picked out for you, you'll find out that the million dollars you wanted to make will be transformed. You'll no longer care about it because you'll see it transformed right before your very eyes into a million dollars' worth of fairy tale, life altering, over flowing love of a lifetime.

I say all of this to tell you that I did find my fairy tale. Shahlo and I married on the Eleventh of November in two thousand five at 11:11 in the morning. Why 11:11? I was told by someone that it's the only time on a digital clock where all digits are the same, and if you make a wish when it reached that time, all of your dreams will come true. I wanted everyone to know that all my dreams had come true in a beautiful woman from Uzbekistan. Some people cry at their weddings, I prayed constantly. I couldn't thank God enough. My mother-in-law would hear, "Thank you, Jesus. Thank you, Jesus!" And being Muslim she'd wonder how a man could talk to God that much. Later when Shahlo accepted Christ, we let her mother know that it was part of the life plan with being a Christian. You have a personal relationship with him, being able to thank him for everything. Blessings and trials alike, it shouldn't matter. To this very day though, my mother-in-law doesn't understand this. But hey, I love this woman. She's been the father and mother to my wife. And I'll brag about my wife until Jesus comes back. I have the absolute best woman in the entire world. You know why I know? Because I flew the miles needed to find her. Remember the Million Miler man from Delta;

I flew so much my arms were getting tired. But it worked out for the great of finding love, too. So to me, it was worth every bird I had to shoo out of my way to get there.

When someone writes a screenplay, it has to have plot points to develop the story and give it substance. So where would this story go without plot point one? It'd suffer wildly and go nowhere! It'd almost certainly flat line into one bad movie, right? In September, I'll have you know that my fairy tale took on even more significance. We were blessed with a healthy baby boy, my little "Babushka", or "Mio Rigazzo" as I call him.

So yes, dreams do come true with or without the million dollars. I found out late in life that if you let the Lord of life lead the love of your life, you'll end up being Mr. Right and Mr. Right Now at the exact same time. And that's exactly where you want to be! My prayer for you is that you find your own little fairy tale. I promise you, it's out there. You don't have to steal someone else's. It's your life and you can define your own. But I'd like to offer some hospitable advice:

A. Do what I did, but tailor it to fit your own individual character. It may not work out for you the way it did for me, but it doesn't have to, because you have the ultimate power to decide what's going to make you happy.

B. Clearly define what you want to see when you look in the mirror. If one doesn't know who they are then how does one expect to be a perfect fit for someone else?

C. Stop settling for mediocrity. I can say this because I was there. Things I thought were productive were seen to others as mediocrity. However, the minute I decided if my ship didn't come in, I'D SWIM OUT TO IT, life ultimately changed.

D. Don't use things in the past to predict your future. I knew two people who experienced extreme circumstances, yet made decisions to move in a positive direction. Yes, they remembered their past, but they refused to let it stop them from living their lives in more progressive and lively manner.

E. Go sit by yourself for a while. Most people don't have a travel benefit like Delta gives its employees. So travel to foreign countries may not be an option. However, by sitting by yourself, you'll be able to look at things objectively. But hey, a little friendly advice, tell them to remove the setting from across the table so that you don't look like a complete idiot.

F. Bring your best. Allowing your best to be on display will indeed bring out the best in others. I'd bring the chocolate delight every time knowing that Mrs. Johnson would bring the best friend chicken in the South. I'm not saying that bringing your best in order to get something in return is the best option. But I am saying that Bringing your best is extraordinarily rewarding. What I'm also saying is to bring napkins because it really could be that good. Don't rush into anything because you're lonely. I did it, so I know what I'm telling you is certifiably true. I said I'd be married at twenty three, and guess what? I was. But I wasn't at all happy being there? In reality, I was demonstratively miserable. What I'm suggesting here is that you take your time in a relationship before making a permanent decision. One more thing you might want to remember. It would behoove you not to decide to do anything in an extremely stressful situation. Just watch the movie Speed. And you'll know exactly what I'm telling you.

G. Don't let depression kill you. It'd be best to just be happy and don't worry about it man. I've seen people ruin their whole lives by depending on what happened in the past. On the other hand, I've seen where some have changed their stars and lived a completely prosperous life. Refer to the Bible verse where God tells you, "Everything works out for the good." If it's in there, you'd better listen to it. If you do, I'd almost guarantee that you'll walk around singing like one of those happy Jamaicans, "Don't worry now, and be happy!"

H. Never let your desire to be loved triumph over the God ordained ability to tell right from wrong. Believe you, me, been there, done that. Let me tell you that spending three days in a Columbia County jail will teach you valuable lessons. It doesn't matter if you've got the fattest cigarette smoking with the reptilian partner detective telling you that you're finished as a productive member of society, because truthfully, that has nothing to do with them, it's entirely up to you. If you're making bad decisions, then what they were saying might end up true! Personally though, I knew conclusively when I turned towards the South end of the law, and did nothing to stop it. And when I recognized that acknowledgement, I apologized, repented, and when facing judgment, I prayed for mercy. Don't let the self-preservation mechanism kick in. Because to me, when that happens, you're sacrificing everything about you for something you thought was love.

I. Don't go out with someone based upon someone else's prodding. Bobby D was persistent in making me feel like a second class citizen. He couldn't believe that I didn't want to go out with Savannah. But I let his constant prodding determine the direction I wanted to go with my love life. If you want a successful relationship then don't let someone else decide who'd be perfect for you. You know what you want, not him. I don't care how many times he calls you a "faggot." When you feel like you don't have a choice, just remember, if you take them out, you're the one who's paying the bill, not him. So, it's up to you to do what you want.

J. Know what you're getting into should you decide that normality is something you want to venture from. Imagine being in the middle of Poland sitting on a park bench and you hear someone tell you, "But this isn't right. If my boyfriend knew what I was doing, he'd kill me." Or what about when you get a letter from a Ukrainian woman who lets you know that she won't leave without her son. And the son's father wouldn't sign off on him leaving anyway. My departure from normality was a progressive learning process. Listen to some of the things being said because frankly, and you may have heard this before, the words will guide you. The normality you're venturing from may offer more to you than what's on the other side of the pond. However, you may find abnormality even though you've been beaten and bruised by ignorance. And if you do, you just may end up with your own wonderful version of Shahlo.

K. Don't let small things like the Russian Mafia stop you from searching. Most Russian block countries are still infiltrated with the Mafia. I was staying at the Radisson Hotel in Tashkent and used the phone fourteen times and when I was handed my bill, I was shocked to see seven hundred and thirty eight dollars for Phone services. I'd saved enough to cover these expenses but I knew where they were coming from. I just didn't let it stop me from following through with my marriage to my self-defined perfection. Don't get me wrong, the Russian Mafia is a group of people who can ruin your life. However, if you mind your business and know that love surpasses all, you'll be fine. But don't stop something wonderful because of fear. One thing to remember is there is an opposite of fear and that would be faith. So, have the faith to know that what you're pursuing is noble and worthwhile.

L. If leaving the comfort zone, make sure you have phone numbers and addresses before you leave. Don't get stuck in a foreign country, or even someplace close without more information in your wallet. I left my comfort zone here in the states with reckless abandon. Didn't pay much attention to the fact that I didn't have her number, or anything with that would help me find her. Never even dreamed she'd stand me up. But hey, it happened, and I learned that you've got to have something with you, and that way you won't feel like a complete dope.

M. Test the water to see if it's hot or cold. Shahlo at first wasn't what I imagined. Keep in mind that I thought she was a little Russian dude. So when I got her letter, I had a choice to make. Was the water I was testing hot or cold? Well, I think you already know. But you know what? I would've never known if I didn't at least try. Bringing me to an appealing line from Meet Joe Black, "To make the journey and not fall in love, well you have to try, because if you haven't tried, you haven't lived." Part of testing the water is putting yourself in a relationship and deciding which aspect fits best.

N. Pick a place with a clear and concise personal meaning. I wanted to make an impression with my marriage proposal. So I thought about different places that Delta flew and chose a place that to me was an awesome place to propose. As I've said before, Ephesus was a place that our Biblical Paul used as a backdrop to teach us how to love our wives. I had a clear and precise location because I wanted my future wife to know that I'd love her as Ephesians said Christ loved his church.

O. Give your all, but only when it's appropriate. You know Shahlo was going to ask me to marry her had I not asked her first. I was giving her everything I had to give. However, there was more that I held back for maximum impact. I felt she'd say, "Yes!" But I wanted to make sure both of us remembered this event for the rest of our lives. So in essence, I gave my all, but only when it was appropriate.

P. When you finally get what you want, thank her or him for choosing you. I sit here today to let you know that when I first received Shahlo's letter, I couldn't believe that a woman that beautiful was writing me. I was sarcastic for the first couple of letters thinking she was the vodka drinking Russian that the man in the Ukraine warned me about. And as time would heal impressions I'd be eternally thankful for her choosing me. What'll happen is that you'll remain thankful, and you just might be amazed at the fact she'd thank you for choosing her.

Q. Don't take life or her/him for granted. Cherish the time God has given you. Crazy Alise loved her husband about as much as anyone could. Unfortunately though, his life was cut short, leaving her in an unstable condition. She moved past her yesterdays but a grinding pain was still there. You want to hear of someone who didn't take him for granted. She'd do anything to have five seconds to be with him again. Maybe she took life for granted, maybe she didn't. It doesn't matter, what does matter though, is that we have an opportunity to treasure life, and not take anything, or anyone for granted.

R. Live spontaneously. Enough said. Do things that give people reason to boast incessantly about your relationship with your partner! Always pack a weekend bag, and be ready to go on romantic rendezvous on a whim. You don't have to leave town for a picnic. So pack the sandwiches and blankets, and head out now. And I'm sure when you get back you'll be rewarded beyond your wildest and craziest imagination.

You can call this my itty bitty disclaimer, if you will. I can't guarantee by following these steps you'll discover the fairy tale ending you're searching for. But I will say that you'll find the things in your life that make you blissfully happy. The one and final point of advice is please, NEVER DEPEND on someone changing anything about them! Personal happiness shouldn't be dependent on someone else's change.

We, as individuals try to maximize expectations almost certainly putting our relationships in immediate danger. But why do we? Because forcing someone to change something about themselves will do nothing but prolong the inevitable. And then you're left realizing the person still isn't the one you're searching for.

Placing them into a box of perfection will do nothing but drive them out as if they were a jack-in-a-box. Ba dunkey dunk, ba dunkey dunk, ba dunkey dunka do, and everything you've done right blows out the top of the box. And then you're left trying to stuff the little clown back in. As a suggestion, never try to stuff someone into a box that small because expectations ultimately drive them out anyway. As if separation needed company, I think it ultimately means you're eventually driving them away from you. And no one wants that to happen, right?

The point of searching for a fairy tale is finding it. But I have to be honest with you. It may take a long time. I had to go through what seemed like hell and high water but I stand here today and tell you that when I found my Shahlo, it was worth every second I spent wading through the water. So go on now, make a list, be specific about what you really want, if you're a God fearing person, pray hard, and as you find what you've progressively searched for . . . **LIVE HAPPILY EVER AFTER.**

www.ingramcontent.com/pod-product-compliance
Lightning Source LLC
Chambersburg PA
CBHW061352280526
45784CB00001B/226